S T I L L

UNSOLVED

GREAT TRUE MURDER CASES

Selected, with an Introduction, by
RICHARD GLYN JONES

GUILD PUBLISHING
LONDON · NEW YORK · SYDNEY · TORONTO

British Library Cataloguing in Publication Data

Still unsolved.
  1. Unsolved crimes, history
  I. Jones, Richard Glyn, 1946–
364.109

  ISBN 1-85480-030-2

This selection and Introduction copyright © 1990
Xanadu Publications Limited

First published 1990 by Xanadu Publications Limited
19 Cornwall Road, London N4 4PH

This edition published 1990 by Guild Publishing
by arrangement with Xanadu Publications Limited

Reprinted 1992

Typeset by Avocet Robinson, Buckingham
Printed and bound in Great Britain by
Biddles Limited, Guildford and King's Lynn

CN 6411

Contents

List of Illustrations

Introduction

This is a book about getting away with murder. In all, there are some seventy-three murders which were committed by approximately twenty-one people, though I cannot be precise about either figure because it is by no means certain that all the victims' bodies were found, and since none of the killers were firmly identified we sometimes do not know whether they were working as individuals, duos or in gangs. Nonetheless, this appalling toll of destruction without a single verdict of 'guilty' offers clear proof that, contrary to popular and comforting views that murder will out, crime does not pay and so forth, it is not merely possible to get away with murder: it happens all the time.

To demonstrate this alarming thesis I have selected twenty cases, some of which are classics of their kind, some less familiar but which perhaps deserve to be more widely known, and others which are just plain bizarre. I have also tried to include as many different *types* of murder as I could, variety being the spice of death as well as life. The Axeman of New Orleans and the so-called Head Hunter of Kingsbury Run are serial killers of the kind that America seems to throw up regularly – as you might when you read of their deeds, but it *is* fascinating to follow the progress of these events as an unknown hand brings mounting terror and panic to a city. In stark contrast to these are domestic murders in small, closed communities like those that feature in 'The Mystery of the Poisoned Partridges' and the case that rocked Hollywood in the 1920s when William Desmond Taylor was shot in the night. Some of the shorter cases that I have designated 'Little Mysteries' are simply unbelievable: a box full of corpses washed up on the seashore, the midnight kidnapping of a headsman, a man trying to avoid notice by wearing blue goggles and a startling red wig? They might seem to have come straight from the mind of Poe or Chesterton, yet they are all true, and once read are not likely to be forgotten.

There are pleasures in the telling of these stories, too. Not merely the satisfaction of an interesting tale well told, but incidental delights such as the author's comment on the habit of the baker's wife of pelting her husband with his own loaves when she was out of sorts ('not significant of either affection or esteem'), or the sudden appearance of Eliott Ness, the famous Untouchable, in what must have been one of his less successful assignments. One or two of the pieces are actually period-pieces, as much of their time as the murders themselves, but this can be helpful, a key element in 'The Mystery of the Village Beauty', for instance, is the moral climate of the 1900s, especially as it manifested itself in a small English village, when it was not just a matter of scandal but of *evil* for an unmarried woman to have any kind of sex life – a view to a large extent shared by the author of this account of the matter.

For readers of these cases there is also the undoubted interest of playing the detective oneself, when there is sufficient evidence to permit it. The Green Bicycle Case is one of the classic 'did-he-or-didn't-he?' puzzles, and it has attracted many different explanations from all sorts of people, while there is also much scope for fruitful speculation in the Camden Town killing, the Errol case (recently filmed as *White Mischief*), the Mystery of Madame X, the Yarmouth murder and several others here. The name of Sherlock Holmes – the greatest of all fictional detectives – is invoked by a number of the writers in passing, and in the case dealing with the German baker ('How to Dispose of a Human Body') may lie the origins of Holmes, tracing fiction back to fact. Michael Harrison has argued brilliantly that when this crime was first reported in the London newspapers in 1882 it was at the precise time when the young Conan Doyle was contemplating a writing career, and he traces remarkable parallels between the real events and Holmes's first exploit in *A Study in Scarlet*, showing the subtle transformation of Wendel Scherer (who appears very briefly in the account given here) into Sherlock Holmes. Fascinating stuff.* Would-be Sherlocks will find their wits tested to the utmost here, though, for these are crimes that have baffled the experts, and remain unsolved to this day.

And the murderers? Some of the suspects did suffer for their suspected crimes, but others appear to have got clean away, and it is also interesting to speculate on *that*. Perhaps the person you pass in the street or who sits next to you on the train is one of them – or are they racked with remorse and haunted by their misdeeds?

Can anyone really get away with murder?

—RICHARD GLYN JONES

* Anyone wishing to know more about this should consult Michael Harrison's 'A Study in Surmise' in *Ellery Queen's Mystery Magazine*. no. 327 (February, 1971).

ROBERT TALLANT

The Axeman of
New Orleans

In 1918 New Orleans like all other American cities was busy
thinking and reading about and devoting itself to the news and
the duties of World War I. In the spring of that year no one
knew it would end in November, although there was hope that
it would not go on much longer and a great deal of optimism
that the Allies would win. Headlines in a New Orleans newspaper
on May 3 read, 'Lull in Flanders; Allies Lines Holding,' yet
by May 23 the same newspaper warned, 'Massed Germans
Awaiting Orders Now To Open Drive,' and Orleanians were
instructed to 'Kill The Germ In Germany—Liberty Bonds Will
Help!' On May 24 another headline announced, 'Senate Rejects
Dry Amendment by 20 to 20 Vote.' At New Orleans moving
picture theatres Charlie Chaplin was starring in *A Dog's Life* and
Theda Bara in *The Soul of Buddha*. Also on that day a woman
was arrested in New Orleans for wearing trousers on the street.
But on the same day there was another headline in all the papers
in the city. A couple named Maggio, who operated a small
grocery at the corner of Upperline and Magnolia streets, had
been attacked during the night before by an unknown assailant
who was armed with an axe. It had begun, although most
Orleanians must have thought of it as a shocking but isolated
case, and they could hardly have dreamed of what lay ahead.

On that morning of May 24, 1918, the *Times-Picayune* devoted
a good portion of its front page to the story, and in the centre
of the page was a photograph of the room where the Maggios
had been sleeping, a room in their living quarters behind their
store, with inset pictures of the couple as they had looked at their
wedding fifteen years before. According to the account, police

1

thought it was just before dawn when someone had chiselled out a panel in a rear door of the apartment and entered. He had struck each of the sleepers once with an axe, then slit their throats with a razor. Mrs Maggio lay on the floor, her head nearly severed from her body, Joseph Maggio was sprawled half out of bed. The razor lay on the floor in a pool of blood. The axe, as bloodstained as the razor, was found on the steps going out into the back yard; it had been Maggio's own property. There was a small safe in the room which was open and empty, yet a hundred dollars or more in cash was found beneath Maggio's blood-soaked pillow and on the dresser in a little pile was Mrs Maggio's jewellery, including several diamond rings. The police were reported to have already stated that they did not believe robbery was a motive, but that the murderer had opened the safe to make it appear that it was.

In rooms on the other side of the house lived Joseph's brothers, Andrew and Jake. They had discovered the bodies. Jake told police that he awakened at about five o'clock and heard groaning and strange noises on the other side of the wall separating his bedroom from that of Joseph and his wife. He aroused Andrew and together they went into the room. Joseph was on the bed then, and still alive. He even tried to rise and fell half out of the bed. Andrew and Jake called the police at once. The police put them both under arrest, after a neighbour who rushed into the house along with them said he had seen Andrew come home some time between two and three in the morning. Later in the morning there was another curious discovery. Chalked on the sidewalk a block away were these words: 'Mrs Maggio is going to sit up tonight just like Mrs Toney.'

The police went to work. In 1911 there had been three axe murders, similar to the Maggio case, all of Italian grocers and their wives. There had been a grocer named Crui, then one named Rosetti, whose wife was murdered with him, finally a Tony Schiambra and his wife. Was the last the 'Mrs Toney' referred to in the sidewalk writing? People began talking of Mafia and of Black Hand. The Italian population was particularly worried and some of them demanded police protection.

In the meantime Andrew and Jake Maggio were in jail

swearing their innocence. Andrew said it was true he had been out late the night before. He had been celebrating for he had just received his draft call. He had come home drunk and he would not have been able to notice anything strange if there had been anything to notice. Jake verified this and said he had had a hard time arousing Andrew. They were respectable, hard-working young men—Andrew was a barber, Jake a cobbler.

Jake was released the following day and Andrew on May 26. Andrew told a *Times-Picayune* reporter with 'tear-filled eyes' that he would never get over this. 'It's a terrible thing to be charged with the murder of your own brother when your heart is already broken by his death,' he said. 'When I'm about to go to war, too. I had been drinking heavily. I was too drunk even to have heard any noise next door.' But he and Jake were free and were cleared of any suspicion.

The papers of May 26 announced that Detective Theodore Obitz had charge of the case and had 'many theories.' On the evening of May 26 Detective Obitz was shot through the heart by a Negro he had arrested for burglary. It had no connection with the Maggio murders.

Weeks passed and nothing more happened. The newspapers informed Orleanians that the Allies had been forced to retire on the Aisne and that the Russian Czar had been murdered. Many citizens probably almost forgot the Maggio case. They were rushing to the Strand Theatre to see James W. Gerard's *My Four Years in Germany* at road show prices and talking about putting New Orleans 'over the top' in the new Red Cross Drive.

Then on June 28 a baker, John Zanca, made his morning call to deliver bread and cakes to the grocery of Louis Besumer. It was after seven o'clock when he arrived, and as Besumer's store was still closed, Zanca went around to the living quarters in the rear to leave his bread there rather than risk having it stolen from the front of the store. When he reached the back door he stopped and stared in horror. A lower panel of the door was neatly chiselled out. Perhaps half-consciously Zanca knocked on the door. He said later, 'There seemed nothing else to do.'

And Louis Besumer opened the door. Blood streamed from a wound in his head. He said, 'My God! My God!'

Zanca rushed past him and found the woman he had always thought Mrs Besumer on the bed covered with a bloodstained sheet, unconscious and with a terrible head wound. He called the Charity Hospital and the police.

The newspapers announced the next day that 'Mrs Besumer' was in a serious condition, but still alive, and that Besumer had been released. Detectives believed the woman had been attacked on the gallery leading across one side of the living quarters, for there was much blood there, then had dragged herself or been carried back to the bed, possibly by Besumer. An axe, Besumer's property, was discovered in the bathroom, still bright, bright red with blood. Besumer, it was said, was Polish, and had lived in New Orleans only three months. He had come to the city from Jacksonville, Florida, and before that had operated a farm in South America.

On June 29 there were further developments. That morning the *Times-Picayune* carried a headline reading, 'Spy Nest Suspected!' It was stated that letters to Besumer written in German, Russian and Yiddish had been found in a trunk in his apartment. The New Orleans *States* the same day asked the question, 'Is Besumer a German Agent' and 'Was the Besumer Grocery a Front for a Spy Ring?' On June 30, a Sunday, a great deal of space was devoted to this, and it was hinted darkly that federal authorities were interested in the case. One reporter did note, however, that Besumer was not Italian and asked, 'What of the Mafia theory in the axe killings?' It was also noted that Lewis Oubicon, a Negro employee of Besumer, was behind held for questioning.

Besumer's own statements were made public on July 1. The first thing he is reported to have said was 'That woman is not my wife.' He said the woman who had been attacked was named Mrs Harriet Lowe and that she had come to New Orleans from Jacksonville with him, and that they had lived together ever since. His own wife was ill, he said, and with relatives in Cincinnati. He swore he did not know what had happened. Someone had struck him while he slept. When he regained consciousness he found Mrs Lowe on the gallery and he had carried her to the bed. He had been about to summon an ambulance when Zanca knocked at the back door. He was not a German, but a Pole, and he had no use for the Germans. He spoke and received mail in a half-dozen languages. He was certainly no spy, he vowed. He offered the police his full co-operation.

But federal authorities did come into the case. Carrying a bathrobe for her, Besumer went to see Harriet Lowe at the hospital. He was refused admittance and the bathrobe was taken away from him and ripped open at the seams by government agents. The next day his grocery and living quarters were ransacked. Nothing was found.

Mrs Lowe made her first statement on July 5, having by then regained consciousness. She said, 'I've long suspected that Mr Besumer was a German spy.' Besumer was arrested at once.

On July 6 Mrs Lowe was interviewed again. She said, 'I am married to Mr Besumer. If I am not I don't know what I'll do.' Then she added, 'I did not say Mr Besumer is a German spy. That is perfectly ridiculous.' A few days later Besumer was freed from government custody.

Mrs Lowe at last talked of the attacks. She said that Besumer was working on his accounts about midnight, sitting at a table with a lot of money before him. She always worried about how careless he was with money, she said, and she warned him and asked him to put it in the safe. Then she smelled some prunes she was cooking in the kitchen and she went into the kitchen to look at them. There her memory left her. She supposed it was the blow on the head. She could not even remember going to bed. Her next memory was of awakening. 'I don't even know what made me wake up,' she told police, 'but I opened my eyes and in the light from outside I saw a man standing over me, making some sort of motions with his hands. I saw the axe. I recall screaming, 'Go away! Don't push me that way!' He was a rather tall man, and heavy-set. He was a white man and he wore no hat or cap. I remember his hair was dark brown and almost stood on end. He wore a white shirt, opened at the neck. He just stood there, making motions with the axe, but not hitting me. The next thing I remember is lying out on the gallery with my face in a pool of blood.'

The story changed on July 15. In another police interview

that day Mrs Lowe said she was not in bed when she was struck. She was on the gallery. Police thought this made more sense and again looked toward Besumer with suspicion. They questioned neighbours. Yes, the Besumers had had violent quarrels, they were told. Besumer was fifty-nine and Mrs Lowe twenty-nine. He was jealous and they quarrelled over money, too. Police began asking one question. Could Besumer's own wound have been self-inflicted! A check with authorities in Jacksonville and in Cincinnati proved that Besumer and Mrs Lowe had never been married and that Besumer had a living wife. That did not help matters, and they were far from convinced that Besumer was not a German agent. Neighbours gossiped about the foreigner who had odd ways and spoke German fluently, as well as other languages, who looked like a simple peasant and had the manners and airs of a cultured gentleman. People began saying that perhaps Besumer had attacked Mrs Lowe, then wounded himself, all in imitation of the Axeman, perhaps because Mrs Lowe knew too much of his activities as a spy.

Then on August 3 the doctors at Charity Hospital performed surgery upon Mrs Lowe. Two days later she died, and, dying, mumbled that Besumer had struck her with the axe. He was arrested at once and charged with murder.

The Axeman chose that night, August 5, to strike again.

Edward Schneider, a young married man, was working late that night, and it was after midnight when he turned the key in the front door of his home in Elmira Street. When he reached his bedroom and turned on the light he was almost paralysed with horror. His wife lay unconscious, her face and head covered with blood.

Mrs Schneider, who was expecting a baby within a few days, was rushed to Charity Hospital. She regained consciousness and remembered awakening to see a dark form bending over her, an axe swung high. She recalled shrieking as the axe fell.

She recovered and a week later was delivered of a healthy baby girl. She was never able to tell more about what had occurred, however, and although the police searched diligently for clues none was found. To add to the general confusion were deviations from the Axeman's habits. No axe was about. The intruder seemed to have entered by a window, for no door panel was chiselled out. As usual, however, nothing was stolen.

The day after the attack upon Mrs Schneider a newspaper for the first time put into a headline what Orleanians had been asking each other for months. The *Times-Picayune* asked, in large and dramatic type: IS AN AXEMAN AT LARGE IN NEW ORLEANS?

Pauline Bruno, aged 18, and Mary, her sister, aged 13, awoke shortly after three in the morning of August 10 when they heard strange noises coming from the next room, where their uncle, Joseph Romano, was sleeping. Pauline crawled out of bed, turned on her light, and opened the door between the rooms. A man, whom she later described as 'dark, tall, heavy-set, wearing a dark suit and a black slouch hat,' was standing by her uncle's bed. Pauline screamed and then the man seemed to vanish. As if it were all a fantastic nightmare, her uncle rose from the bed, staggered through a door at the other side of the room, and crashed to the floor there, which was the parlour. Pauline ran after him.

Later she told the following story to an *Item* reporter: 'I've been nervous about the Axeman for weeks,' she said, 'and I haven't been sleeping much. I was dozing when I heard blows and scuffling in Uncle Joe's room. I sat up in bed and my sister woke up too. When I looked into my uncle's room this big heavy-set man was standing at the foot of his bed. I think he was a white man, but I couldn't swear to it. I screamed. My little sister screamed too. We were horribly scared. Then he vanished. It was almost as if he had wings!

'We rushed into the parlour, where my uncle had staggered. He had two big cuts on his head. We got him up and propped him in a chair. "I've been hit," he groaned. "I don't know who did it. Call the Charity Hospital." Then he fainted. Later he was able to walk to the ambulance with some help. I don't know that he had any enemies.'

Romano died two days later in the hospital, without being able to make further statements. Police reported that this time there were all the Axeman's signatures. An axe was found in

Romano's back yard, bloodstained and fearful. The panel of a rear door had been cut out. Nothing in the house was stolen, although Romano's room seemed to have been ransacked. The only thing that made it unlike some of the other cases was that Romano was a barber, not a grocer.

Now there was a new wave of hysteria among the Italians in New Orleans. Some of the familes set up regular watches, taking turns standing guard over their sleeping relatives. A few were said to be leaving the city.

Police began to be flooded with reports about the Axeman after the Romano incident. Al Durand, a grocer, reported finding an axe and a chisel outside his back door on the morning of August 11. Joseph LeBeouf, a grocer at Gravier and Miro streets, only a block from the Romano home, came forward with the story that someone had chiselled out a panel of his back door on July 28, a day when he was not home. Still another grocer, Arthur Recknagel, told of finding a panel in one of his doors removed back in June, and of finding an axe in the grass of his rear yard. Recknagel lived only a half-dozen blocks from the Romano home. On August 15 several persons called police to tell them the Axeman was wandering around in the neighbourhood of Tulane Avenue and Broad Street disguised as a woman!

On August 21 a man was seen leaping a back fence at Gravier and South White streets. A woman reported she clearly saw an axe in this man's hand. Immediately the neighbours formed a kind of posse, as other people ran from their houses screaming that the Axeman had just jumped their fence! A young man named Joseph Garry vowed he had fired at the Axeman with his shotgun. Police arrived on the scene, but no one was apprehended, and the excitement quieted down about midnight, although it is doubtful if many people in the vicinity slept well that night or for several nights thereafter. The New Orleans *States* reported the next day:

> Armed men are keeping watch over their sleeping families while the police are seeking to solve the mysteries of the axe attacks. Five victims have fallen under the dreadful blows of this weapon within the last few months. Extra police are being put to work daily.

An least four persons saw the Axeman this morning in the neighbourhood of Iberville and Rendon. He was first seen in front of an Italian grocery. Twice he fled when citizens armed themselves and gave chase. There was something, agreed all, in the prowler's hand. Was it an axe? . . .

On August 30 a man named Nick Asunto called the police to tell them he had awakened and heard strange noises downstairs. He lived in a two-storied house. He went to the head of his stairs and saw a dark, heavy-set man standing below, an axe in his hand. When Asunto yelled at him the Axeman ran out the front door. On August 31 Paul Lobella, a notions store proprietor at 7420 Zimple Street, found an axe in his alley. There were a dozen similar reports.

Now police made statements to the effect that they did not believe the Besumer case was of the now ordinary variety. They made public Mrs Lowe's confession. Her memory cleared after the operation, they said, and she had told them that Besumer struck her with an axe after she had asked him for money. He chased her down the gallery, screaming, 'I am going to make fire for you in the bottom of the ocean!' She had reiterated, too, that Besumer was a German spy. Therefore they were sure this was not the Axeman at work, although they believed all the other attacks, including that upon Mrs Schneider, were the crimes of a single person, perhaps a homicidal maniac.

Joseph Dantonio, a retired detective, long an authority on Mafia activities, was questioned by a *States* reporter, and was quoted in that newspaper as saying, 'The Axeman is a modern "Dr Jekyll and Mr Hyde." A criminal of this type may be a respectable, law-abiding citizen when his normal self. Compelled by an impulse to kill, he must obey this urge. Some years ago there were a number of similar cases, all bearing such strong resemblance to this outbreak that the same fiend may be responsible. Like Jack-the-Ripper, this sadist may go on with his periodic outbreaks until his death. For months, even for years, he may be normal, then go on another rampage. It is a mistake to blame the Mafia. Several of the victims have been other than Italians, and the Mafia never attacks women, as this murderer has done.'

Then, as if he were exactly as Detective Dantonio had

theorized, the Axeman did disappear. After the Romano killing
and the other unauthenticated attacks and scares, nothing
happened at all for a long time. Weeks and months passed, the
fighting of World War I ended, Christmas came and then the
New Year and no more attacks occurred. Orleanians, even the
Italians, breathed freely again, and the police, still mystified,
found nothing more to work with in solving the crimes. From
time to time suspects were arrested, but all had to be released.
Only Besumer remained in jail awaiting trial, the only real
suspect they had in connection with any of the crimes.

Then, on March 10, 1919, Iorlando Jordano, a grocer in Gretna,
just across the river from New Orleans, heard screams coming
from the living quarters of another grocer across the street, a
man named Charles Cortimiglia. He rushed over and into the
Cortimiglia apartments. Mrs Cortimiglia sat on the floor, still
shrieking, blood gushing from her head and the body of her two-
year-old daughter Mary clasped in her arms. Also bleeding
frightfully, Charles Cortimiglia lay on the floor nearby.

Jordano tried to take Mary from her mother's arms, but she
wouldn't let him, so he got wet towels from the bathroom and
tried to bathe her face and that of her husband. Cortimiglia
groaned, but did not regain full consciousness. Then Frank
Jordano, young son of Iorlando, rushed in and began assisting
his father. The father sent him to call an ambulance. Both the
Cortimiglia parents had to be taken to the Charity Hospital with
fractured skulls. Little Mary was dead.

When the police searched the property they found the familiar
Axeman pattern—the back door panel chiselled, the bloody axe,
Charles Cortimiglia's own, on the back steps, nothing stolen.
Reading the newspapers the next morning Orleanians and the
citizens of Gretna all knew the worst. The Axeman was back!

As soon as she could talk coherently Rosie Cortimiglia told
of awakening to see her husband struggling with a large white
man wearing dark clothes, who was armed with an axe. The
man tore himself loose from Cortimiglia, sprang backward and
struck once with the axe. When her husband fell to the floor
and the Axeman swung around Mrs Cortimiglia seized Mary,

who was asleep in her crib beside the parents' bed, clasped her to her and screamed, 'Not my baby! Not my baby!' The Axeman struck twice more, then fled. Mary was killed instantly.

Both the Cortimiglias were badly injured, but Charles recovered first and left the hospital. A few days later Rosie made another statement, an accusation that amazed the police. 'It was the Jordanos!' she said. 'It was Frank Jordano and the old man helped him. It was those Jordanos!'

Charles Cortimiglia was questioned. He looked as astounded as the police. 'It was not the Jordanos,' he said. 'I saw the man well and he was a stranger. No, it was not Frank Jordano.'

Nevertheless, both Jordanos were arrested, charged with the murder of Mary Cortimiglia and placed in the Gretna jail.

Both protested their innocence fervently. Frank, who was only eighteen and about to be married, said at first he had been home all night, then admitted he had been to a dance with his girl and that he had lied because he did not want her name brought into the affair. The elder Jordano, sixty-nine and in poor health, told his story of finding the Cortimiglias over and over again.

Yet Rosie Cortimiglia told her story over and over, too. Frank and Iorlando had both been in the room. It was Frank who had struck them all, had murdered her baby. She said the Jordanos had hated her husband and herself a long time because both familes were in the grocery business in the same block. It was jealousy, she said. She gave the police everything they needed—eyewitness identification and motive. Charles Cortimiglia continued to deny it all.

'My wife must be out of her mind,' he said. 'It was a stranger.' Rosie retaliated, 'He is afraid for his own neck, that husband of mine. It was the Jordanos.'

One thing seems to have bothered detectives working on the case more than anything else. For all his youth Frank Jordano was more than six feet tall and weighed over two hundred pounds. Making a test with a man of similar size, they admitted a man that size could not squeeze through the panel of a door. A giddy reporter on the *Times-Picayune* wanted to know if it were possible the Axeman was really a midget.

When Rosie was released from the hospital she was taken to

the Gretna jail. There she identified the Jordanos again. Pointing a finger at them she screamed, 'You murdered my baby!' and fainted. It was announced that the Jordanos would go to trial for the murder in May.

But before that Louis Besumer went on trial. The trial opened on April 30. It was brief and few witnesses were called. District Attorney Chandler Luzenberg summoned Coroner Joseph O'Hara for the State, who described Mrs Lowe's wounds and the cause of her death. Zanca, the baker, said that Besumer did not seem to know what he was doing that morning when he had opened the door or even to realize Mrs Lowe was hurt. Federal officers admitted they had no evidence that Besumer had ever been a German agent. Besumer's attorney, George Rhodes, said it was a reflection on the United States Secret Service to say that Besumer had been a spy, and that Besumer was not being tried on that charge in any case and, besides, the war was over. The police to whom Mrs Lowe had made her accusation of Besumer admitted that even then she had not been very coherent. Dr. H. W. Kostmayer said that only a very powerful man could have inflicted himself with the wound Besumer had received and he did not consider the accused strong enough to have accomplished it.

The next morning the jury debated but ten minutes and Besumer was found not guilty. Released, Besumer told reporters that he believed the same Axeman had attacked Mrs Lowe and himself as had attacked the others and that his imprisonment had been due almost entirely to 'war feeling,' because he had been thought to be a German, although he was really a Pole and had never been a German sympathizer.

In the meantime the Cortimiglia case had brought on a new series of Axeman reports. Immediately after the attack upon the Gretna family New Orleans police received numerous reports of chiselled panels, axes being found, dark, heavy-set men lurking in neighbourhoods, particularly around grocery stores, and many Orleanians, particularly Italian grocers, appealed once more for police protection. The newspapers reviewed all the cases of 1918 and editorialized upon the mystery. It was announced that Police Superintendent Frank Mooney had again assigned special men to the task of uncovering the perpetrators of the crimes, despite the fact that the Jordanos were in the Gretna jail and that Superintendent Mooney had expressed the opinion that he '. . . was sure that all the crimes were committed by the same man, probably a bloodthirsty maniac, filled with a passion for human slaughter.'

A *States* editor wrote, on March 11:

> Who is the Axeman; what are his motives?
>
> Is the fiend who butchered the Cortimiglias in Gretna Sunday the same man who committed the Maggio, Besumer and Romano crimes? Is he the same who has made all the attempts on other families?
>
> If so, is he madman, robber, vendetta agent, sadist or some supernatural spirit of evil?
>
> If a madman, why so cunning and careful in the execution of his crimes? If a robber, why the wanton shedding of blood and the fact that money and valuables have often been left in full view? If a vendetta of the Mafia, why include among victims persons of nationalities other than Italian?
>
> The possibilities in searching for the motives in this extraordinary series of axe butcheries are unlimited. The records show no details of importance which vary. There is always the door panel as a means of entrance, always the axe, always the frightful effusion of blood. In these three essentials the work of the Axeman is practically identical.

But the reaction of Orleanians to the 1919 outbreak of the Axeman was by no means all fearful and grim. Probably because the war was over and people were in a gayer mood than they had been the year before, there were some who joked about him and even found a kind of humour in the situation. There were reports of 'Axeman parties' and a New Orleans composer wrote a song entitled 'The Mysterious Axeman's Jazz' or 'Don't Scare Me, Papa!' which Orleanians played on their pianos. Then, on March 14, a letter purporting to be from the Axeman appeared in a newspaper, which read as follows:

> Hell, March 13, 1919
>
> Editor of the *Times-Picayune*
> New Orleans, Louisiana
>
> Esteemed Mortal:
> They have never caught me and they never will. They have never seen me, for I am invisible, even as the ether that surrounds your earth. I am not a human being, but a spirit and a fell demon from the hottest hell. I

am what you Orleanians and your foolish police call the Axeman.

When I see fit, I shall come again and claim other victims. I alone know who they shall be. I shall leave no clue except my bloody axe, besmeared with the blood and brains of him whom I have sent below to keep me company.

If you wish you may tell the police not to rile me. Of course I am a reasonable spirit. I take no offence at the way they have conducted their investigations in the past. In fact, they have been so utterly stupid as to amuse not only me, but His Satanic Majesty, Francis Josef, etc. But tell them to beware. Let them not try to discover what I am, for it were better that they were never born than to incur the wrath of the Axeman. I don't think there is any need of such a warning, for I feel sure the police will always dodge me, as they have in the past. They are wise and know how to keep away from all harm.

Undoubtedly, you Orleanians think of me as a most horrible murderer, which I am, but I could be much worse if I wanted to. If I wished, I could pay a visit to your city every night. At will I could slay thousands of your best citizens, for I am in close relationship to the Angel of Death.

Now, to be exact, at 12.15 (earthly time) on next Tuesday night, I am going to visit New Orleans again. In my infinite mercy, I am going to make a proposition to you people. Here it is:

I am very fond of jazz music, and I swear by all the devils in the nether regions that every person shall be spared in whose home a jazz band is in full swing at the time I have mentioned. If everyone has a jazz band going, well, then, so much the better for you people. One thing is certain and that is that some of those people who do not jazz it on Tuesday night (if there be any) will get the axe.

Well, as I am cold and crave the warmth of my native Tartarus, and as it is about time that I leave your earthly home, I will cease my discourse. Hoping that thou wilt publish this, that it may go well with thee, I have been, am and will be the worst spirit that ever existed either in fact or realm of fancy.

THE AXEMAN

The Tuesday on which this 'Axeman' promised to visit the city was March 19, St. Joseph's Night, a night when many Orleanians, and even more in 1919 than now, give parties and dances to celebrate a break in Lent.

That St. Joseph's Night in New Orleans seems to have been the loudest and most hilarious of any on record. All over the city Orleanians obeyed the instructions in the letter. Cabarets and clubs were jammed and friends and neighbours gathered in homes to 'jazz it,' according to the letter's edict. Bands and phonographs and inner-player pianos all over the city created bedlam, and every owner of a piano seemed to have on hand sheet music of 'The Mysterious Axeman's Jazz' or 'Don't Scare Me, Papa!'

Young men living in a fraternity house at 552 Lowerline Street even inserted an advertisement in the *Times-Picayune* inviting the Axeman to call. Appearing in the morning of Tuesday, March 19, the advertisement was signed by 'Oscar Williams, William Schulze, A. M. La Fleur and William Simpson,' and it informed the Axeman that a bathroom window would be left open for him, so that it would not be necessary for him to mar any doors; and that all doors would be left unlocked if he would stoop to making such a conventional entrace. He was told there would be, however, no jazz music, but only a rendering of 'Nearer, My God, To Thee,' which his hosts considered more suitable for the occasion. They concluded the advertisement by stating: 'There is a sincere cordiality about this invitation that not even an Axeman can fail to recognize.'

But the Axeman failed everybody that night and made no appearances. Apparently he was satisfied with the amount of jazz music being played all over the city.

Frank and Iorlando Jordano went to trial on May 21 for the murder of Mary Cortimiglia. The Gretna courtroom of Judge John H. Fleury was packed with friends and neighbours of both the victims and the accused.

The first witness was Coroner J. R. Fernandez, who went through the routine of describing the cause of Mary's death. In the front row sat Rosie Cortimiglia, dressed in black, tense and obviously near hysteria from the moment the proceedings began. Not far away sat her husband, but they did not look at each other or speak, for they had separated immediately after their disagreement over the identification of the Jordanos. Besumer was in the room, having been called because he was a survivor of a visisitation of the Axeman. He was summoned to the stand early in the trial. He said he could not identify either Frank or Iorlando Jordano as the man who had attacked him and Mrs Lowe. He could have identified no one, he concluded, because he had not seen the Axeman.

Rosie burst into tears when she took the stand, but she reiterated her identification, pointing to the men again. Some of the people in the courtroom hooted her and Judge Fleury had to ask for order and threaten to clear the room. Still whispering and angry noises could be heard from friends of the Jordanos.

Charles Cortimiglia once again flatly denied the man with whom he had struggled was either of the Jordanos. He could not understand his wife's insistance on placing the blame on them, he said. He had seen the man. He had not been Frank; he had not been Iorlando Jordano. No! It was all wrong!'

Defence Attorney William F. Byrnes summoned a stream of character witnesses for almost all of two days. All testified both the accused were respectable men of fine reputation in the town. Mrs Iorlando Jordano took the stand. She was nervous and tense and she was kept only a moment. She said, 'My old man was home all night and my boy was out with his girl.'

During the second day Andrew Ojeda, a *States* reporter, was called by the defence. He testified that he had interviewed Mrs Rosie Cortimiglia soon after she regained consciousness. At that time she had said, 'I don't know who killed Mary. I believe my husband did it!'

This caused another commotion in the courtroom. A woman screamed in the rear. People who must have been friends of the Jordanos applauded; friends of the Cortimiglias hooted and hissed. Again the judge had to threaten to clear the room. Charles Cortimiglia sprang to his feet, then sat down again.

The defence summoned Dr Jerome E. Landry, who had treated Mrs Cortimiglia. Did Mr Landry consider Rosie Cortimiglia's mental condition such that she would make a reliable witness? He stated that in his opinion it was. District Attorney Robert Rivarde summoned Dr C. V. Unsworth. Did he consider Rosie Cortimiglia sane? He did. The defence then brought Dr Joseph H. O'Hara to the stand and asked the same question. Dr O'Hara stated that in his opinion she was suffering from paranoia.

As the trial went on more and more people fought their way inside, bringing small children, babies, and box lunches. Several times a day Judge Fleury had to issue threats because of the bedlam in the room.

On the fourth day the defence issued new character witnesses for the Jordanos, one another Gretna grocer, Santo Vicari, who testified that someone had tried to chisel through a panel in one of his doors only two nights before the attack upon the Cortimiglias and at a time when he knew the wereabouts of the Jordanos. When Iorlando Jordano took the stand he said that he thought Rosie was not in her right mind. He had loved little Mary. She had called him 'Grampa.' Only a lunatic could imagine he would have harmed her. He had been as shocked and grieved by the cruel attack as if he had been the child's grandfather. He had run to the Cortimiglias' home in answer to Rosie's screams, then his son had come, later his wife. All they had tried to do was help. Now they were accused of the attack. His boy was a good boy.

Frank Jordano was on the stand two hours. He answered Mr Byrnes's questions in a strong clear voice and he did not waver under the district attorney's cross-examination. He had been at a dance with his girl that night. He had lied about that, yes, but it had been to protect his sweetheart and to keep her out of this. He had been home in bed a little while when he heard Rosie Cortimiglia's shrieks. He had followed his father to the Cortimiglias'. His father had been trying to help. His mother had bathed Charles Cortimiglia's face.

Sheriff L. H. Marrero testified that Rosie Cortimiglia had accused the Jordanos at once. There had been no hesitation on her part to do so, he said, no doubt in her mind. She had been positive.

On the fifth day the jury had the case in their hands. They were in consultation forty-five minutes. The Jordanos were found guilty. The courtroom resounded with angry shouts of protest.

A few days later sentence was passed. Frank Jordano was sentenced to be hanged. Iorlando Jordano was sentenced to life imprisonment.

The Axeman went back to work on August 10.

Early that morning a New Orleans grocer, Steve Boca, tottered out of his room in Elysian Fields Avenue and staggered down the alley next door to the entrance of the room where his friend Frank Genusa slept. When Genusa opened the door he caught Boca in his arms. The man's skull was split and he was drenched with blood. A Charity Hospital ambulance was called.

Boca recovered but he could tell nothing. He had awakened, seen the form over his bed and the blow coming. When he was conscious once more he had gone to Genusa for refuge. He could give no description of his attacker.

Police found all the usual signs of the Axeman's visit: the door panel was removed; the axe was in the kitchen; there had been no theft. Using a method that seemed usual with them, they then arrested Genusa. Boca himself defended him and he was released after a few days.

It was announced in the papers that William F. Byrnes was taking the Jordano case to the Supreme Court. It was said that most of the citizens of Gretna believed the father and son innocent, considered their conviction a miscarriage of justice. Rosie Cortimiglia was reported in hiding in New Orleans.

On September 2 William Carlson, a New Orleans druggist, heard a noise at his back door while he was reading late in the night. He got his revolver, called several times, then fired through the door. When he went outside no one was visible, but police rushing to the scene found what they believed were the marks of a chisel on one of the panels of the door.

On September 3, Sarah Laumann, a girl of nineteen, who lived alone, was found by neighbours who broke into her house when she failed to answer her bell. She was unconscious in her bed, several teeth knocked out, her head injured. A bloody axe was found beneath an open window. This time the Axeman had not used a door panel for entry. Was this another of his victims? It was thought so. Miss Laumann had a brain concussion, but recovered. She could recall nothing. Evidently the attack had taken place while she slept.

There were no more Axeman appearances until October 27. Early that morning Mrs Mike Pepitone, wife of a grocer, awoke to hear sounds of a struggle in the room next to her own, where her husband slept. She reached the door between the rooms just in time to see a man disappear through another exit to her husband's room. Mike Pepitone lay on his bed covered with blood. Blood splattered the wall and a picture of the Virgin above the bed. Mrs Pepitone shrieked and the six small children were awakened by their mother's screams. When the police arrived they found the signatures—the chiselled door panel was there and the axe lay on the back porch. Pepitone was dead. His wife could tell police little or nothing. She had seen the man, but her description was no less general than others they had received. It seemed as hopeless a case as the rest. By now they had a feeling that there was nothing to do but wait for the Axeman to strike again. Would it go on for ever?

But it did not go on for ever. No one knew it then, but it was over. Mike Pepitone was the last victim. Calls continued to reach the police from frightened citizens night after night, but all turned out to be scares and nothing more.

Throughout the months that passed and became a year a number of arrests were made, but in vain. New Orleans began to relax again and discussion of the Axeman cases became infrequent. Only the Jordanos languished in the Gretna jail, awaiting the new trial their attorney had promised them—or the hanging of Frank.

Then, on December 7, 1920, Rosie Cortimiglia appeared in the city room of the *Times-Picayune* and asked to speak to a reporter. Later accounts of her visit were highly dramatic. Rosie was utterly changed. Thin and ill, clothed in black, her face almost unrecognizable as that of the pretty young woman of a year before, she fell to her knees before the reporter assigned to interview her, screaming, 'I lied! I lied! God forgive me, I lied!'

Everyone in the offices gathered about. This was it, great, sensational copy.

Rosie remained on her knees, tears streaming down her cheeks. 'I lied,' she said. 'It was not the Jordanos who killed my baby. I did not know the man who attacked us.'

Helped to her feet and then to a chair, Rosie leaned forward, her hands clutching her now scarred and pitted cheeks.

'Look at me!' she cried. 'I have had smallpox. I have suffered

for my lie. I hated the Jordanos, but they did not kill Mary.
St. Joseph told me I must tell the truth no matter what it cost
me. You mustn't let them hang Frank!'

Rosie was taken to the Gretna jail at once. On the way she
babbled incessantly of her suffering and that she had lied. She
said Sheriff Marrero had forced the accusation of the Jordanos
from her. Then she said she had made it simply out of hatred
for the Jordanos.

In Frank Jordano's cell she threw herself to the floor and kissed
his feet, crying, 'Forgive me! Forgive me! You are innocent!'

Raising her head, she said, 'God has punished me more than
you. Look at my face! I have lost everything—my baby is dead,
my husband has left me, I have had smallpox. God has punished
me until I have suffered more than you!'

The Jordanos were soon free. There had been no real evidence
against them but the testimony of Rosie Cortimiglia, and so there
was no reason to hold them longer.

Frank Jordano visited the offices of the *Times-Picayune* on the
day of his release. He said he would marry his sweetheart at
once. He had always known God would not let him die for a
crime of which he was innocent. He stood at a window of an
office in the newspaper building and looked out into Lafayette
Square just across the street, where the sun was bright on the
greens. 'Ain't it fine!' he said. 'It all looks fine!'

But nothing had been solved about the Axeman crimes. It was
almost as if the cruel attacks had been committed by a
supernatural being, by a 'fell demon from the hottest hell,'
as the letter purporting to be from the Axeman had put it.
Many had been charged and all had been freed. No proof of
the criminal's identity existed. With the freeing of the Jordanos
the Axeman returned to the conversation of Orleanians and,
briefly, to the editorial pages of the newspapers. Who was the
Axeman? Had there been one Axeman or several—or many?
Had each attack been the work of a different person? Or all
of one?

Then, almost simultaneously with the confession of Rosie
Cortimiglia, New Orleans police learned of a strange occurrence

in Los Angeles. At first the news seemed almost unbelievable. Later they seem to have been anxious to believe it.

On December 2, 1920, an Orleanian named Joseph Mumfre was walking down a Los Angeles business street in the early afternoon. A 'woman in black and heavily veiled' stepped from the doorway of a building, a revolver in her hand, and emptied the gun into Mumfre. He fell dead on the sunny sidewalk and the woman stood over him, making no attempt to escape or even to move.

Taken to the police station, the woman in black said at first that her name was Mrs Esther Albano and refused to say why she had shot Mumfre. Days later she changed her mind and told Los Angeles detectives that she was Mrs Mike Pepitone, the widow of the last victim of the New Orleans Axeman.

'He was the Axeman,' she said. 'I saw him running from my husband's room. I believe he killed all those people.'

Immediately New Orleans police were drawn into the case. They knew a lot about Mumfre. He had a criminal record and had spent much time in prison. Dates were checked carefully. He had been released from a prison term in 1911, just before the slaughter of the Schiambras, of Cruti, and of Rosetti. Then he had gone back to jail and had been freed only a few weeks before the Maggio attack began the latest series of such crimes. In the lull between the end of August 1918 and March 1919 he had once more been in jail on a burglary charge; this was the span of time between the attack on Mrs Lowe and the others of that period and the next outbreak that began with the Cortimiglia family. It was known that Mumfre had left New Orleans just after the slaying of Mike Pepitone.

That much fitted. It was almost too perfect. Yet there was no proof that Mumfre was the Axeman. As the newspapers pointed out, the dates might be mere coincidence. It was thought he was the man who had attacked Mike Pepitone. All else remained a matter of conjecture.

Mrs Pepitone was tried in a Los Angeles court in April. She pleaded guilty and the proceedings were brief. Her attorney's plea was justifiable homicide. This did not hold, but there was much sympathy in her favour. She received a sentence of ten years, but in little more than three she was freed, and subsequently vanished from sight.

Were the Axeman mysteries solved?

Most Orleanians did not think so and do not think so yet. Of course no one will ever know now if Mumfre was guilty of all the crimes, of some of them, or only of the murder of Mike Pepitone. Probably the most general consensus of opinion in New Orleans, both among the police and the citizens, always remained that there was no one Axeman at all, but at least several.

Was the Mafia responsible?

Mumfre was not known to be a member of any such organization, but that in itself meant nothing. Membership was always secret. Yet, as Detective Dantonio said, the crimes never fitted the Mafia pattern. The Mafia did not attack anyone but Italians and they never murdered women. Besides it was thought the Mafia had passed from New Orleans for ever with the apprehension of the kidnappers of little Walter Lamana.

If the Mafia did still exist and the Italians who were attacked were its victims, what of Mrs Lowe, Mrs Schneider, Sarah Laumann, and the others who were not Italians yet had also been the Axeman's prey?

It is true that in all these cases the exact pattern of the Axeman's technique was not followed. Often one or more of his habits were omitted. He chose a different means of entry, for instance. Did this prove the assailant was not the same? Did it then mean that when the steps were followed carefully—when the door panel was chiselled out, the axe borrowed from the victim himself and left behind, and nothing was stolen—that the same murderer had called?

Was the following of that pattern indicative of the fact that the killer was a homicidal maniac, the 'Doctor Jekyll and Mr Hyde' of Detective Dantanio's theorizing? Adherence to such a pattern is thought to suggest the insane killer, who kills for pleasure and no other motive.

It must also be remembered that most of the victims were alike—Italian grocers. Did someone hate Italian grocers? Did someone want to kill all the Italian grocers in New Orleans—

perhaps in the world? If that is so, we come full circle again. What of the others who were not Italian grocers?

Confusion did much harm in all cases. Then there were the false accusations—of Harriet Lowe against Besumer, of Rosie Cortimiglia against the Jordanos. There were lots of lies, without a doubt. There was fear. Probably some of the victims and their relatives did not tell all they knew, either for fear that the Mafia still existed and that they might be further punished, or because they knew the Mafia did exist and that one of its members would extort reprisals from someone in their family if they talked.

All we know now is that the Axeman did vanish from New Orleans about the time Joseph Mumfre left the city and that he never returned after Mumfre was killed. It is extremely doubtful that anyone will ever know more. The Axeman came and struck and went away. The citizens of New Orleans can only hope that they never hear the sound of the chisel at work on the door panel again.

Little Mysteries No. 1

NGAIO MARSH

The Hand in the Sand

Truth may or may not be stranger than fiction. It is certainly less logical. Consider the affair of the severed hand at Christchurch, New Zealand, in 1885. Late in the afternoon of December 16 of that year, the sergeant on duty at the central police station was visited by two brothers and their respective small sons. They crowded into his office and, with an air of self-conscious achievement, slapped down a parcel, wrapped in newspaper, on his desk. Their name, they said, was Godfrey.

The sergeant unwrapped the parcel. He disclosed, nestling unattractively in folds of damp newsprint, a human hand. It was wrinkled and pallid like the hand of a laundress on washing day. On the third finger, left hand, was a gold ring.

The Godfreys, brothers and sons, made a joint announcement. 'That's Howard's hand,' they said virtually in unison, and then added, in explanation: 'Bit off by a shark.'

They looked significantly at a poster pasted on the wall of the police office. The poster gave a description of one Arthur Howard, and offered a reward for information as to his whereabouts. The Godfreys also produced an advertisement in a daily paper of two months earlier:

Fifty Pounds Reward. Arthur Howard, drowned at Sumner on Saturday last. Will be given for the recovery of the body or the first portion received thereof recognisable. Apply *Times* Office.

The Godfreys were ready to make a statement. They had spent the day, it seemed, at Taylor's Mistake, a lonely bay

24

not far from the seaside resort of Sumner, where Arthur Rannage Howard had been reported drowned on October 10. At about two o'clock in the afternoon, the Godfreys had seen the hand lying in the sand below high-water-mark.

Elisha, the elder brother, begged the sergeant to examine the ring. The sergeant drew it off the cold, wrinkled finger. On the inside were the initials A.H.

The Godfreys were sent away without a reward. From that moment they were kept under constant observation by the police.

A few days later, the sergeant called upon Mrs Sarah Howard. At sight of the severed hand, she cried out—in tears— that it was her husband's.

Later, a coroner's inquest was held on the hand. Three insurance companies were represented. If the hand was Howard's hand, they were due to pay out, on three life policies, sums amounting to £2,400. The policies had all been transferred into the name of Sarah Howard.

The circumstances of what the coroner called 'the alleged accident' were gone over at the inquest. On October 10, 1885, Arthur Howard, a railway workshop fitter, had walked from Christchurch to Sumner. On his way he fell in with other foot-sloggers, who remembered his clothes and his silver watch on a gold chain, and that he had said he meant to go for a swim at Sumner, where, in those days, the waters were shark-infested.

The next morning a small boy had found Howard's clothes and watch on the end of the pier at Sumner. A few days later insurance had been applied for and refused, the advertisement had been inserted in the paper and, as if in answer to the widow's prayer, the Godfreys, on December 16, had discovered the hand.

But there also appeared the report of no less than ten doctors who had examined the hand. The doctors, after the manner of experts, disagreed in detail, but, in substance, agreed upon three points.

(1) The hand had not lain long in the sea.

(2) Contrary to the suggestions of the brothers Godfrey, it

had not been bitten off by a shark, but had been severed by
the teeth of a hacksaw.

(3) The hand was that of a *woman*.

This damaging report was followed by a statement from an
engraver. The initials A. H. on the inside of the ring had
not been made by a professional's tool, said this report, but
had been scratched by some amateur.

The brothers Godfrey were called in and asked whether,
in view of the evidence, they would care to make a further
statement.

Elisha said that in his former statement he had withheld
certain information which he would now divulge. Elisha said
that he and his brother had been sitting on the sands when,
from behind a boulder, there appeared a man wearing blue
goggles and a red wig and saying: 'Come here! There's a man's
hand on the beach!'

This multi-coloured apparition led Elisha and his brother
to the hand, and Elisha had instantly declared: 'That's
Howard's hand.'

The goggles and wig had then said: 'Poor fellow . . . poor
fellow.'

'Why didn't you tell us before about this chap in the goggles
and wig?' The police asked.

'Because,' said Elisha, 'he begged me to promise I wouldn't
let anyone know he was there.'

Wearily, a sergeant shoved a copy of this amazing deposition
across to Elisha. 'If you've still got the nerve, sign it.'

The Godfreys read it through and angrily signed.

The police, in the execution of their duty, made routine
inquiries for information about a gentleman in blue goggles
and red wig in the vicinity of Sumner and Taylor's Mistake
on the day in question.

To their intense astonishment they found what they were
after.

Several persons came forward saying that they had been
accosted by this bizarre figure, who excitedly showed them
a paper with the Godfreys' name and address on it and told
them that the Godfreys had found Howard's hand.

The police stepped up their inquires and extended them the length and breadth of New Zealand. The result was a spate of information.

The wig and goggles had been seen on the night of the alleged drowning, going north in the ferry steamer. The man who wore them had been run in for insulting a woman, who had afterwards refused to press charges. He had taken jobs on various farms. Most strangely, he had appeared at dawn by the bedside of a fellow worker and had tried to persuade this man to open a grave with him. His name, he had said, was Watt. Finally, and most interesting of all, it appeared that on December 18 the goggles and wig had gone for a long walk with Mrs Sarah Howard.

Upon this information, the police arrested the Godfrey brothers and Mrs Howard on a charge of attempting to defraud the insurance companies.

But a more dramatic arrest was made in a drab suburb of the capital city. Here the police ran to earth a strange figure in clothes too big for him, wearing goggles and a red wig. It was the missing Arthur Howard.

At the trial, a very rattled jury found the Godfreys and Mrs Howard 'not guilty' on both counts and Howard guilty on the second count of attempting to obtain money by fraud.

So far, everything ties up quite neatly. What won't make sense is that Howard did his best to look like a disguised man, but came up with the most eye-catching 'disguise' imaginable.

No clue has ever been produced as to the owner of the hand. Of eight graves that were subsequently opened in search for the body to match the hand, none contained a dismembered body. But the hand had been hacked off by an amateur. Could Howard have bribed a dissecting-room janitor or enlisted the help of some undertaker's assistant? And if, as seemed certain, it was a woman's hand, where was the rest of the woman?

Then there is Howard's extraordinary masquerade. Why make himself so grotesquely conspicuous? Why blaze a trail all over the country? Did his project go a little to his head? Was he, after all, a victim of the artistic temperament?

The late Mr Justice Alper records that Howard's lawyer

told him he knew the answer. But soon after this the lawyer died.

I have often thought I would like to use this case as the basis for a detective story, but the material refuses to be tidied up into fiction form. I prefer it as it stands, with all its loose ends dangling. I am loath to concoct the answers. Let this paradoxical affair retain its incredible mystery. It is too good to be anything but true.

EDMUND PEARSON

The Green
Bicycle Case

There was a murder case in England which not only needed a
Sherlock Holmes but seemed as if it had been devised in solemn
conclave by Conan Doyle, Holmes, and Watson themselves. It
could be entitled The Mystery of the Green Bicycle; or, The
Curious Incident of the Dead Raven.

Unfortunately, there was no great hawk-faced detective from
Baker Street in it. Only, at the beginning, a local constable
named Hall. Perhaps that is why one of the men best informed
on this case says that it has 'considerable claims to be regarded
as the most fascinating murder mystery of the century.'

Bella Wright was twenty-one and lived with her father and
mother in a tiny place called Stoughton. This is within a mile
or two of the city of Leicester, and in that city she was employed
in a rubber factory.

She was a girl with good looks and good character, and was
engaged to be married to a stoker in the navy.

The country round about Leicester is full of little villages
connected by old Roman roads or by lanes with high hedges.
to the north is the famous hunting center of Melton Mowbray.

The lanes are charmingly picturesque and lonely, but were
made for a less motorized age. They are sometimes full of
surprises and excitement for the pedestrian or the cyclist. At a
curve he may suddenly be confronted by a flock of sheep just
as an enormous motor bus, brushing the hedge on either side,
comes up behind him.

Miss Wright was accustomed to go to and from her work on
a bicycle, and sometimes, in the long daylight hours of the
English summer evenings, to cycle from one hamlet to another

Ronald Light, accused of Bella Wright's murder

to do errands or to call on her friends. Her uncle, a man named Measures, lived in the village of Gaulby, three miles from her home.

She was on the late shift at the factory, and one Friday evening in July rode home from her work at eleven o'clock, going to bed soon after. Next day seems to have been a holiday, so she thoroughly made up her sleep, not getting up again till four o'clock Saturday afternoon. Then, after writing a few letters, she rode with them to the post office at Evington. Again she came home, but finally, at 6:30 P.M., set out on her cycle in the opposite direction, away from Leicester. Her mother had seen her start for Evington, and never after that saw her alive.

At nine twenty that evening (still daylight) a farmer named Cowell was driving cattle along the old Roman road called the Gartree Road or *Via Devana*. At a point about two miles from Gaulby, where the way is very lonely and the hedges, at that season, more than eight feet high, Cowell found Bella Wright lying dead in the road. Her head was covered with blood, and her cycle lay askew, with its front wheel pointed toward Stoughton—that is, toward home.

The farmer supposed that she had been killed by a fall or similar mischance. He placed her on the grass at the side of the road. Her body was still warm. Close to the spot where it was found—and this may be important—there was an opening in the hedge: a field gate which led into the grassy meadow beyond.

Constable Hall and a doctor came later, after it was dark. the doctor's hasty examination led to nothing more than a general impression that Miss Wright, being thrown from her bicycle, had fractured her skull on a stone. Cowell's statement as to his discovery of the body seems to have been accepted as quite satisfactory. This was due, I suppose, to his good reputation, since the only witnesses he could call to prove his story were his cows.

Miss Wright's body rested that night in a cottage nearby. Early next morning Constable Hall decided to make further investigation. He carefully examined the road; and seventeen feet from the bloodstain which marked the spot where the girl's head had lain in the dust he found a bullet, caliber .45, partly embedded in the road as if it had been stepped on or run over.

He made another exceedingly curious discovery: the gate which led into the field was painted white, and on the top bar were marks of claws—marks in blood. There were tracks of these claws, also in blood—twelve such sets of tracks, six going and six returning—leading from the body to the gate. In the field the constable came across a large bird with black plumage—dead. This bird was found to be gorged with blood. Indeed, that surfeit of blood was supposed to have killed it.

In England everybody is keen about birds and their habits. As soon as the Leicester police said that this bird was a raven, other folk flew to the defense of ravens. They said that (a) there were no ravens around Leicester; and (b) if there were, they had never been known to drink blood.

(The bird of which the Book of Job says 'Her young ones also suck up blood' is not the raven but the eagle.)

This creature, said the bird experts, must be a rook or a carrion crow.

Whatever bird it was, there are two schools of thought about it, and all the authorities, Messrs. H. R. Wakefield, Edward Marjoribanks, and others, have discussed it. There are the severely practical ones, who think that the raven (or rook) had no connection with the death of Bella Wright; and there are the romantics, who believe there was a very close connection.

At all events, how did the bird obtain so much blood from the poor dead or dying girl as to cause its own death? Was that really the cause of its death? How did it chance to be in that vicinity at the moment? Since the body is supposed to have been found within a few minutes of death, how was there time for all this gruesome feasting and tracking back and forth from road to gate?

Let's return now to Constable Hall and the bullet. He and the doctor made another examination of the body. After the blood had been washed from the girl's face, they found a small bullet wound one inch below the left eye, and another slightly larger, the mark of the exit of the bullet, in her hair. Thus it seemed that this heavy bullet had passed through the girl's head, yet had gone no farther than seventeen feet from her!

At all events, this was murder; and it was the duty of the

police to inquire where she had been, and with whom, between six thirty and nine twenty of that summer evening—daylight all the time.

At seven thirty she had ridden up to the cottage of her uncle, Mr Measures, in Gaulby. Calling on Measures at the time was his son-in-law, a man named Evans. So both of them were important witnesses to her arrival and departure. With her, when she came, was another cyclist, a young man. Bella Wright went in, leaving the young man outside. She remarked that he was 'a perfect stranger,' and added:

'Perhaps if I wait a while he will be gone.'

Yet she did not ask her uncle to drive him away, as if he were objectionable. And when, an hour or more later, they came out again, the young man was still there—having either returned or waited. This time, he greeted her, so said Measures and Evans, with the remark:

'Bella, you *have* been a long time. I thought you had gone the other way.'

Evans had some friendly conversation with the stranger about his bicycle. And finally, the girl and the young man pedalled away together—at, say, eight forty. Forty minutes later, or thereabouts, Cowell, the farmer, was finding Bella's dead body in the Gartree Road.

Now, as the reader has noticed, there are some contradictions in this. If the man was 'a perfect stranger,' how had he progressed so far as to call her Bella? This has been answered by the statement that what he really said was 'Hello!' And that certainly goes more reasonably with the rest of his remark.

How is this for an explanation of the incident? That he was a stranger, as she said, who had joined her as she rode along; and that, while his company was perfectly tolerable to her, she had offered a little tribute to strict propriety when she said to her uncle that if she waited around a bit he would go away. Girls do not, today—if they ever did—scream and say, 'Sir, I have never met you!' when a presentable stranger starts conversation, while riding along a country road. They may welcome it, or they may simply bear it, not wishing to make a fuss, and knowing that, in most cases, the man will soon go away without becoming an annoyance.

Measures and Evans had had a good look at this man and his cycle, and so in a few days the police were offering a reward for a man of thirty-five, about five feet seven to nine inches in height, hair turning grey, and with rather a high-pitched voice. They gave a description of his clothes and various other particulars.

The notable thing was that he rode *a green bicycle*.

And for the next few months each man in Leicestershire unfortunate enough to own a green bicycle wished to heaven that he had never bought it. After he had satisfied the police as to where he had been on that July evening, he had to encounter the jeering remarks of his friends as to his diversions and his murderous disposition.

But the man really sought—the last man alive with Miss Wright—was not so easily discovered. Scotland Yard had a try at it, but could do nothing with the murder, the missing green bicycle, or the dead raven.

Half a year went by, and Bella Wright had long been lying in the churchyard, past which she rode that evening. Then, one day in February, something happened: a most peculiar chance, which, for a time, probably revived faith in the ancient falsehood, 'Murder will out.'

A canal boat was passing through Leicester, carrying a load of coal to the rubber works where the dead girl had been employed. A boatman named Whitehouse was idly watching his towrope when he saw it slacken down into the water and then tighten. As it became taught it brought up part of a bicycle, which hung in plain sight for a moment—long enough to change the whole current of a man's life—then slipped back into the water. Whitehouse had not forgotten all those police advertisements and the reward: he came back next day and dragged the canal. He hauled up the bicycle frame again, and, as he hoped, it was green.

The police were soon busy—dragging the canal for other interesting objects and examining the one the boatman had found. From the canal they fished other parts of the machine; also a revolver holster with twelve ball and seven blank cartridges in it.

The green bicycle was of a special model, made in

Birmingham, and from it the name and number plate and other identifying marks had carefully been removed. But, in an obscure place, was found the number 103,648—and this was the number of a bicycle sold years before to a Mr Ronald Vivian Light.

This gentleman was found teaching mathematics at a school in Cheltenham. He was a good-looking, rather earnest man; a little prematurely old in appearance, possibly as a result of his experiences in the war. He was a Rugby School boy; a civil engineer, who had served four years in France, part of the time with an officer's commission. Shell-shocked and slightly deaf since the great German attack in 1918, he had been discharged in 1919. For about a year thereafter (the year 1919, in the summer of which Miss Wright was killed) he had been out of work and living in Leicester with his mother. His present position dated only from January, 1920, the month before the discovery of the green bicycle.

Invited by a police inspector to explain how the fragments of his bicycle happened to be at the bottom of the canal, Mr Light proceeded to tell a pack of lies. He said he had never owned a green bicycle; he had never seen Bella Wright; he had never been in the village of Gaulby—certainly not on that crucial evening last July.

Naturally, there was nothing to do but arrest him—especially as Bella's uncle, Mr Measures, and Evans also, positively identified him as the mysterious man who rode away with her so shortly before the murder. And two little girls, Muriel Nunney, aged fourteen, and Valeria Caven, twelve, believed they recognized him as a man who had followed and frightened them, about five thirty on the day of the murder, and in the same vicinity. They remembered this many months after the event. Some of the cartridges, by the way, found in the holster suspiciously near the sunken bicycle, had bullets like the one found in the road. But of course Mr Light denied the holster as firmly as he did all the other relics.

Now, here was a beautiful case of circumstantial evidence. The net was drawn tight around the poor young man, ·who would, of course, be convicted—as in the detective novels.

About three months after his arrest, Ronald Light was placed on trial. The Attorney General stated the case against the prisoner in all its deadly detail. He began to prove by his witnesses that the bicycle belonged to Light; that he was with the girl shortly before her death; that he had concealed evidence, and lied about it, over and over again.

In the middle of this testimony, the prisoner's counsel quietly interrupted. This was Sir Edward Marshall Hall—the famous defender of accused persons, for whom everybody sent in time of great trouble. Sir Edward courteously intimated that the learned Attorney General was going to unnecessary pains. He need not prove that the bicycle belonged to the prisoner; they admitted it. He need not prove that his client rode up to Mr Measures's house that evening, with Bella Wright; they admitted that. Most of the Crown witnesses would not be cross-examined by the defense; only one or two points did they deny.

The Attorney General and the police were probably somewhat disgusted. Here was the defense conceding three quarters of the case at the outset. What about the other quarter?

Sir Edward denied, and his client would deny, that his client had used the name 'Bella.' He had said 'Hello.' And Sir Edward took in hand, very kindly and gently, the two little girls, who said they had met Ronald Light near the scene of the murder, and who described him going about the lanes seeking to molest unprotected damsels.

When he got through with Miss Muriel and Miss Valieria, they no longer looked like two little angels of justice, but rather more like two busy little brats who, feeding for months on sensational newspapers and pictures, had suddenly begun to remember something which *might* have happened to them on some day or other—but which they obligingly fixed for a *certain* day, after the police had suggested the date.

At the end of the trial the judge advised the jury not to trouble themselves at all with the testimony of Miss Muriel and Miss Valeria.

When he began to present his case, Sir Edward played his ace. He called the prisoner to the witness stand. Ronald Light was serious, calm, and dignified. He was what we call 'a shell-shocked veteran,' who had, moreover, become partially deaf as the result of an exploding shell. There was no attempt to emphasize Light's wartime services, except in so far as his shattered nerves might explain some of his conduct.

Light now testified that he had never had a revolver or pistol since he had been sent home from France on a stretcher. On the evening of the murder he left home at about five forty-five for a bicycle ride, expecting to return at eight o'clock. He rode through Gaulby, a district he did not know very well, and at six forty-five he was near a place called Little Stretton. He did not see the two small girls anywhere. As it was still early, he turned about to go home by the long route, and this led him again toward Gaulby.

He met a girl, who was a stranger to him, standing at the roadside examining her bicycle. She asked if he had a wrench. He had not, but he looked at the front wheel, which seemed merely to wobble a little. There was nothing he could do for it. They rode on together, chattering as they went. She said that she was going to see some friends in Gaulby, and added:

'I shall only be ten minutes or a quarter of an hour.'

Light then testified:

'I took that as a sort of suggestion that I should wait and we should ride back together. I waited for ten minutes or more, then walked my machine up the hill to the church. Here I got on the bicycle to ride back to Leicester, when I found the rear tyre flat. I pumped it up, and sat down on a gate; but the tyre went down again and I had to mend the puncture. By this time it was eight fifteen, and I knew I was late anyhow. I thought I would ride back and see if this girl had come out. She came out the gate as I rode along, and I said, ''Hello, you've been a long time. I thought you'd gone the other way.'' I talked with Evans, and all that he says is correct, except that I did not say ''Bella.'' '

He further testified that they rode together for only about ten minutes; that he had still more trouble with his tyre; and that the girl left him at a crossroads. He kept on the upper or more direct road; she took the lower, the Gartree Road. He had to walk nearly all the way home and did not arrive till nearly ten. On the following Tuesday he heard of the death. He read the description of Bella Wright and of his own bicycle and came to the conclusion that he was the man wanted.

He was utterly terrified. Both for his own sake and for his mother's, who was an invalid, he wanted to escape the horror of an investigation, perhaps a trial. Foolishly, as he now admitted, he refrained from going to the police at once, and drifted into a policy of silence, then of concealment, and finally of falsehood. He never went out on the green bicycle again, but hid it and at last broke it up and threw it (together with the holster) into the canal. He now frankly admitted all the lies told when the police came to him.

'I see now, of course,' he said to the judge, 'that I did the wrong thing.'

He must have been astounded again when the evidence rose against him from the canal. It is recorded that he had looked at this water from his cell, while he was awaiting trial, and exclaimed:

'Damn and blast that canal!'

Ronald Light's story, as he now told it, could not be contradicted or disproved in any detail. Five hours of cross-examination failed to trip him once.

His lawyer, who was himself an expert on firearms, sharply questioned the Crown witnesses who testified on technical points: about the wound, and about the bullet. Sir Edward maintained that such a heavy bullet, fired, as they thought, from a distance of seven feet, would have blown out the back of the skull. It was absurd that it should not have travelled farther. The only explanation would be that she was shot as she lay on the ground, and even this was not wholly satisfactory.

That it was the same caliber as bullets found in Light's holster meant nothing: bullets like this one had recently been made in England by the thousand million. Sir Edward suggested that the bullet found in the road might not be the fatal one at all, and that she might have been killed by an accidental shot fired from the neighbouring field. It could be a rifle bullet.

No one had appeared who could testify that Light and the girl were together on the Gartree Road; he was never placed at or even very near the scene of the crime.

The Crown had shown no motive. It was not a lovers' quarrel;

the two were strangers. There had been no sexual assault. Why should Light have shot her?

The defense, of course, slid over the fact that certain kinds of murders, particularly of women and children, are committed for no apparent motive whatever.

The judge, in his charge, seemed rather to lean to the side of the defense. The jury argued the case for three hours, standing nine to three in favour of the prisoner. Then the three were won over, and they reported Ronald Light 'not guilty.' The verdict was cheered.

But who did kill Bella Wright? Probably we shall never know. Probably, also, we shall never know whether we ourselves, if innocent, but in a predicament like that of the rider of the green bicycle, would behave any better.

Now to come back to our raven. A gentleman named Trueman Humphries went down to the Gartree Road, took pictures, and looked about. At the end he wrote, for the *Strand*, an entertaining bit of fiction. He imagines a scientific detective challenged to solve the mystery of the green bicycle. This detective organizes, in the neighbourhood of Gaulby and Little Stretton, a shooting match. A prize is offered and all the boys and men in the region are drawn in.

There are various targets: disappearing images of deer, running rabbits, or the like. All of them are sprung upon the contestants suddenly and as a complete surprise. Before one of these sportsmen—a young lad— as he lies on the ground, firing, there rises what seems to be a dark hedge cut in the middle by a white gate. And on this gate sits a raven!

The boy tumbles over in a faint. When he comes to, he is ready to make his confession. He was in the field near the Gartree Road that July evening. He had sighted a bird of some kind on the white gate. He lay behind a sheep trough two or three hundred yards away (there is really such a trough) and fired. He killed the raven—but the bullet also killed the girl who rode by the gate at that moment.

Far-fetched? Very likely. But it's not unworthy of the great Sherlock!

CRAIG RICE

Death of the
Black Dahlia

Beth Short was known as the Black Dahlia. Why? Perhaps because of the lovely hair that fell over her shouldrs. Perhaps because of her love for the black dresses she wore so well. Or perhaps because a fortune-teller might have picked out a card that said: 'The colour for you is—black!'

Her story has always fascinated me—not only because I was so intimately connected with it from the time the city editor of the Los Angeles *Herald Express* called and said: 'This one is for you,' not only because I saw her tortured and mutilated body— but because of the strange and mysterious character of the Black Dahlia herself.

It was an anonymous telephone call that sent Los Angeles police to a vacant lot near the corner of Crenshaw and Santa Barbara Boulevards, where two officers found the nude body of a young girl, cut in two at the waist, and bound with rope. A beautiful girl, with black hair and grey-green eyes.

There was nothing, not even a scrap of clothing, to provide a clue to her identity, let alone the identity of her murderer. The Los Angeles *Examiner* arranged for her finger-prints to be sent by sound photo to the F.B.I. in Washington. If she had ever worked in a defence plant, or been in trouble with the law, her prints would be on file. The report came back quickly. The murdered girl was Elizabeth Short, last known address Santa Barbara, California. Born July 29, 1924, in Hyde Park, Massachusetts.

The call went out for information on Elizabeth Short, twenty-two, dark hair, eyes green, five foot three. The hunt for the Black Dahlia slayer had begun.

It was a Long Beach druggist who introduced Beth Short's nickname into the case. 'She'd come into our drugstore frequently,' she said. 'She'd usually wear a black two-piece beach costume which left her midriff bare, or she'd wear black lacy things. Her hair was jet-black. She was popular with the men who came in here, and they got to calling her the Black Dahlia.'

Police questioned everyone who had been in her company, or even remembered seeing her, but the results were baffling. Many people had known Beth Short—but nobody knew very much about her.

The crime itself was an unusually hideous one. Beth Short had been tortured before death put an end to her agony. The torturer had then severed the body at the waist, bound it with ropes, and transported it to where it had been found.

It was learned that Beth Short—penniless and homeless—recently had spent a month at the home of a girl friend in San Diego, and that from there she left to meet a former bandsman in the Air Force who was known only as 'Red'.

In two days' time, Red was in police custody. He readily admitted that he knew Beth Short and sometimes called her the Black Dahlia, but without further evidence he was exonerated as a suspect.

Several people had seen and talked with Beth in the days before her death. All told the same story—that the girl was a lost soul, obviously sick in heart and mind, wandering about town aimlessly, and scared of something she refused to talk about.

Something of Beth's life was told in letters that police found tucked away in her luggage located at a bus station in Los Angeles. These were love letters, neatly tied in ribbon, and revealing a story of men, heart-break, more men, and more heart-break.

A sense of guilt which plagued Beth's unfaithful heart revealed itself in letters which she wrote but never mailed. Desperation was their keynote. They revealed her as a beautiful, passionate girl, desperate for love and for protection.

In the days after the discovery of the Black Dahlia's tortured and mutilated body, tips poured in.

A girl who worked as a dancer in Hollywood night spots said she saw Beth Short sitting alone in the 'Gay Way' bar on South Main Street six days before she was murdered. Another girl acquaintance repeated that she saw her that same night, sitting in the lobby of an apartment hotel embracing a young man 'dressed like a petrol-station attendant'. The head bar-tender at a Hollywood Boulevard bar said he saw her five days before she died in the company of two girls of 'dubious reputation', looking 'seedy, as if she had slept in her clothes'.

Four days before the Black Dahlia's death, a South Main Street bar-tender had seen her and an unidentified blonde girl in an argument with two sailors. The next morning, another tip revealed, she took a room with an unidentified man in an East Washington Boulevard hotel. That evening she was seen alone again by the same dancer who had seen her before, and in the same bar, the 'Gay Way'.

The day before the murder, a bus-driver saw the Black Dahlia board his bus in the Santa Barbara bus terminal and alight at the Los Angeles terminal. On the same day, late in the afternoon, she was in a café in San Diego with a man dressed in a green suit.

There the trail ended. Nobody seemed to know where the Black Dahlia was between that afternoon and the next morning—January 15, 1947—when her dismembered body was found in the vacant lot.

The police recalled that Beth Short had failed to pick up her bags at the bus station during the last five days of her life. Had she been prevented from doing so? Had she been held prisoner during those days, free to move around only as long as she was under guard or the surveillance of others?

Investigation of this angle was hardly under way when an anonymous letter seemed to crack the case wide open. Soaked in petrol and addressed with lettering clipped from newspapers, it was found to contain a note reading: 'Here is Dahlia's belongings. Letter to follow.'

In the envelope police found a black address-book known to have been carried by the murdered girl, a newspaper clipping telling of the marriage of a former sweetheart, Beth Short's birth certificate, and a baggage claim check for the suitcases the police already had found and examined. There was no doubt that these things had been taken out of the Black Dahlia's purse.

The following day another letter came. It read: 'Here it is. Turning in Wed., Jan. 29, 10 a.m. Have had my fun at police— Black Dahlia Avenger.'

Authorities knew that the Avenger might be a prankster. On the other hand, it is not unusual for the psychotic killer to taunt the police with such notes and eventually give himself up; and in this case vengeance might well have been the motive, because it was known that the Black Dahlia lived in constant fear.

It was obvious that the Avenger had access to Beth's purse, so if he was not the actual killer, he was someone who could throw some much-needed light on the case. Would he give himself up Wednesday as he had promised?

On Tuesday night a man giving his name as Voorhees gave himself up because he couldn't 'stand it any longer' and signed a one-line confession. In twenty-four hours his 'confession' was discredited as the fantasy of a mentally sick man. He could never have known Beth Short. His was not the first 'confession' nor the last, all the work of cranks.

As for the Avenger, apart from a last note saying: 'Have changed my mind', that was the last anybody ever heard about him. All other leads have proved equally fruitless.

Who killed Beth Short, the Black Dahlia? The police are still working to find out. They will never give up. I don't know, either, but I have made some interesting deductions.

Everybody knows that the body of Elizabeth Short was cut in two at the waist—but what everybody does *not* know is that the job was done with precision and every evidence of professional skill.

Elizabeth Short was only five feet three inches in height, and weighed no more than 105 pounds. Why did the killer bisect the body? For more convenience in transporting it?

If the killer was a man, he would have had little difficulty in carrying the body. But suppose he were an under-sized man— a cripple—or a woman?

It seems likely that the mad killer must have been a doctor, a trained nurse, an undertaker or an undertaker's assistant.

Of the four, I would bet on one of the last two. Here are my reasons. A doctor's office or even a private hospital is not a handy place to mutilate a girl and then cut her body in half. Patients, nurses, anybody can drop in. On the other hand, an undertaking parlour offers privacy.

I believe that someone working in an undertaking parlour tortured and killed the Black Dahlia.

ERLE STANLEY GARDNER

The Case of the
Movie Murder

To those who are familiar with the psychology of Southern California, it will come as no surprise that when this section came to make its contribution to classic murder mysteries, it should bring forth a case which Hollywood itself could only label 'super-colossal.'

The William Desmond Taylor case runs true to form throughout. Not only is the main thread of the plot so weird and bizarre as to challenge the credulity of the reader, but it is to be noted that it had its inception at a time when at least one of the witnesses described the weather as 'unusual.'

On the night of February 1, 1922, William Desmond Taylor was seated in a rather modest, two-story, bungalow-court residence eating dinner. The hour was approximately 6:30.

At this particular time, there was much in vogue in Los Angeles the type of construction known as the 'bungalow court.' Bungalows were constructed side by side, not fronting on the street but on a walk or driveway which ran the length of a deep lot. In this way it was possible to crowd productive rentals on every inch of a relatively deep lot.

The bungalows in the court where William Desmond Taylor lived had been largely rented by people who were connected with the motion-picture industry. While newspaper accounts present some conflict as to the exact location of some of the neighbouring tenants, it would seem from a reading at this late date that Taylor's bungalow was a double, and in the other side of this bungalow lived Edna Purviance, at the time Charlie Chaplin's leading lady. The bungalow opposite was occupied by Mr and Mrs Douglas MacLean.

45

Taylor's dedication reads: 'Yours, now and forever, Mary...

It was a period of transition in the picture industry. The early days, when pictures floundered around with train robbers and bandits, had given way to the adaptation of drama. It was the era of increasing salaries, of the silent film with its dramatic subtitles. One of those most frequently used at the time has become immortalized, *Came the Dawn of a New Day*. This subtitle was usually shown with a background of drifting clouds, gradually lighting up, and accompanied by appropriate inspirational music on piano or organ.

William Desmond Taylor, while an important director, was working for what would today be considered a mere stipend in the industry; but at that time, he was in the big-money group.

The income tax of the period was at the rate of four per cent and there were, even then, mumblings and grumblings on the manner in which the tax hogs were gathering around the trough in an orgy of wasteful spending. The point is mentioned because it appears that Taylor was in the process of performing a very disagreeable task. He was making out his income tax for the year 1921. His partially finished statement showed an income of $37,000.

Henry Peavey, Taylor's coloured houseman, announced that dinner was served, and the motion-picture director left his income-tax work to go to the table where a simple meal was served to a lonely bachelor.

This was the period in Hollywood's development when it was unnecessary for the famous to stroll into the night spots and be photographed by reporters for the fan magazines.

Here was an important director dining alone at 6:30 in a relatively small bungalow court. The furnishings, however, were in exquisite taste. The bookcases were filled with books which were well chosen and well read. Such art objects as were in the room were those which could only have been selected by a connoisseur. These surroundings give us a clue to the man's character. They indicate a modest, simple man with a large income living a simple, unassuming life.

So far there has been nothing to indicate that the life of this man is other than an open book. His associates see in him a grave, dignified, thoughtful executive. Yet he has vision and

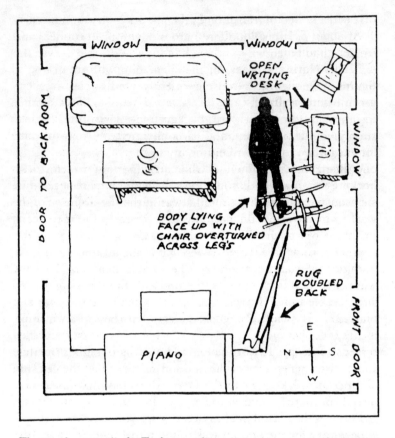

The murder scene in the Taylor townhouse

imagination. His face lights up with a kindly smile. He is a
practical philosopher with something big-brotherly in his grave
manner.

Adela Rogers St. John, one of the most articulate of the
associates of film celebrities, and a famous writer in her own right,
was later to say of him: 'William D. Taylor was the sort of man
that revived your faith in the sex. . . . He had a breadth of vision
and a businesslike understanding of what the screen needed.'

So here is a dignified, magnetic executive sitting down to
dinner on this cold February night, his income-tax statement

on his desk, his mind occupied with the destiny of the screen.

At about 6:45, Mabel Normand was driven up to the court by her chauffeur.

Mabel Normand was one of the most glamorous, colourful figures of the silent screen. It needs only a glance at the publicity given her to realize something of her dynamic character. For instance, it was mentioned at a somewhat later date that she simply couldn't be bothered to set her watch backward and forward when, on a transcontinental train trip, she passed from one time zone to another. So she carried several watches with her, presumably set according to the different time zones. When she passed from one time zone into another, she disposed of the watch which was no longer accurate by the simple expedient of tossing it out of the window.

Under cold and careful appraisal, this story bears the unmistakable stamp of the press agent. Mabel Normand certainly was not travelling by day coach. Pullman windows of the period were double and of heavy glass. This was before air conditioning on trains and, while the windows were frequently raised a few inches at the bottom, there were permanent, heavy, close-meshed screens to keep out as much of the dust as possible. But this watch-throwing episode is indicative of the period, of the thinking of the people, and of the star. The mere fact that this would have been considered good publicity at the time is interesting. Nowadays, if a star had the habit of tossing watches out of a train window merely because she couldn't be bothered to set the hands forward or back, her public relations men would tear their hair in agony lest the idiosyncrasy be discovered and publicized. But in those days this was all a part of the temperament which one associated with a great actress.

On this night of February 1, 1922, Mabel Normand had been sitting in the back of her chauffeur-driven car eating peanuts and dropping the shells on the floor. As she left the car to call on Taylor, she instructed her chauffeur to clean up the car. Then she hurried through the cold chill of the early evening to the rear of the court and the bungalow occupied by the director.

Taylor was engaged in talking over the telephone when Mabel Normand was admitted by the houseman.

Mabel Normand visited with Taylor while the houseman served dessert to the director. Then apparently the house-man went out to visit with Miss Normand's chauffeur, perhaps helping him to clean up the peanuts. His recollection is that he left around 7:30 and when he left, Miss Normand and Taylor were *drinking cocktails*.

There is an almost pastoral simplicity about the scene. The motion-picture director, having had his dessert served at around seven o'clock, is now engaged in drinking cocktails with Mabel Normand, who apparently must have dined before she arrived. Therefore the Normand stomach must have contained dinner, peanuts, and cocktail, ingested in that order. William Desmond Taylor, progressing from dinner to cocktails was spared the ordeal of the peanuts.

Now it appears that Taylor was very anxious that Mabel Normand should read a book. In some unaccountable manner an impression seems to have been created that this book was by Freud. There were, it seems, two books that Taylor was very anxious Miss Normand should read, and he had sent one of them over to her house that day. But the other was one for which he had asked her to call in person. On February 11th the newspapers were to contain a statement by Mabel Normand that this book was *Rosmundy* by Ethel M. Dell, and she is at a loss to understand how a rumour started that this was a book of Freud's.

Did Miss Normand and Taylor discuss this book while they were chatting in the bungalow? It is worthy of note that while Taylor had sent one book over to Mabel Normand's apartment that day, he had asked her to call for this book in person. Why?

And it was to develop, moreover, that when she left him at 7:45 it was understood he was to telephone her at nine o'clock and find out how she liked the book. Again, why?

Be that as it may, at 7:45 Mabel Normand says she left Taylor alone in his bungalow, and it is to be noted that according to the statements of both Mabel Normand and her chauffeur, Taylor escorted Miss Normand out to her car, a gallant gesture on the part of the director which may have cost him his life; for one of the police theories was that he left the door of his bungalow open while he was escorting Miss Normand and that a shadowy figure who had been lurking in the alley took advantage of this opportunity to slip into Taylor's little bungalow.

Taylor, blissfully unconscious of what was so soon to happen, stood at the curb, watched the car drive away, turned and walked back to keep his appointment with death.

On the morning of February 2, 1922, Henry Peavey, the houseman, came to the house at 7.30 A.M. ready to begin his day's work.

He opened the door and stood petrified at what he saw. The body of William Demond Taylor lay stretched out on the floor, lying on its back with the feet toward the door. Over the legs was a chair which had overturned.

Henry Peavey ran out of the door, screaming that Mr Taylor was dead. In his own words, 'I turned and run out and yelled. And then I yelled some more.'

E.C. Jeessurum, the proprietor of the bungalow court, responded to the alarm.

What happened after that is very much of a blur. Apparently, from the first newspaper reports, the police were promptly notified and imediately took charge in a routine manner. A physician appeared and diagnosed the death as from natural causes—apparently a hemorrhage of the stomach. The coroner's office put in an appearance, and it was then found that Taylor had been shot by a .38 caliber revolver. The bullet, of ancient vintage and obsolete design, had entered the left side at about the place where the left elbow would have rested if the hands were hung normally at the side. The bullet had travelled upward until it lodged in the right-hand side of the neck just below the skin.

Later on, two peculiar points were noticed. One, that the body was lying neatly 'laid out,' the limbs stretched out straight, the tie, collar, cuffs unrumpled—what was, apparently, a most unusual position for a corpse. There never was any explanation of this, if we can discount the statement of one of the officers, who said the deceased may have done this 'in his death struggles.'

The second point, which developed a little later, was that the holes made by the bullet in the coat and vest did not match up.

With the arms at the sides, the hole in the coat was considerably lower than the hole in the vest; and it was only when the left elbow was raised that the bullet holes came into juxtaposition.

It was because of this fact that the police promptly advanced the theory which, for the most part, they seem to have stuck with through thick and thin, that there was something in the nature of a holdup connected with the crime and preliminary to it, and that Taylor was standing with his hands up at the time he was shot.

Apparently the bullet was fired from a weapon held within a very few inches of the body.

Searching Taylor's body, police found jewellery and money of over two thousand dollars in value. There were seventy-eight dollars in cash in his pocket, a two-carat diamond ring on his finger, and a platinum watch on his body. The watch had stopped at 7:21; and nearly three weeks after the murder, the police suddenly decided this might be a clue. On February 21st they rushed the watch to a jeweller to find out whether it had run down or had stopped because of the concussion of the fall of the body. The newspapers blazoned this shrewd but somewhat tardy idea of the police to the public.

On the twenty-second they carried the answer. The watch had run down.

On the desk was an open checkbook. Near-by was a pen. Also there was the half-completed income-tax blank previously mentioned.

Edna Purviance, Charlie Chaplin's leading lady, and apparently a close friend of Mabel Normand's, stated that while she knew William Desmond Taylor, the acquaintance was a casual, nodding acquaintance and that was all. She had noticed that there was a light on in the Taylor side of the bungalow when she returned home somewhere around midnight on the night of the murder.

At sometime between 8:00 and 8:15 that evening Douglas MacLean, who occupied bungalow 406-B (Taylor occupied 404-B), noticing the 'unusual' cold, went upstairs to get an electric stove. While there, he heard what he refers to as a 'shattering report,' muffled, yet penetrating to every corner of the room.

His wife went to the door of 406-B and was just in time to see a figure emerge into the light from the Taylor bungalow. This figure paused on the porch, turned back toward the oblong of light from the half-opened door and stepped inside briefly, as though to say some word of farewell. He was smiling. Then he stepped back to the porch, quietly and normally closed the door, walked directly toward Mrs MacLean for a few steps until he came to the opening between the houses, then turned, walked down between the two houses and vanished into the night.

In her first statement, Mrs MacLean described this figure as being that of a man with a cap, and a muffler around his neck. she couldn't be absolutely certain whether the man did or did not wear an overcoat. She was, however, sure of the cap. Then later on, she said that the figure *might* have been that of a woman instead of a man. A woman dressed in man's clothing.

At approximately 7:55 P.M., however, Howard Fellows, who was driving Taylor's automobile and who had been told to get in touch with Mr Taylor that evening, called him on the telephone and received no answer. At 8:15 he went to the Taylor bungalow, rang the doorbell, and got no response. On the other hand, he stated that he had telephoned Taylor two or three times before 7:30 in the evening and had received no reply.

He put up Taylor's automobile for the night and walked home. He was wearing a cap and a raincoat and so far as he is concerned, he is satisfied he is the man Mrs MacLean saw. But apparently he did not open the door nor was the door open when he was standing on the porch. So, if he was the man Mrs MacLean saw, then she must be mistaken in her recollection of what the man did. Incidentally, it is to be noted that Mrs MacLean apparently is not the type to be hypnotized by her own recollection. It was exceedingly cold and there is probably no doubt but what the figure wore an overcoat. A less scrupulous witness would have said she saw an overcoat. A less painstaking one would have visualized the fact that the man must have worn an overcoat, and so gradually have built up the conviction that he was wearing one. Not so Mrs MacLean. She is sure of the

cap, she is fairly sure of the muffler, and there she stops being
sure. A most commendable sign. But bear in mind that she is
certain that she saw this figure on the porch step back to the lighted
doorway. She saw him step out and 'quietly and normally' close
the door.

There were the usual stories of puzzling clues. Mysterious
figures slithered through the pages of the newspapers. A streetcar
conductor said a man who answered the description given by
Mrs MacLean had boarded a car on Maryland Street, at either
7:54 or 8:27 the night of the murder. He was about five feet
ten inches, fairly well dressed, weighed about a hundred and
sixty-five, had a cap of light colour, and the conductor remembers
that he wore something tan. He can't remember where the man
left the car. There was also a man who insisted that shortly before
the murder he had been stopped on the street by someone who
asked first for a fictitious address and then asked to know where
William Desmond Taylor lived. The information was given.
There were two men at a service station who remembered that
shortly before six o'clock a man answering the description of
the man seen by Mrs Douglas MacLean had stopped at the
service station and inquired where W. D. Taylor lived. The man
was described as about twenty-six or twenty-seven, a hundred
and sixty-five pounds, with dark suit and a light hat or cap. They
directed him to the bungalow court and this was the last they
saw of him.

A Mrs C. F. Reddick, a neighbour, stated she was awakened
by a shot or a backfire between one and two o'clock in the
morning. Police fixed the time of death as between 7:40 and 8:15
P.M., Wednesday, February first.

At nine o'clock Mabel Normand had been lying in bed with
her book, waiting in vain for William Desmond Taylor to call.

He had then been dead for approximately an hour.

It is to be noted that in the room where the body was found
were three framed pictures of Mabel Normand. On February
18th there was publicity given to a locket with a photograph of
Mabel Normand and bearing the inscrpition, 'To my dearest.'

For a while the investigation followed routine lines. There was
some indication that a mysterious man had stood back of the

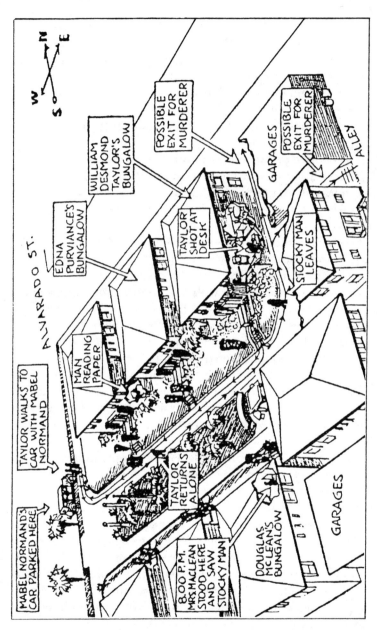

Taylor's bungalow plan

Taylor bungalow waiting for an opportunity to slip in through
the door. He was apparently someone who had reason to believe
that by waiting in that position an opportunity would present
itself—perhaps someone who knew that Taylor had or was going
to have a woman visitor and that he would quite probably escort
this woman out to her automobile. In any event, there was a
litter of cigarette stubs indicating that someone had stood there
waiting for some little time.

It is reported that there was a mysterious handkerchief bearing
the letter 'S' lying near the body. One of the police detectives
picked this up and rather casually left it lying on a table. When
he looked for it again, it had disappeared, and apparently has
never been heard of since.

This ushers in the now-you-see-it-now-you-don't phase of the
case. With bland, disarming casualness, 'authorities' and others
toss off statements which make the reader dizzy.

We may as well begin with the Mabel Normand letters.
Apparently Mabel Normand's first knowledge of what had
happened was when Edna Purviance (who, it will be
remembered, occupied the other side of the William Desmond
Taylor bungalow) telephoned her on the morning of February
second and told her that Taylor was dead. Miss Normand seems
to have gone directly to the bungalow and asked for certain letters
and telegrams which she had sent to Taylor. She was very anxious
to have them returned to her and said that she knew exactly where
they were.

From a study of the newspapers it is not always easy to
reconstruct exactly what happened and the order in which it
happened. In the *Los Angeles Examiner* of February 10, 1922, it
is stated that when Peavey found Taylor's body, the first person
he telephoned was Charles Eyton, manager of the Lasky Studios.
Eyton and other picture people seem to have been on the scene
nearly an hour before the police arrived. Some eight days after
the murder a writer was to state boldly in the press, 'The mad
effort being made by the powers in the Hollywood motion picture
colony to block the investigation will avail them nothing now
that Woolwine has assumed command.' Woolwine, it is to be
noted, was at the time the district attorney.

The day before that statement, a newspaper had printed that, 'It is suspected that both of them [picture actresses] are revealing only half truths because the complete disclosure might affect their professional interests. And it is also is suspected that pressure has been brought to bear on them from others in the industry not to make disclosures which would injuriously affect the sales value of their pictures.'

It is therefore understandable that against such a background we will find rumours and contradictions, naïve explanations which fail to explain. Facts are to be glossed over with a smear of whitewash, evidence will vanish from under our noses.

But piecing together the facts solely from what the public was able to read in the press, we proceed to consider the rather remarkable history of these Normand letters.

In an interview on February 5th, Mabel Normand stated to a reporter, according to the published account, 'I sought those letters and hoped to get them before they reached the scrutiny of others. I admit this, but it was for only one purpose—to prevent terms of affection from being misconstrued.'

However, on February 7th we find a published quotation from Miss Normand to this effect: 'There have been insinuations made that I went to Mr Taylor's house after the inquest Saturday to seek some of my letters to him. That is grossly erroneous. I went to the bungalow at the request of the detectives and in their company and solely for the purpose of showing to them the exact location of the furniture as it was placed in the room before I left. It was to show how disordered the place had become after the intrusion of the murderer.'

In any event, it seems that Miss Normand arrived at the house and made a request for her letters and was given permission to take them. It is not clear from whom she made this request, exactly when it was made, or who gave her the permission. But she is reported to have said that she knew where they were and to have gone immediately to the top drawer in Taylor's dresser in his upstairs bedroom.

The letters weren't there.

Under date of February 7th it was stated in the press that it is believed a man of high position and influence in the motion-

Mary Miles Minter

picture world may have taken the Mabel Normand letters, and perhaps others too, in order to protect the fortunes of actresses in whom he had a business interest.

Public Administrator Frank Bryson claims that when his representatives arrived at the Taylor home Thursday morning, the room was filled with detectives, motion-picture people, and reporters, and the premises were warming with them.

The *Examiner* of February 9, 1922, contains the following: ' "It is very evident," one of the officers said, "that someone who entered the house shortly after Taylor's body was found made a thorough search and took all letters which Taylor had received from women, or men, which might aid in solving the mystery of his death." '

Now then, surprise, surprise! On February 10th, Frank Bryson, the Public Administrator, stated that he had found the Normand letters concealed in Taylor's apartment, 'under a double lock.' Where were these letters between February first and February 9th. Is it possible that the officers in searching the house did so in such a slipshod manner that these important letters, 'under double lock,' were not discovered for a period of more than a week? 'Under double lock' is slightly reminiscent of the subtitles of the period. Figuratively it is an expression which hints at impenetrable security. Taken literally it means two locks. There is no specific interpretation given of how it was used in the quoted statement.

On February 11th Mabel Normand's attitude toward these letters discovered 'under double lock' seems to have been almost casual. She is quoted as saying, 'My letters to him—I would gladly set them before the world if the authorities care to do that. I have nothing to conceal. . . . I have been charged with trying to recover those letters; with trying to conceal them. That is silly. If those letters are printed you will see that they are most of them casual. . . .'

And on February 10, 1922, the district attorney, Thomas Lee Woolwine, stated that the Normand letters contained nothing helpful in the investigation. Another official who had read them said that they were not the burning missives which they had been imagined to be. Apparently these letters were returned to Miss

Normand. On February 14th Miss Normand admitted that she now had the letters.

There seems to be no explanation as to why letters which had been 'under double lock' in Taylor's residence had been overlooked for a period of some eight days.

In fact, the William Desmond Taylor murder case as reported in the press has some of the Alice-in-Wonderland qualities which leave the thoughtful reader rubbing his eyes.

There is yet another letter to figure in the investigation. Police opening a book in the library some time after the murder noticed that a letter fell out. The letter had the crest of M. M. M. and read: 'Dearest, I love you. I love you. I love you,' followed by several cross marks and one big cross mark and signed, 'Yours always, Mary.'

On August 14, 1923, the press stated that Mary Miles Minter, declaring that the time had come to reveal the true relationship that existed between William Desmond Taylor and herself, had announced they were engaged at the time of Taylor's death. She is also reported to have set forth her reasons why the engagement had not been disclosed immediately after the murder.

In fact one of the peculiar developments of this case is the manner in which important facts are to be published for the first time years later. In the press of March 26, 1926, four years after the crime, the public learned, apparently for the first time, that two 'strands of blonde hair' found on the body of William Desmond Taylor were being safeguarded by the district attorney's office and were forming the basis of a new probe for the slayer. And it is in May of 1936 that we find Captain Winn in a newspaper interview disclosing that in the toe of one of William Desmond Taylor's riding boots were found a dozen fervent love letters written in a simple code, all signed 'Mary.' These letters were described as the outpouring of a young girl's heart to the man she obviously loved.

But this is no ordinary murder mystery. Probably no other murder case has existed in history where every feature was so touched with bizarre mystery.

William Desmond Taylor, the simple, kindly motion-picture director as Hollywood knew him, had managed to preserve the secret of his identity. But now that he had been murdered and an investigation was started into his background, it was disclosed that the famous director had a complex past filled with checkerboard patches of mystery that would have done credit to one of the movie plots of the period.

William Desmond Taylor, it developed, was really William Cunningham Deane Tanner. In 1908 William Deane Tanner had, it seemed, carried on a business in New York from which his share of the profits amounted to a cool twenty-five thousand dollars a year, and in those days that was a very considerable sum of money—particularly when one remembers that the income tax had not as yet been discovered and applied to our economic life.

For some undisclosed motive William Cunningham Deane Tanner, after having attended the Vanderbilt Cup Race in the fall of 1908, returned to New York, sent a message to a hotel where he evidently maintained a room asking to have clothing sent to him, drew five hundred dollars from his business, and vanished.

One minute here was a prosperous businessman with wealth at his finger tips and influential friends and connections. He had a charming wife, a beautiful daughter, an established business, a rosy future. The next moment he had vanished into thin air.

There follows a hiatus which has never been satisfactorily filled. there are rumours of this and that. Apparently he was in Alaska for a while. And it is certain that sometime along in 1917 he drifted into Hollywood where he became William Desmond Taylor and rapidly climbed the ladder of fame and influence.

But prior to that time, in 1912, his brother, Dennis Deane Tanner, also suddenly vanished into thin air, leaving a wife and two children.

The wife of this brother subsequently secured a divorce. She moved to Southern California and while there saw a motion picture of some of the screen notables. Watching those flickering figures on the silver screen, she suddenly gripped the arms of her chair, leaned forward, and stared incredulously. The picture of William Cunningham Deane Tanner, her long-missing brother-in-law, was before her startled eyes. She saw the man's familiar figure, his gestures, his smile. And the man was William Desmond Taylor, the noted motion-picture director who was fast winning wealth and fame in the world's motion-picture capital!

She immediately notified her sister-in-law, telling her what she had seen, and was calmly advised that this was no news as her sister-in-law knew it already. Yet apparently there had been no attempt made by Mrs William Cunningham Deane Tanner to communicate with her husband.

Thereafter, to complicate the situation, the ex-Mrs Dennis Deane Tanner went to William Desmond Taylor and accused him of being William Cunningham Deane Tanner who had disappeared in 1908. And the man who was her brother-in-law blandly asserted that the woman was suffering from a case of mistaken identity. Yet apparently he kept an eye on her and when her health broke down, he sent her every month an allowance which she received regularly up to the time of his murder—all of the time, however, insisting that this woman was a total stranger to him.

Nor is this all. As William Desmond Taylor had hurried through the chill of that early February evening to keep his appointment with death, he had in his pocket an assortment of keys which fitted no doors the police were ever able to discover. Moreover, in his bungalow, if we are to believe the testimony of his houseman, was a mysterious pink silk nightgown which was to figure prominently in the murder case.

No less an expert than Arthur B. Reeve, famous author of mystery stories of the time, is authority for the statement that Taylor's employee (referring perhaps to Taylor's former secretary, Edward F. Sands), doing a bit of amateur sleuthing on his own, made it a habit to take this silk nightgown from the bureau drawer where it was neatly folded, fold it over again and in a certain distinctive manner, then return it to the drawer. The next morning he would find that the folds of the nightgown had been changed, indicating that it had been worn and refolded. The amateur detective would unfold it, fold it once more in his distinctive manner, only to find that the next morning it had been used and refolded. Later on, everyone concerned is to minimize the importance of this nightgown. The houseman is to say he paid no attention to it; police are to push it out of the case as of no importance. Arthur Reeve doesn't say where he got his information, and the press is to be very coy about the initials which may or may not have been embroidered on the garment.

There was much gossip around Hollywood as to those initials, and we find Miss Normand referring to the nightgown in the press as having initials on it. But the issue is confused by the manner in which the authorities shrug the matter off. As one of the papers said: 'Little importance was attached to the pink silk nightgown found in the director's apartments. This, it was learned, had been laundered only once or twice and bore no initials or other marks by which its ownership might be determined.'

Despite the fact that William Desmond Taylor was drawing an excellent salary, his money seemed to disappear into thin air. His bank accounts melted away as by magic.

On January 31st he is asserted to have gone to the bank and drawn $2500 in cash. And then the following day, the day of his death, he had reappeared at the bank and deposited $2500 in cash. No explanations offered, no subsequent reason found by the police. Apparently on January 31st he had felt he would need $2500 in cash. The next day the need had passed and the money was returned to the bank. However, later on, after this withdrawal and deposit have been accepted as a fact in the case (and apparently the report originated from the public administrator who had taken charge of Taylor's property after his death and certainly should have known), we are to find a sudden flurry of explanations and alibis. Taylor, it seems, was going to buy some diamonds. So, quite naturally, he went to the bank and withdrew this money. Then he changed his mind about the diamonds and so redeposited the money. Simple, just like that. Then, some two weeks after the murder, there is another puzzling statement to account for this mysterious withdrawal and deposit. This one really should win a prize. On February 15th the newspapers blandly asserted that although it had been stated that Taylor withdrew $2500 from the First National Bank on

January 31st and made a deposit of that sum, or of $2350, on February first, it had been disclosed the day before (evidently February 14th) that he had not withdrawn any large sum from the bank within the last two weeks before his death.

Now you see it and now you don't. These peculiar 'reports' and the charming naïveté of the police – a whole two weeks. Tut, tut!

On February 6th, Miss Normand is reported as having said that when she visited Taylor on the night of the murder, Peavey answered her ring at the doorbell and told her Mr Taylor was telephoning. Not wanting to interrupt, Mabel Normand waited outside. When Taylor heard her voice, however, he hurriedly cut off his phone call and rushed to her.

Now notice what Miss Normand is reported to have said at that time about that telephone conversation. 'If there is a possibility that the jealousy of another woman enters into the mystery, I feel certain that the phone call which he was receiving as I entered his apartment had something to do with it. Whoever it was calling him seemed intensely absorbed in what he had to say.'

Naturally the question arises, How did Mabel Normand know this person had called Taylor instead of Taylor having been the one to place the call? How could Mabel Normand, entering the room, and seeing Taylor hastily terminating a telephone conversation, know that the person at the other end of the line was intensely absorbed in what Taylor had to say?

Did Taylor tell her about this call during the visit which followed when he and Miss Normand were sitting there alone? Did Miss Normand's naïve statement show that she knew a great deal more about that call than she told police? It is an interesting field for speculation.

Let us digress at this point for just a moment to mention an article which appeared in the February 1, 1929, issue of *Liberty* in which Mr Sidney Sutherland, the author, states that he had talked with Mabel Normand the year before (apparently 1928) about the Taylor murder. And at the time of this conversation she is reported to have said, 'When I reached Bill's open door, I heard a voice inside; he was using the telephone. So I walked around the flower beds a few minutes until he had quit talking and hung up. Then I rang his bell. He came to the door, smiled, and held out both hands. "Hello, Mabel darling," he said. "I know what you've come for—two books I've just got for you." '

Sometime after that fatal night, one of Taylor's friends was to express it as his opinion that he was the one with whom Taylor was talking on the telephone at the time Mabel Normand arrived. But a cautious reader, thinking over those several statements of Miss Normand's, will wonder what Taylor said to her about that telephone conversation during the period when they were seated side by side on the davenport sipping their cocktails. And why did Miss Normand apparently try to point out to the police the possible significance of that telephone conversation?

Moreover, William Desmond Taylor had been the victim of mysterious burglaries. In fact, only some two weeks before his death his place had been burglarized and someone had stolen some jewellery, also a large number of specially made cigarettes which the director had had tailored to his individual taste. Then pawn tickets *in the name of William Deane Tanner* had been placed in an envelope and mailed to William Desmond Taylor so that he could, by using his right name and paying the amount of the loan, redeem the jewellery which had been stolen from him.

Some six months or so prior to his death, Taylor had returned from a trip abroad and had accused his secretary, a man by the name of E. F. Sands, of forgery. Apparently the charge was that while Taylor was abroad, Sands had forged checks, charged bills for expensive lingerie and women's clothing and had generally looted the apartment. At about this time Sands disappeared, vanishing into thin air, and has never since been located by the police although every effort has been made to find him.

Keep this man, Sands, in mind. On February 10th, newspapers asserted that a Denver man who 'asked that his name be withheld' declared that Sands was none other than Taylor's brother! This man was reported to have known both brothers well. Sands, it seems, was engaged to a beautiful girl and the older brother won the love of that girl. Years later the younger brother entered the office of this mysterious informant and tried to find out about the whereabouts of the older brother. This mysterious informant is reported to have said, 'I will stake my life that when Sands is caught the mystery of Taylor's murder will be cleared up and a number of events and elements in the man's life which now seem obscure will be made plain. Revenge is the motive behind the murder of William Desmond Taylor.'

Mabel Normand's testimony at the inquest, as reported in the *Los Angeles Times* of February 3rd, and which purports to give the gist of her statement, is that a certain 'Edward Knoblock had Mr Taylor's house while Mr Taylor was in Europe last summer, and that Mr Taylor had Mr Knoblock's London house. Sands apparently stayed right along in Mr Taylor's service in Los Angeles, and also assisted Mr Knoblock. Two or three days before Mr Taylor was to arrive from London, Sands told Mr Knoblock that he thought he would take two or three days leave of absence, but would be back again Sunday. He never showed up again. When Mr Taylor arrived from London, he said he found that Sands had stolen everything, had forged his name to checks and had gone to Hamburgers and bought lingerie . . . A few weeks ago Mr Taylor's house was robbed again. Then from Stockton he kept getting anonymous letters, and he received a pawnbroker's ticket, showing that things had been pawned in the name of a Mrs Tennant, who is Mr Taylor's sister-in-law. The way Mr Taylor knew it was really Sands was because he had always spelled Mrs Tennant's name wrong, and the wrong spelling was on the ticket. Mr Taylor knew that Sands wasn't out of California by this fact.'

Apparently there is some confusion about the name on these pawn tickets. This may have been due to the fact that there were several pawn tickets and more than one burglary. In the 1936 interview previously referred to, Captain Winn is authority for the statement that at Fresno on the record of a pawnshop where the names of all borrowers were kept, there appeared 'in handwriting that was readily identified by experts as that of Edward Sands, the name of "William Deane Tanner." '

There is evidence that William Desmond Taylor felt very bitter toward his former secretary. Apparently when Taylor was asked by the police whether he would be willing to go to the trouble of having Sands extradited from another state, Taylor replied,

Mabel Normand, who expected to become Mrs Taylor

'I would go to any trouble or expense to extradite him not only from a neighbouring state but from any country in the world. All I want is five minutes alone with him.'

In the *Examiner* of February 4th, Claire Windsor recalled a conversation she had had with Mr Taylor about a week before his death. Apparently that was only about a week after the mysterious burglary of Taylor's house. And according to Miss Windsor, Taylor had said, 'If I ever lay my hands on Sands I will kill him.'

There were, of course, the usual reports and rumours. Sands was reported to have been arrested in various parts of the country; he was called upon by the officials to appear and establish his innocence. He was even offered immunity by the district attorney if he would establish his innocence of the murder of William Desmond Taylor and furnish information which would assist the authorities in locating the actual murderer.

Sands made no move.

Since we have previously mentioned this 1936 newspaper story about Captain Winn's impression of the case, we may as well incorporate some other things which were in that interview. For instance, Captain Winn's statement, 'From another source, a source that even now I do not wish to reveal, we learned that Sands, within twenty-four hours of the time of Taylor's murder, had made the statement: "I came back to town to get that — — — Taylor." The same person who heard Sands make this rash threat emphatically declared that he again saw Sands—he could not be mistaken in his identification—within a block of the Alvarado court less than an hour before the fatal shot was fired.'

In this interview Captain Winn also takes up the claim that Edward Sands was none other than Dennis Gage Deane Tanner, the mysterious missing brother. 'Clear, distinguishable photographs of Sands were virtually nonexistent,' Winn is reported to have declared. 'Pictures of Dennis Deane Tanner were even scarcer, one faded print of the man being the only likeness ever turned up. It was hard to say that a similarity existed between the pictures of Sands and the faded print of Dennis Deane Tanner. But it was as hard to say they were dissimilar.

. . . Our investigation revealed that William Deane Tanner had made no less than three trips to Alaska in quest of gold, and that, on at least one of these trips, his brother, Dennis, accompanied him.'

A peculiar conflict developed in connection with the testimony of William Davis, Mabel Normand's chauffeur. A moving-picture machinist, George F. Arto, insisted that either on the night of the murder or on the preceding night he saw Peavey talking to some man in the alley back of Taylor's house. Two days after that statement, Arto was reported to have said that on the night of the murder a man other than Davis was talking with Peavey in front of the court where Taylor lived. Davis, Arto is reported to have said, was sitting in his (presumably Mabel Normand's) car at the time. Davis and Peavey both denied this. For a time newspapers mentioned this conflict in the stories of witnesses, then seem to have let it drift into oblivion.

This was during a period of relative normalcy as far as the case is concerned. For a few days one could read the newspaper reports and forget that he was dealing with anything other than the usual mysterious murder. The Alice-in-Wonderland quality was apparently all finished.

Then of a sudden the whole case skyrocketed once more into fantasy.

There entered into the picture a motion-picture executive who told a story that could well have graced one of the pictures of the time.

It seems this person had employed Taylor some years before, and that during that time Taylor had told him of having been imprisoned in England for three years. Taylor was perfectly blameless. He had, it seems, been arrested while holding money in his hand which he wanted a woman to put back in the safe. The husband of this woman unexpectedly appeared upon the scene and accused Taylor of theft; and Taylor, like a gallant gentleman, had kept silent, protecting the good name of the woman at the expense of three years in jail.

There are elaborations of this story, some of them going to the extent of putting together a plot containing a wicked gambler, a scheming husband, a betrayed woman, the gallant Taylor, and at the dramatic moment, Taylor stepping forward to stand between the woman and disgrace, bowing his head in silence and going to jail for three years rather than do anything which would cast a reflection upon the character of the woman. It was typical of the silent drama of the time.

On the 24th, one Tom Green, an assistant United States Attorney, disclosed that Taylor had wanted him to 'clean out' a certain place. Taylor, it seems, was protecting a woman from drugs. She was a woman who was paying two thousand dollars a week for dope.

The newspapers gravely published this story, with no explanation as to why no disclosure had been made earlier.

Two thousand dollars a week was a lot of dope.

Then suddenly came the weirdest development of all. A rancher living near Santa Ana, some forty-five miles from Los Angeles, announced that he had picked up two hitch-hikers, rough characters, who confided to him that they had been in the Canadian Army where they had suffered under the harsh discipline of a captain whom they referred to as 'Bill.'

It was at least intimated that this 'Bill' had been responsible for one of these men being 'sent up.' Both hitchhikers avowed their intention of 'getting' Captain Bill who was living in Los Angeles whither, apparently, they were making their way on a mission of vengeance. One of the hitchhikers happened to drop a gun. The Santa Ana rancher saw that it was a .38 caliber revolver.

To add to the importance of this clue, police now disclosed that they had received a letter from a former Army officer in London who stated that sometime after the Armistice was signed he was dining with Captain Taylor in a London hotel. As a stranger in the uniform of the Canadian Army crossed the dining hall, Taylor suddenly exclaimed, 'There goes a man who is going to get me if it takes a thousand years to do it.' Taylor then went on to explain that he had reported and court-martialled this man for the theft of Army property. A description was contained in this letter to the police which tallied exactly with that given by the Santa Ana rancher of one of the hitchhikers, a man called 'Spike.'

Apparently police had some reason to believe that these hitchhikers might be found at resorts near the Mexican border, and they immediately proceeded to comb Tijuana which is south of San Diego, and Mexicali which is just south of Calexico in the Imperial Valley.

Fortuituously enough, they located a man in a bar in Mexicali who was named Walter Kirby and who, at the time of his arrest, was reported to have been wearing a cap similar to that worn by the figure seen by Mrs MacLean leaving the Taylor bungalow. Moreover, this Kirby was reported to have been 'positively identified' by the rancher who had picked up the hitchhikers as one of the men to whom he had given the ride. It was also reported that when Kirby's room was searched, a pair of Army breeches was found with leggings to match and several .38 caliber bullets. It was asserted he had admitted serving in a Canadian regiment in which William Desmond Taylor was serving as captain. Moreover, detectives are reported to have said they recognized Kirby as a chauffeur known in Los Angeles as 'Slim' and 'Whitey' Kirby. Then it is asserted that he had worked for Taylor for one day and was acquainted with him.

A pretty good case one would say.

Twenty-four hours later, Kirby, questioned by police, seems to have produced an air-tight alibi. And then comes the most interesting and amusing sequence of all. The Santa Ana rancher, solemnly asserted the newspaper, 'could not identify him positively as the man to whom he had given a ride in his car. . . . He also said that the man arrested was many years younger than the one who had ridden in his car, as well as several inches shorter.'

This man Kirby, promptly released from custody however, seems destined to add another page to this chapter in the mystery. Early in May of 1922, two small boys who were out rabbit hunting in the swamp bottoms of New River, west of Calexico in the Imperial Valley, discovered Walter Kirby's body.

This time the identification was positive.

Newspapers reported that shortly before his death Kirby had confided to a friend in Mexicali that someone was after him and would 'end him quick.' Under a dateline of May 2, 1922, the

newspapers posed the question whether Kirby died of an overdose
of drug, exposure and lack of food, 'or was he killed by means
only known to the underworld of the border?'

It is to be noted in passing that it was asserted that Kirby was a
drug addict. Habitual drug addicts, as any reader of mystery fiction
well knows, are peculiarly vulnerable to murderous machinations.
The drugs of underworld commerce are greatly diluted. It becomes
only necessary to deliver to an habitual drug user a dose of 'the pure
quill' and the man, thinking he has his usual diluted dose, is
conveniently removed from the scene of operations.

However, there is too much more to be written about the
Taylor case to permit ourselves to be diverted over the death
of Walter Kirby.

Incredible as it may seem to the reader, the fact seems to be
clearly established that by the sixth of March, 1922, more than
three hundred people in the United States alone had confessed
to the murder of William Desmond Taylor, and there was one
confession from Paris and one from England. These confessions
were for the most part embellished with the most astounding
detail, ranging from the plausible to the riduculous. One person
who swore he was a friend of a certain motion-picture actress
is reported as stating that he passed the Taylor bungalow on the
night of the murder where he observed the director and this
actress in a heated argument. Slipping into the house, he saw
that Taylor had a gun, struggled with him to get possession of
the gun and in the course of that struggle, shot him.

In addition to these confessions, there were solemn statements
by 'witnesses.' One convict 'confessed' that he entered the Taylor
bungalow for the purpose of burglarizing it; surprised by the
unexpected appearance of Taylor, he hid in the only place which
was available, to wit, behind the piano. And while he was hiding
there, he witnessed a quarrel between Taylor and a woman who
was dressed like a man, the quarrel culminating in the shooting
of the director.

It is, indeed, some murder case which brings in confessions
at the rate of virtually ten a day for thirty days.

But don't think you've seen anything yet. These are just the
preliminaries. The Taylor case was not allowed to die.

Seven years later, in December of 1929, Friend W. Richardson, ex-governor of the state of California, exploded a bombshell by announcing that he knew who had killed William Desmond Taylor, that he had positive proof that a motion-picture actress had committed the crime and that Asa Keyes, Los Angeles district attorney, had blocked the case. Asa Keyes, the ex-district attorney, promptly issued a denial and demanded to know, among other things, why the governor had not disclosed his information sooner. Richardson retorted that he had approached the Los Angeles grand jury and had been advised that there was nothing he could do because 'Keyes would never prosecute the case.'

Inasmuch as these disclosures came during the heat of a political campaign, it is easy to imagine the commotion which was aroused in the press.

Pressed for an amplification of his statement, ex-governor Richardson is reported to have said that he received his information from a Folsom convict now paroled, whose name he had 'forgotten, and wouldn't tell if he did remember it, because it would mean the man's death.'

Newspaper reporters were not so reticent. They promptly decided that the source of the governor's information was one Otis Hefner.

On January 13, 1930, one of the Los Angeles papers which seems to have been rather unsympathetic politically toward ex-governor Richardson has this to say: 'Mr Hefner is the resourceful young man whose twice-told tales of what he knew about the murder of the Hollywood movie director created a big stew when former governor Friend W. Richardson threw it into the political pot several weeks ago. He did most of his talking in 1926, and was rewarded with a parole from Folsom. Now that he has been uprooted from his job and attempts to stage a comeback and support his little family, he would just as soon be left alone. But if Mr Fitts must have the facts, there is what Hefner says he will tell the Los Angeles district attorney: That most, if not all, he ever said about the case was hearsay with him; that he never stated to anybody he could identify a woman he once said he saw leave the Taylor bungalow on the night of the murder; that he does not know where Edward F. Sands, Taylor's old valet, and now suspect in the case, is at the present time, and that the story he told Governor Richardson and saw published in San Fancisco newspapers in the last few days is the old tale which the Los Angeles authorities discarded as unworthy of consideration.'

With interest in the murder thus revived, newspaper reporters instituted a search for Peavey and finally located him in Northern California. What happened next is reported in the press of January 8, 1930, as follows: 'Two long statements were forthcoming from Peavey during the day. As usual, they contradicted one another.

'In the first he declared flatly that a famous film actress killed the equally famous director—the same actress named by Hefner in his story Monday. He added that he would welcome a return to Los Angeles and an appearance before the grand jury, and that he had been silenced by the authorities and told "to get out of town" shortly after the murder.

'But in his second statement, Peavey was not so certain. Later in the day, he declared that he had forgotten most of the details of the killing. He believed he knew who did the killing, but even of this he was not then altogether certain. And he didn't desire a return to this city and least of all a call to appear before the grand jury.

'In both statements, however, he fixed the time of the murder at about 7:30 P.M. Peavey, found in the Negro quarters at Sacramento, explained that the case was "getting on my nerves" and that he couldn't remember distinctly that far back. A few hours earlier, however, he seemed to remember everything.'

The name of the motion-picture actress apparently referred to by Hefner and Peavey never found its way specifically into the columns of the press but was, perhaps, intended to be a political bombshell if one can judge from the reports of the time, and failed to have sufficient explosive force to cause the case to be reopened.

Down through the years, the red thread of mystery in the William Desmond Taylor murder case has wound its way in and out of the press. Various circumstances have 'recalled the Taylor murder case.' And now and again incidental sidelights have appeared in the newspapers.

During the time when Asa Keyes was district attorney, there was a flare-up over two diaries which had apparently been taken from a safe-deposit box and found their way into the possession of the district attorney. There was quite a bit of newspaper comment about these diaries but the young woman who had authored them retained shrewd counsel who advised the district attorney that if any hint of their contents became public property, the district attorney would be held strictly accountable. Apparently the threat served as a sobering influence and while the newspapers hinted a bit here and there, no quotations, excerpts, or purported summary of the contents were ever published.

Those diaries, in connection with other things, caused Keyes to rush around the country making an investigation. Once more people were interrogated—and then the thing died down again.

As 1923 went out and 1924 was ushered in with a blare of noise and the usual celebrations, Mabel Normand and Edna Purviance were at a New Year's party.

Trying to unscramble all that happened at that party is like trying to follow the directions given by a well meaning, you-can't-miss-it friend for finding some house in a strange countryside.

Suffice it to say that one of the men at the party was shot by Mabel Normand's chauffeur (not the same one she had employed at the time of the Taylor murder). For a while it was expected the victim would die. Then he recovered physically although the newspaper reported that his memory was 'still sick.' The preliminary hearing on this case was scheduled to open on March 19, 1924. On March 17th newspapers mentioned that Miss Normand had left the day before for New York. On April 16th the district attorney's office announced that it would not go to trial on a shooting charge against Miss Normand's chauffeur without the presence of Mabel Normand. The trial was continued until June 16th. On June 15th, the newspapers stated that the grand jury was making an investigation, trying to find out how

it happened that the victim of the shooting had succeeded in
leaving the jurisdiction of the California courts and also taking
with him the $5000 that he had put up as security that he would
be on hand to testify.

The chauffeur was acquitted.

All in all, Hollywood's contribution to murder mysteries at
a time when the silent film was at the zenith of its popularity,
is fully in keeping with what one might expect—a murder
mystery which is 'super-colossal.'

At this late date it is impossible to 'solve' the William Desmond
Taylor murder case from the facts as presented by the press.
It is, however, interesting to speculate upon lines which the police
inquiry could have taken some years ago. In the first place, it
seems to me that the police theory of a 'stick-up' has several
very big holes in it.

Let us suppose a man did slip through the door and
commanded Taylor to raise his hands. The movie director
complied—then why shoot him? If a man is perpetrating a
robbery and the victim raises his hands, the next move is for
the robber to go through his clothes and take his personal
possessions. The use of firearms is resorted to when the victim
refuses to comply with the order to stick up his hands. Moreover,
apparently robbery was not the motive because of the money
and jewellery found on the director's body.

It occurs to me that the police have either overlooked or
deliberately failed to emphasize a far more logical theory than
this stick-up hypothesis.

There was a checkbook on the desk, a fountain pen, also the
income-tax statement. When a person is writing, if he is right-
handed, he rests his left elbow on the desk and slightly turns
his body. That would have the effect of raising the coat just about
the amount that would be required to match up the bullet holes
in Taylor's coat and vest.

Let us assume, therefore, that Taylor was writing at the time
he was shot.

What was he writing?

Obviously it was not a check. He may have offered to write

a check, but the person who shot him didn't want a check. He wanted something else *in writing*.

If William Desmond Taylor had *refused* to write a check, the checkbook wouldn't have been there on the desk with the fountain pen near-by. If he had written a check, then it was to the interest of the person receiving that check to see that Taylor lived long enough for the check to be cashed. A man's checking account is frozen by his bank immediately upon notification of his death.

It seems to me, therefore, that some person wanted, and quite probably obtained, a written statement from Taylor. Once that statement had been properly written out and signed, the person had no further use for Taylor and probably through a desire for vengeance, or else with the idea of sealing his lips, pulled the trigger of a gun which had been surreptitiously placed against the side of the director's body.

It is interesting to speculate whether some woman may not have been concealed in the upstairs portion of the house at the time the shot was fired. The presence of a pink silk nightgown indicates that at some time previously women, or at any rate a woman, had been there.

Notice the manner in which the body had been 'laid out.'

If the person in an upstairs bedroom had heard voices below, followed by the sound of a shot, and then the noise made by a body falling to the floor, then the opening and closing of a door . . . Perhaps, after ten or fifteen minutes of agonized waiting this person tiptoed down the stairs and found the body of the director sprawled on the floor. It is quite possible that this woman, before slipping out into the concealment of the night, would have bent over the lifeless body, wept a few tears, and arranged the clothing as neatly as possible.

The most interesting lead of all was offered by Mabel Normand in her comments about the telephone conversation. Quite obviously she was trying to impress upon the police that in her opinion this telephone conversation had some probable bearing upon the death of the director. It is almost certain that this was no mere casual conversation and that Taylor discussed it with her while they were talking together. How else could Mabel Normand have know that the person had called Taylor, not vice versa? How did she know that the person at the other end of the wire was very interested in what Taylor was saying? And why was her subsequent recollection of the telephone conversation so widely at variance with her original statements to the press?

Is it possible the police failed to appreciate the significance of Miss Normand's statement, or did Miss Normand, after thinking things over, decide that she had gone too far and that it would be better to forget all she might have been told about that telephone conversation?

It is to be borne in mind that the police were undoubtedly subjected to great pressure at the time. They were also confused by confessions which were arriving at the rate of ten a day for a period of thirty days. That's an average of better than one an hour for each hour of the working day.

One thing is certain, no dyed-in-the-wool mystery fan would have let Miss Normand's significant statement about the telephone conversation pass unnoticed. And I think most really intelligent mystery readers would have given an interpretation other than the stick-up hypothesis to the fact that the course of the bullet indicated the left shoulder had been raised at the time of death.

As time passes, it becomes less possible that the case will ever be solved by the police. Yet there is an interesting field for speculation in the fact that police have the fingerprints of Edward Sands. It is becoming more and more common nowadays for all classes of people to be fingerprinted and the prints passed on to the F. B. I. Imagine what a furor there will be if some day the F. B. I., making a routine check of some fingerprint, comes upon that of the missing secretary of the murdered motion-picture director. That is a very distinct possibility, one which may once more bring the case into the limelight. So one can hardly write the murder of William Desmond Taylor off the books—not yet.

NANCY MITFORD

The Mystery of the Missing Arsenic

This week the trial of Marie Besnard re-opens at Poitiers after having been adjourned for exactly one year. The French newspapers, with their usual lack of inhibition, have called her the Lafarge or Brinvilliers of our age, after those two famous female poisoners. Her neighbours are convinced that she is a mass murderess and so was the whole of France until, suddenly and dramatically in the middle of her trial, the case for the prosecution seemed to crumble away to nothing. Here is the story of Marie Besnard, but we must take into account the fact that it is told by her deeply prejudiced neighbours. She seems to be without one friend in the world and nobody has a good word for her.

Marie Besnard was born in 1898; her parents were well-to-do peasants, what we should call smallholders. They sent her to school at the local convent, where the other children disliked her so much that, when she made her first communion no little girl could be found to walk up the aisle with her. In 1920, she married Auguste Antigny, a poor creature, said by her to be tubercular. Nine years later he got very thin and died. Now, widows, in provincial France, are expected to mourn. They envelope themselves in a huge black vail, yards and yards of crêpe, and may not go to any place of amusement or even play the piano for at least two years. To the horror of her neighbours, however, the Widow Antigny threw her black veil into a bed of nettles and went gallivanting off to the circus with a new acquaintance, Léon Besnard. Worse still, she was heard to call him 'tu', the equivalent of our 'darling'. She then married him quite respectably and they appear to have been perfectly happy. Her new in-laws, however, hated her from the beginning; in 1930 her sister-in-law wrote of her as 'this horror of a woman'. The Besnards were comfortably off. They owned two farms and a vineyard and bred horses. 'We were not Rothschilds, but we lived well'. Today Marie Besnard owns about £15,000, three hotels at Loudun, two farms and 50 hectares of land. The Besnards came through the war without inconvenience, except for the difficulty of getting help on the farm. In 1947 they engaged a German prisoner, Dietz, a handsome boy of twenty-four, to work for them. He was not, he said, a Nazi. The neighbours thought that Marie Besnard was falling in love with Dietz; she took to rouge, considered a terrible sign of wickedness in the provincial bourgeoisie; she shortened her skirts. (This piece of evidence is not very convincing since it refers to the year of the New Look when most women were frantically adding false hems to all their garments.) She certainly must have needed a little relaxation since for ten years she seems to have spent most of her time at sick-beds, death-beds and the graveyard. Except for her mother and husband, all her relations and her two closest friends had now died. She had looked after them herself; worn out with nursing, she had then been obliged to arrange and pay for their funerals (first-class), because it so happened that she and her husband were heirs, direct or indirect, of each and all of these loved ones. The declared value of the legacies, it is true, was not very much, varying from £3 to £500; however nobody in rural France declares their money and everybody has a stocking more or less filled with gold. The Besnards probably inherited a few thousands pounds in all. While the neighbours were gossiping about Marie and Dietz, Léon Besnard became very thin. He is supposed to have said to a friend: 'If I die, see there is an autopsy'. He did die, soon to be followed to the churchyard by his mother-in-law. Marie Besnard and Dietz were now alone in the house together, but not for long. They were arrested; Dietz was set free again the same day, and Marie was tried for having forged the signature of some deceased relation on a money order. She was found guilty and sent to prison for two years.

Meanwhile, the loved ones were being dug up out of their graves, and their remains were packed off to Marseilles. There they were analysed by Dr Béroud, who found that every single body contained a heavy dose of arsenic. They were:

Aunt Louise, who died in 1938. When Besnard learned at the funeral that she had left her money to his mother and sister and not to him, he flung a little holy water on her grave and went off in a rage.

1939: The great friend, Toussaint Rivet, who spent every Sunday with the Besnards. Marie Besnard was his wife's heiress.

1940: Marie's father. Died after taking a purge administered by her.

1940: Léon's father. He left £227. Marie said, 'I can't imagine how the doctor found arsenic in him; I was not even there'.

1941: Léon's mother.

Two months later, Léon's sister Lucie was found hung up and strangled. Verdict of suicide. She was a fervent Roman Catholic, and had a happy life with her flower garden, her poultry and her rabbits.

1941: Marthe Rivet, widow of the great friend. She had made over her house to the Besnards in return for £2.10s. a year and free lodging, and died almost immediately afterwards.

1945: Pauline and Virginie Lalleron, cousins of Léon, both over 80. Virginie only left £3 but was supposed to wear a little bag of gold round her waist day and night. She told a policeman that Léon was trying to take it away from her, but the policeman does not seem to have pursued the matter. Pauline and Virginie were both rather simple.

When the analyst's report was delivered, Marie Besnard was brought to trial and accused of having murdered all these people. In the dock she presented the classical appearance of a poisoner. She was dressed in shiny black and wore a black lace mantilla: her hideous face was chalk white. Though a sturdy, masterful looking woman, she spoke in a sinister little voice, thin and high as a reed. 'I pray for my dead every day'. As the prosecution told the story of these deaths and spoke of 36, 48, 50 milligrams of arsenic (over ten is a fatal dose), nobody doubted for a moment that she was guilty. But then came the turn of maître Gautrat, counsel for the defence. Almost at once things began to look quite different. There had clearly been a great deal of carelessness in the Marseilles laboratory and the various exhibits were hopelessly mixed up.

Maître Gautrat's cross-examining the doctor:

'Marie Besnard's mother's remains were put into ten tubes, duly sealed and inventoried. Why, then, did 11 tubes turn up at Marseilles, of which two were different from those that were sent?' . . . 'You say that Virginie contained 24 milligrams of arsenic; but did not Virginie's body crumble into dust?'

The doctor soon became flustered and then angry. 'All you Parisians have a down on Marsilles'. This is rather true. The Northern French love the people of Provence, but never take them very seriously. 'But my methods were undisputed and my instruments are pure.'

Maître Gautrat: 'Now here are six tubes which you say contained traces of arsenic. Which of these contains arsenic? Between ourselves, they contain no arsenic at all; three of them contain antimony.' Collapse of the doctor. Commotion in court.

The case was immediately adjourned so that the bodies could be analysed again, this time under the auspices of Professor Fabre, head of the faculty of Medicine in Paris. He and his three assistants have now finished their work, and we shall know next week what they have found. Meanwhile, Marie Besnard sits in a little cell looking over the gardens, waiting. She is said to be perfectly cheerful and confident.

WILLIAM RITT

The Head Hunter of Kingsbury Run

It would be difficult to find a less enchanting spot than Kingsbury
Run. It is a dusty, sooty gully, the dried bed of a creek which
once flowed through what is now the heart of Cleveland, toward
the Cuyahoga River, in some long-forgotten time. Today the
Run lies like a scar across the face of the city. In the light of
day it is a drab and colourless place, traversed by railroad tracks
and hemmed in by crumbling cliffs where, in summer, a few
hardy sunflowers stand above the decay of countless rusting tin
cans, broken bottles, and other debris. Oddly enough, this
ancient ditch, cluttered with strings of railroad freight cars and
spanned by an occasional rude wooden bridge, is the gateway
to one of Cleveland's finest suburbs, for through here speed the
Rapid Transit passenger trains which connect downtown
Cleveland with Shaker Heights, a plush community of handsome
streets and beautiful homes.

At night Kingsbury Run is lost in Stygian blackness, relieved
only by the winking red or green eye of a railway trackside signal
or the brief glow from the windows of passing Rapid Transit
cars rushing homeward to the cleaner air of the suburban heights.

Only youth could feel the spirit of adventure in such an
unlovely spot as Kingsbury Run, but since time began hills have
been a challenge to boyhood and it must have been some such
urge which brought sixteen-year-old James Wagner to the
shapeless and weedy mound which is known as Jackass Hill in
Kingsbury Run that day of September 23, 1935. Jimmy stood
for a brief moment and stared down the sixty-foot slope of the
hill, then decided to climb down it. He scrambled and stumbled
through the weeds and rocks until finally he stood at the foot

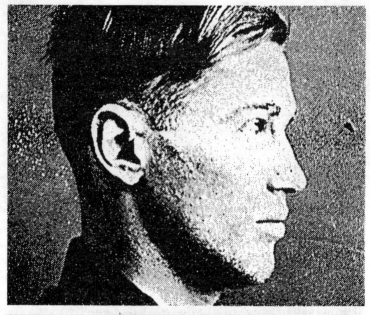

Kingsbury Run victims

of the hill. And there he saw something, partially hidden by a bush.

His heart beating wildly, Jimmy brushed back the branches of the bush, took one look and, suddenly, the spirit of adventure was gone from the boy and the world was a cold and frightful place. Jimmy was staring with popping eyes, his throat dry, at the nude, headless body of a man.

'Oh, gosh,' he gulped. 'Oh, gosh!' And then he fled, wildly and with trembling legs, to find someone, someone alive, to whom to tell his horrible discovery. 'There's a man down there,' the boy gasped to the first person he encountered, 'and—and he—he hasn't got any head!' Jimmy was still pale when the first police squad car drove up, its siren wailing, and officers scrambled down the hill to find the bush and what Jimmy said it hid.

The body was there, right enough, and not only lacked a head but had been emasculated as well. Believing that the missing head probably was buried somewhere near by, the police officers began a systematic search of the area. The search had not gone far when a cry from one of the patrolmen brought his fellow officers rushing to him.

'Find the head?' one of them asked, eagerly.

'No,' said the officer, 'I've found another body!'

He pointed to the partially concealed torso of the second victim. This body, too, lacked a head, and, again like the first, had been emasculated. The search for the heads belonging to the two bodies was redoubled and before darkness fell the seekers were rewarded. The missing heads were found in shallow graves nearby.

What added another fillip of horror to the newspaper account which made many a Clevelander's breakfast the next day suddenly unpalatable was a statement made by the coroner's office after an examination of the two bodies. The heads had been skillfully removed. The decapitations had been made with swift, sure strokes which could have been performed only by someone skilled in dissection. The instrument had been a knife, sharp and so heavy it would naturally have been cumbersome in the hands of anyone not accustomed to its use.

One of the bodies was obviously that of a middle-aged man

of stocky build. The torso was stained by some solution which suggested there had been a possible attempt at preservation. Death had apparently taken place some three weeks before discovery of the murder.

The body of the second victim was that of a much younger man. He had been dead about four days. Through fingerprints this second body was identified. It had been that of one Edward Andrassy, twenty-eight years old, who had lived at 1744 Fulton Road, N. W. Andrassy, it was learned, had at one time been employed at Cleveland City Hospital as an orderly. He had been something of a minor police character, having been arrested some four years before his death on a charge of carrying concealed weapons. There was no apparent motive for his murder nor did any of the clues found point to his killer. The body of the older man who, because his death took place prior to that of Andrassy, must be regarded as the first of the Head Hunter's victims, was never identified.

The twin torso murders appeared, at first glance, not too difficult a mystery to solve. But it was to prove a most baffling case. The emasculated condition of the two bodies indicated the work of a pervert. The skillful manner in which the bodies had been dissected pointed to the probability that the murderer was adept with a dissecting knife or, at least, a butcher's knife.

Cleveland police were still diligently searching for further clues when, four months later, they were distracted by the discovery of a third torso murder. This time the victim had been a woman. What excited investigators was that the discovered parts of the third body were found in an area not far from Kingsbury Run.

January 26, 1936, dawned raw and bitter, a typical Cleveland January day. Pedestrians in East Twentieth Street buried their ears under upturned overcoat collars and shoved hands deep into pockets against the wind that whistled icily along the sidewalks. Along with the wind an eerie cry rose and fell, a cry with a note of terror in it that made the passersby shiver but not with the cold. It was the howling of a frightened dog.

'Just listen to that hound,' said a pedestrian to his companion. 'That dog sounds mighty excited.' Excited the dog was, indeed, and uneasy—for he stood in the rear of the Hart Manufacturing plant at 2315 East Twentieth Street beside two burlap bags and a half bushel basket. Curiosity finally brought someone to investigate the dog's frantic barking. One of the burlap bags was opened and a few minutes later the police were on the scene. The bags and the basket contained dismembered parts of about half of a woman's body.

The bloody parcels held a severed right arm, right hand, and thighs. Immediate search for the missing parts was launched and was rewarded thirteen days later with the finding of the left arm and lower legs in the rear of a vacant building on Orange Avenue, S. E., near East Fourteenth Street. The head was never found. By means of finger prints of one hand, detectives were enabled to identify the woman. She was Mrs Florence Sawdey Polillo, forty-one years old, a resident of 3205 Carnegie Avenue. The police identification was later verified by the woman's former husband who recognized an abdominal scar. As in the case of the two Kingsbury Run torsos, the severed parts of Mrs Polillo's body indicated some degree of skill in dissection.

No motive for Mrs Polillo's murder seemed to exist and, save for the similar skill shown in the dissection of the three bodies, there appeared at the time to be no connecting link between Mrs Polillo and the Kingsbury Run victims. Three years later, however, some evidence was brought forward that suggested the possibility that Mrs Polillo and Andrassy may have been acquainted.

The scene now shifts from that cold and clammy January day when the first parts of Mrs Polillo's body were found to the beautiful, bright morning of June 5, 1936. The day was so lovely that two small Cleveland school boys decided to play hooky and, since their homes were not far from Kingsbury Run, what more enchanting place could two lads find to spend their stolen holiday? Their rompings brought the boys eventually near a willow bush in the Run.

'Hey, lookit!' one of the boys suddenly called to his companion, pointing. 'Somebody left an ole pair of pants under that bush!' The trousers had not been cast aside or folded but were rolled into the shape of a large-sized ball.

'Aw, who cares about an old pair of pants! Bet they were left there by some old tramp! Come on!'

'Let's see if there is anything in the pockets, huh? Come on, now, let's look!'

The trousers were lifted from the ground and the severed head of a young man rolled into view. Two small human comets went plunging in abject terror through the underbrush of the Run to bring to the world news of their frightening find.

What was unique about the discovery of this fourth murder was that this time, not a headless body had been found but a head without a body. However, the torso was unearthed by police the next day near the intersection of Woodland Avenue and East Fifty-first Street. The body was heavily tattooed, which led to the belief that it was that of a sailor. No sailor was missing locally. Nor did anyone come forward to indentify the body or claim it as that of a relative or friend. Despite its distinguishing tattoo marks the body was never identified.

Discovery of the fourth torso murder victim brought to Cleveland realization that the city was experiencing a veritable plague of torso murders. The newspapers recalled, to the increasing discomfort of the more jittery Clevelanders, the grim sagas of other mass murderers—Landru, the French Bluebeard; Haarmann, the German Butcher, and that wraith who once stalked through London's Whitechapel, Jack the Ripper.

Clevelanders read how the Ripper had raged at night through the East End area of London during the period between April and September of the year 1888, slaying and mutilating ten women. And then he vanished, uncaught and unpunished. Kingsbury Run is on Cleveland's East Side. The torso murderer had mutilated two of his victims. To add to these uncomfortable comparisons was the uneasy thought: the Head Hunter, like the Ripper, had not been caught.

Like the Ripper, Henri Landru specialized in the killing of women. The number who fell victim to the dapper but blood-thirsty Frenchman will never be known; estimates range from eleven to twenty, though it is possible the total may have reached a much higher figure. The French Bluebeard lured the women to his villa in a Paris suburb, killed them for their valuables, and cremated the bodies in a furnace in his home. Eventually caught, Landru died beneath the guillotine.

Fritz Haarmann, the third notorious killer in this gallery of human monsters, was the operator of a butcher shop in Germany. His crimes were committed shortly after the close of World War I. He enticed into his shop homeless children, orphaned by the war—there were many in Germany at that time. After killing his young victims Haarmann is believed to have disposed of the flesh through his butcher shop. Caught, he confessed to fifteen killings. Like Landru, Haarmann expiated his crimes beneath the guillotine.

Cleveland's torso murderer has often been compared to this savage European trio but he appears to have been a far shrewder criminal than they. Landru and Haarmann were careless enough to use their own homes as human abattoirs and were caught. The Ripper contemptuously left his victims' bodies strewn about the streets of Whitechapel. The Head Hunter had taken care to dispose of and hide the fragments of his victims' bodies. The deeds and shadowy personality of Cleveland's uncaught killer, it would seem, could be more aptly compared to those of Tezcatlipoca, who was not a man at all but a dreaded deity in the ancient Aztec pantheon of gods.

Like the Head Hunter, who has also been called the Torso Killer, the Mass Murderer and the Uknown, Tezcatlipoca, the Lord of the Night Wind, was known by many other names. He was Zezahualpilli, the Hungry Chief; Toveyo, the Doomster, and Yaotzin, the Enemy. The Head Hunter presumably prowled the Cleveland streets at night in search of human prey and it was death to encounter Tezcatlipoca on the moonlit roads of ancient Mexico. In his role of Doomster, the Cleveland killer, like the Mexican satan, preyed on men and women alike.

The series of torso murders made grim stuff to read, indeed, and even grimmer thoughts to plague one while walking down a dark street. If Clevelanders, especially those who lived in poorly lit streets of the area near Kingsbury Run, now made a point of returning home earlier or not venturing out at all at night, it is understandable. That man, standing there so motionless on the corner, is he really waiting for an owl street car or—? And that shadow, in yonder doorway, is it really a shadow or—? The whole city felt the cold grip of fear and was to know it for many months to come.

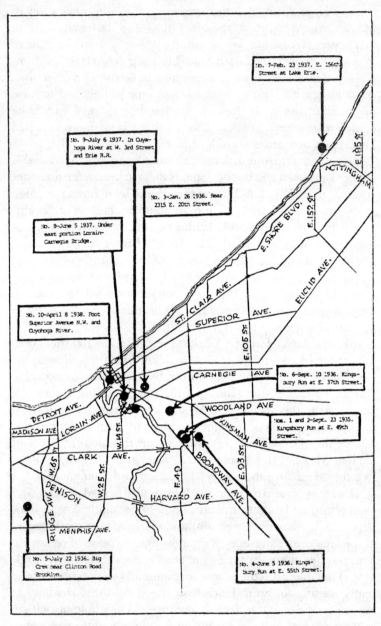

The Mad Butcher's trail

What was most annoying to Cleveland boosters was that the torso murders should occur coincidentally with other local events, planned to bring greater fame and imporance to the city. In 1936, of all years, the community could indeed ill afford such notoriety, for 1936 was to have been the year of Cleveland's glory, the year of the opening of the Northwest Territory Exposition, one of the most ambitious projects in the history of the Lake Erie metropolis. The Exposition was intended to call national attention to the city's industrial and mercantile prominence and to their town's fine summer climate.

The national political spotlight also burned brightly on Cleveland in this summer of 1936, for the city had been chosen as the site of the Republican National Convention, staged in Cleveland's tremendous Municipal Auditorium. This was the Convention that was taken by storm by Governor Alf Landon of Kansas, the triumph of the Sunflower. A number of other but minor national political party conventions also chose to meet in Cleveland that year.

The Exposition drew many large non-political conventions to the city and throughout the summer Cleveland streets, hotel lobbies, and restaurants teemed with conventioneering World War I veterans, lodge brothers of every degree and dignity—or lack of it—and the more sober-minded representatives of numerous industrial and business groups. Music and laughter filled the air and many a gay and colourful parade clattered its way down Euclid Avenue to the sound of drums. Who would be spoil sport enough to remind anyone, especially a visitor, that the Head Hunter still prowled the city's street, unidentified and uncaught?

In the midst of all this gaiety, glamour and good-fellowship, the remains of a fifth torso victim came to light. This time the killer, if he was the same, had crossed the Cuyahoga River which separates the city's East and West Sides. On July 22nd, the completely nude and headless body of a man was found floating in Big Creek near Clinton Road in Brooklyn, a West Side suburb. The fifth victim was never identified and could have been a non-resident drawn to the city by the festivities that marked that summer.

One more torso victim was discovered before 1936's

memorable summer came to an end. On September 10th, a pool
of stagnant, weed-lined water beneath the East Thirty-fourth
Street bridge in Kingsbury Run gave up a grisly find. This
consisted of two neatly severed parts of the body of what had
been a man. The fragments of bone and flesh were so meager
that identification was not possible. The year ended with no
further discoveries of torso murder victims however, much to
the vast relief of understandably nervous Clevelanders.

One of the most extraordinary angles of the Cleveland torso
murders case had now become apparent. Though six persons had
been killed and their bodies or parts of bodies recovered, only two
of them were identified. Four of them still remained unidentified
because, apparently, they had never been reported as missing!
This naturally led to the assumption that they had been vagrants,
without permanent homes and local relatives, neighbours, or even
friends close enough to become curious about their
disappearances. They would appear to have been carefully chosen
as victims by their killer who wanted no hue and cry set upon his
trail by a missing persons report before he successfully disposed
of the remains of his human prey. Since the severed parts of the
various bodies were innocent of clothes, that source of clues was
denied police—further proof of the great care the killer had taken
to make certain his victims would never be named.

What infuriated Cleveland detectives was the sheer audacity
of the Mass Murderer in returning to Kingsbury Run. Four of
the first six victims in the torso killings had been found in the
Run. If the later murders were committed by the same hand,
the Head Hunter must have grown more cautious, for after
disposing of the two fragments in the Thirty-fourth Street pool
the Unknown quiet the place forever.

The hacked upper torso of a young woman was found on
February 23, 1937, on the beach of Beulah Park, where it had
been washed up by the ice-strewn waters of Lake Erie. The beach
is at the foot of East 156th Street, which is on Cleveland's extreme
East Side, miles from Kingsbury Run. This seventh victim was
never identified, though examination of the remains showed that
she had been a mother. Similar fragments had been discovered
on the beach two years earlier. This had occurred on September

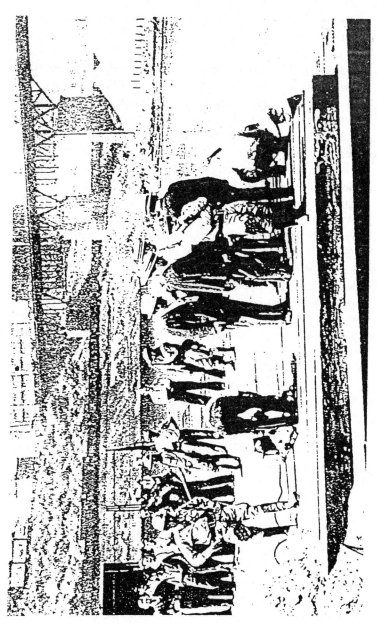

Inspecting the evidence

5, 1934, more than a year before Jimmy Wagner had found the first of the Kingsbury Run victims. This fact makes it possible that the woman may, actually, have been the first one to die at the hand of the killer. Another part of the body had been found two days later, on September 7th, near North Perry, Ohio, some thirty miles east, suggesting that the murder might have taken place there.

It was after the discovery of this torso victim that Cuyahoga County County Coroner Samuel Gerber came forward on the following March first with a report of what had been determined in the examination of the seven murdered persons.

'All seven of the cases,' the coroner's report said, in substance, 'indicate dissection by someone showing keen intelligence in recognizing anatomical landmarks as they were approached.' Absence of blood clots in the heart or larger blood vessels in four of the victims, the report said, indicated death by decapitation or decapitation immediately after being slain. This report was considered of great significance for it gave strong support to the belief that all seven of the murdered persons had probably fallen victim to the same cunning but lethal hand. However, the Cleveland police were no nearer than before to identifying that hand.

No torso but a skeleton was discovered on June 5, 1937. The skeleton, that of a woman, was found beneath the huge Lorain-Carnegie bridge which spans the Cuyahoga River and is one of the main links between western and eastern sections of Cleveland. With only the woman's teeth as a possible clue to her identity police launched a relentless search for the dentist who might be able to recognize the bridgework. For weary months the hunt seemed hopeless and then, nearly a year after the discovery of the body, Detective Peter Merylo, who had been one of the most indefatigable pursuers of the killer, was able proudly to tell reporters that the woman was no longer nameless.

'The skeleton,' the detective announced, 'is that of a Mrs Rose Wallace, forty years of age. She was a resident of Scoville Avenue which is in the area not far from where the skeleton was found. Identification was made by means of her bridgework.'

Mrs Wallace, it was revealed, had last been seen alive nearly a year before her skeleton had been found and nearly two years before identification had been possible. The identification was made by her son, who said the dental work had been done by a Cincinnati dentist who had since died. As a result, positive identification for the police records was not possible.

Exactly one month and one day after the discovery of Mrs Wallace's skeleton, on July 6, 1937, the dismembered parts of a man's body were fished up from the sluggish waters of the Cuyahoga River at West Third Street and the Erie Railroad tracks. The remains were apparently those of a man about thirty-five years of age. Identification proved impossible. With the finding of this body, the killer apparently went into a long hibernation for a tenth victim was not discovered until the following spring.

The severed leg of a mature blonde woman was found in the Cuyahoga River near Superior Avenue on April 8, 1938. Later, on May 2nd of the same year, other parts of the same body were found in the river. These second remnants consisted of the left foot, thighs, and headless torso, wrapped in a burlap bag. It will be recalled here that portions of Mrs Pollilo's body, the third victim, had been similarly wrapped. The original find of the tenth victim, the severed leg, had been cleanly cut at knee and ankle and while the cuts showed evidence of haste as though dissection had taken place immediately after death, the dissection indicated the work of one familiar with the use of the knife.

From the remains it was theorized that this latest victim was a woman of perhaps twenty-five to thirty years of age, possibly weighing some one hundred and fifteen pounds and judged to have been about five feet and four inches in height. Police believed that the finding of the leg had occurred probably less than seventy-two hours after the murder took place. The woman was never identified.

Though it would be years before the more apprehensive of Clevelanders could be persuaded of the fact, the career of the torso murderer was drawing to a close. The bloody drama was ending but the shadow of the slayer was not to withdraw from the stage until two more killings were revealed.

James Dawson, aged twenty-one, chanced on August 16, 1938,

to be passing a dump near the intersection of Lake Shore Drive and east Ninth Street, which is close by the heart of Cleveland's downtown business area, when he spied a mound of rocks. Removal of some of the rocks revealed the dismembered torso and blonde head of a woman perhaps thirty-five years old. The head was wrapped in brown paper. She had been approximately five feet and five inches in height and her weight was about one hundred and twenty-five pounds. Search of the area revealed remains of a second victim. These were the haircovered skull and about forty bones of a male, estimated to have been between forty and fifty years of age and rather short in stature.

Near the woman's remains a copy of *Collier's* magazine was found. It bore the date of March 5, 1938. This clue, if it was one, proved of no value. Of greater interest to the police was a tattered quilt in which the bones of the twelfth victim had been wrapped. After newspaper publication of a photograph of the quilt, a barber came forward and identified it as one he had given to a junkman a month or so before the discovery of the bones on the dump. The junkman told police he had sold the quilt to a rag and paper company, from which it must have been stolen, for here the trail ended.

The discovery of the remains of the last two torso murder victims spurred the police into a new kind of activity. Since the victims had apparently never been missed, it was natural to assume that they had been vagrants. Therefore, the police decided to raid the shanty colony that infested the city's notorious 'Flats' section on a hillside at Commercial and Canal Roads near Kingsbury Run. The raid was launched at one o'clock in the morning of August 18th. Safety Director Eliot Ness led the raiders in person, the invading party consisting of some twenty-five detectives in eleven police cars. A spear-head group of ten detectives, led by Sergeant James McDonald, preceded the main body and took up posts at the six approaches to the raiding zone to prevent any alarm being given.

The police closed in. With a searchlight mounted on a fire truck illuminating the scene, the detectives, carrying flashlights, smashed into the shanties. In an instant the entire shanty colony was in a fearful uproar. The din was terrific. To the screaming and cursing of the surprised vagrants was added the howling of their pet dogs. As fast as the vagrants could be captured they were hustled into patrol cars and were sent speeding jailward. Those of the captured who were without jobs or visible means of support were sent to the workhouse.

When the shanties were swept clear of all human inhabitants, the shacks were fired. This action later brought newspaper protests but no one could deny the fact that one of the city's worst 'eye-sores' had vanished into the smoke that hung above Shantytown and that downtown Cleveland was a cleaner place for it. The police were quick to point out that the arrests had not been made as torso killer suspects but that the removal of the vagrants was for their own protection since, had they remained there, they might well have become potential victims of the Mass Murderer.

The series of torso murders were at an end—but Clevelanders, official and civilian, naturally were unaware of that fact. There continued to be scares that a thirteenth victim had been found. That same August the body of a man was washed ashore onto Gordon Park Beach, on the city's East Side. Though the hands and feet were missing and strands of a rotting rope were entangled with the leg stumps, it was pointed out that this mutilation might have been caused by contact with the sharp rocks on the floor of the lake during the body's long immersion. Condition of the torso indicated the man had been in the water for at least a year.

Another scare shook Cleveland with the discovery of an amputated right foot on a city dump shortly after finding the bodies of the last two victims. However, Detective Merylo and his able associate, Detective Martin Zalewski, assured the public through the newspapers that instead of this being evidence of a thirteenth torso killing the foot most probably was part of hospital refuse, result of some perfectly legal and beneficial surgical operation.

The less tough-minded of Cleveland residents were apt to see 'evidence' of a fresh torso killing down the spine-chilling stretch of every dark alley, amid the weed-clogged hillocks of any long vacant building lot or in the basement of deserted tenements, now fallen into decay. Once the police received a report that a human skeleton had been found in a clogged sewer. Investigation revealed the stoppage in the sewer pipe had not been caused by human remnants but by some sheep bones, thrust there by a thoughtless but far from murderous citizen. Another report of a 'skeleton' sent detectives into the basement of an East Side residential building. The 'skeleton' proved to be a mound of chicken bones and the remnants of some spare ribs discarded by a former resident who apparently had little faith in the city's vaunted system of garbage collection and disposal.

The fame or, rather, infamy of the Head Hunter of Kingsbury Run had spread far beyond the confines of Cuyahoga County and the State of Ohio, making front-page news throughout the world. It was good reading—for Nazi purposes—in the Hitler-controlled press of Germany, firmly under the thumb of Propaganda Minister Josef Goebbels. Gleefully, the *Beobachters* and *Tageblatts* pointed out editorially how decadent life must be in a democracy where a mass murderer could stalk the streets without fear of capture. It made good reading in the Fascist press of Benito Mussolini.

It made interesting reading, spine-chilling reading in the United States too, and as result numerous communities throughout the country began to claim murderous visitations of the Head Hunter. Torsos and parts of torsos made news throughout the East and Middle West. No matter how distant a torso find might be from Cleveland the fatal hand of the Ohio city's master murderer was suspect in the business.

In March of 1938 a dog trotted out of a wood near Sandusky, Ohio, dragging a human leg and foot. The animal had found his prize in the underbrush. Intensive search failed to uncover the missing parts of the body. The leg had been neatly severed just below the knee. Sandusky's Coroner E. J. Meckstroth said that the amputation looked like a 'professional' job. This was enough to make Sanduskians wonder if the Head Hunter might not have become a most unwelcome neighbour.

In May of that same year a severed leg and arm were recovered from the Mohawk River near Albany, New York. The remains were believed to be those of a middle-aged woman, heavily built but of medium height. Police verdict: 'A clean job.' The Head Hunter, again? Parts of a woman's mutilated and decapitated body were found in Lake Ontario near the city of Oswego, New York. It was at first thought the remains might be those of a Cleveland torso victim which had somehow floated that far from the Lake Erie metropolis. A headless torso was found in a swamp near New Castle, Pennsylvania, in October of 1938. The head was found several days later. Pennsylvanians shivered to read that the police authorities had concluded the manner in which the body was dismembered bore a similarity to many of the Cleveland killings.

Local clues by the hundreds were investigated by the Cleveland police without result. In March of 1938 an attendant at a refinery pumphouse near Kingsbury Run reported he had seen an expensive motor car stop on the Jefferson Street bridge. A man emerged from the car and threw a large, seemingly heavy bundle into the river. Nothing came of this clue. In April of the same year two men told police they had seen a heavy-set man walk into a storm sewer beneath the High Level bridge. The man did not reappear nor could the two who saaw him give any clearer description of him. Since this occured at the time of the finding of the remains of the tenth victim a possible connection was seen. Since no further trace of the man could be found this possible clue, too, had to be dropped.

After the finding of the twelfth victim National Guard pilots of the One Hundred and Twelfth Observation Squadron, Thirty-seventh Division, came to the aid of the Cleveland police in an effort to find the mass murderer. The Thirty-seventh Division, incidentally, is one of the outfits that fought so brilliantly in the Pacific Theatre during World War II. The squadron made four reconnaissance flights photographing the area in which the torso and other parts of the body of the eleventh victim were found in May of 1938. Police naturally had high hopes that the aerial photographs might reveal some hidden path or paths which might lead the manhunters closer to their elusive quarry.

One naturally wonders whether the unknown killer might not have watched the skies anxiously as the reconnaissance planes droned back and forth across the blue. Perhaps he stood on some city sidewalk and rubber-necked with the curious crowd, to all appearances just another citizen gawking at planes in the sky.

While the search for the Head Hunter was the concern of every peace officer in the community, the efforts of Detectives Peter Merylo and Martin Zalewski stand out as exceptional. For pure persistence their manhunt was remarkable. Javert's relentless tracking down of Jean Val Jean in Victor Hugo's *Les Miserables*, is matched with the diligence with which Merylo and Zalewski hunted for the torso killer.

The two detectives were assigned the torso-killing case, on which they were to work exclusively, following the discovery of the sixth victim, the third one to be found in Kingsbury Run. Merylo and Zalewski were tireless in pursuit of their quarry. Not only were they assigned full time to the case but they devoted countless off-duty hours to the chase, willingly sacrificing their leisure.

The trail took them through the festering jungles of the city's underworld. They often wore filthy clothes, posing as tramps or worse so that they might ferret out some nugget of information, some chance, unguarded word dropped by one of the habitués of the dives they visited. Through the human rabbit-warrens that make up a great metropolis' underworld they made their way, ears alert and eyes wary for the little clue that might prove the one big clue that would lead to the killer. On occasion they even crawled through rat-infested sewers.

Suspects by the hundreds fell into the dragnet spread by the two detectives. By March of 1938 more than 1,500 persons had been questioned by Merylo and Zalewski. This figure, though staggering, did not compare with what was yet to come. By the end of that year more than 5,000 persons had been questioned by the Cleveland police! Never before and perhaps never again will so many individuals be questioned in a murder case.

The wholesale roundup of vagrants and stumble-bums for questioning led to no solution of the case but had, at least, one very salutary effect. Cleveland was swept nearly clean of criminals, both small fry and some pretty big fish. Among the suspects gathered in by Merylo and Zalewski scores were found guilty of offences ranging from misdemeanors to such major crimes as robbery, burglary, and assault. Among the prizes plucked from Cleveland's underworld were not only the host of wanted criminals but the police also bagged forty-seven insane persons, a number of these being unquestionably of the potential killer class; seven unregistered aliens; and a number of sex perverts.

It began to appear that the inseparable pair of manhunters— Merylo and Zalewski—would continue their search for the mass murderer until either they caught him or they reached the age of retirement from the police force. And then the blow fell. Merylo and Zalewski quarreled bitterly. The break was revealed publicly on April 13, 1938. The two men had toiled unceasingly together in their search for eighteen exhausting months and mutual friends blamed the long, fatiguing manhunt for frayed nerves which may have led to their parting of the ways.

The split between the two partners in pursuit came over Detective Merylo's determination to question a man about his friendship with the late Edward Andrassy who was, it will be remembered, one of the first of the Head Hunter's victims and the only identified among the seven masculine victims. Zalewski's contention was that it would probably prove a better plan to release the man and then keep him under surveillance. When neither would agree to the other's plan, Zalewski heatedly asked that he be taken off the case. Merylo later resigned from the police force and set up shop as a private detective.

And now we come to the most interesting figure in the torso murder case: Frank Dolezal, the bricklayer from Bohemia.

During the summer of 1938 a private investigator by the name of Lawrence J. Lyons, better known to his associates and friends by the nickname of 'Pat' Lyons, became interested in the torso mysteries. After careful study of police and coroner reports, Lyons developed a theory, based on the fact that so many of the bodies were found in a given area of the city and also that the bodies showed a certain skill in dissection. Lyons' hunch was that the murders and dissections probably took place in a well-equipped 'laboratory' and this laboratory most likely was situated somewhere within or very near the Kingsbury Run area.

'This "laboratory," as I visualized it,' Lyons said later in outlining his theory, 'had to be sound-proof, easily cleaned and must, of a necessity, have some sort of storage facilities, probably refrigerated. There couldn't be many places like that in the

Kingsbury Run area. If one existed, it should not be difficult to find.'

As a private investigator Lyons could not explore the possibilities without official permission and aid, so he took his idea to Cuyahoga County Sheriff Martin L. O'Donnell. The sheriff was enthusiastic and immediately assigned John Gillespie, chief deputy sheriff in the civil branch, and Deputy Sheriff Paul McDevitt to work with Lyons.

The three men made an exhaustive canvass of the murder area. However, no such 'laboratory' as Lyons visualized was uncovered. Reluctantly, the investigators abandoned the idea. Meanwhile, they developed a second theory. This was that some of the murder victims may have been known to each other and that there might be a mutual acquaintance who, in the guise of friendship, had won the victims' confidence and had slain them, one by one, to satiate some incomprehensible blood lust.

Investigation finally centered on a nondescript group of some twenty persons, men and women, who frequented a cheap saloon in the neighbourhood of East Twentieth Street and Central Avenue. This tawdry clique was made up largely of prostitutes, beggars, and other riff-raff plus a few others who were gainfully employed.

In casually discussing the murders with the habitués of the bar, Lyons uncovered an interesting fact. Mrs Florence Polillo and Mrs Rose Wallace, two of the murder victims, had been not only frequenters of the saloon but were very friendly with each other. They also were acquainted with some of the men who hung around the bar. The jubilant investigators, now hot on the trail of the unknown, or so they believed, uncovered still another clue – Edward Andrassy had also been a frequenter of the saloon!

Lyons, Gillespie, and McDevitt, felt they were really closing in on their quarry when a fruit dealer, who had an establishment in the area under scrutiny, told of a man he knew as 'Frank' who had a penchant for carrying knives and brandishing them, sometimes 'threatening' to use them on his acquaintances. 'Frank,' further investigation indicated, was a certain Frank Dolezal, a middle-aged bricklayer, who had lived in a small apartment house on Central Avenue, not far from where parts of some of the Head Hunter's victims had been recovered.

The sheriff's investigators gained entrance to the bricklayer's vacated four-room apartment and subjected the place to a microscopic scrutiny. Their mission was fruitless until they reached the bathroom. Here their painstaking search was richly rewarded. In the cracks of the floor and the baseboard were long-dried, black stains. The three men stood up and stared at each other. In their minds one word formed: 'Blood?' If the stains were actually blood, then of this they felt certain: This dilapidated, unkempt little bathroom in which they stood was the grim murder chamber for which they had so long sought, the 'laboratory' of the Head Huntger of Kingsbury Run!

The missing bricklayer was quickly located but no arrest was made. Sheriff O'Donnell wanted as much evidence as possible, evidence which would stand up in a trial, before he closed in on his man. Lyons took scrapings of the stained wood of the floor and baseboard of the Central Avenue bathroom to his brother, G. V. Lyons, a chemist, for analysis. Chemist Lyons reported back: the discolourations were bloodstains.

'Then,' said Lyons, in discussing the later investigations conducted by himself with Gillespie and McDevitt, 'we managed to uncover some startling facts. We found that Mrs Polillo had lived with Dolezal for some time. We also learned that the bricklayer had on occasion visited Mrs Wallace. one informant told us of having seen Dolezal and Mrs Polillo together on the evening of January 24, 1936.'

More evidence began to pile up. Stains on two of four knives said to have once been in Dolezal's possession were discovered to be dried blood. Statements were obtained from neighbours who told of seeing both Mrs Polillo and Mrs Wallace frequenting the Dolezal apartment at 1908 Central Avenue, S. E. They also told of seeing a sailor enter the Dolezal apartment. One of the torso victims, it will be remembered, was heavily tattooed. Though never identified, police believed this body was that of a sailor.

Sheriff O'Donnell now had considerable evidence in his hands, evidence strongly connecting the bricklayer to at least one and possibly more of the torso murders. However, it was not only the evidence uncovered that decided Sheriff O'Donnell to put

Dolezal under arrest. Deputy Sheriff McDevitt walked into the sheriff's office on the morning of Wednesday, July 5, 1939, a worried frown on his face. What he said spurred Sheriff O'Donnell into action.

'Sheriff,' McDevitt said, 'I've just discovered that Merylo has been checking up on my activities lately.'

'Checking up on you?'

'Right. I've learned that Merylo has even called at my home when I was absent. Sheriff, the police know something!'

'It was then,' Sheriff O'Donnell told reporters later, 'that we decided to make the arrest that very night!'

The arrest was made by John Gillespie, the chief deputy sheriff, who had helped Lyons and McDevitt in the investigation which brought the trail to the doorstep of Frank Dolezal. Dolezal was placed under arrest at six o'clock that Wednesday night and he was taken to Cuyahoga County jail for questioning.

Two days later, Sheriff O'Donnell called in newspapermen. The sheriff was apparently in a high state of excitement.

'Boys,' he said, 'we have a signed confession to one of the torso murders!' He then revealed that at two o'clock that afternoon, Friday, County Detective Harry S. Brown had wrung a confession from a prisoner under custody, Frank Dolezal, to the dissection of the body of Mrs florence Sawdey Polillo. He then gave the significant details of the confession. The newspaper reporters and cameramen filed in to get their first look at the prisoner. Their excitement was high. Were they at last to come face-to-face with the Head Hunter himself?

What they saw was a short, stockily built man of 52, of Bohemian extraction, who stared back at them with pale, wide eyes. His ruddy face was badly in need of a shave. He wore a perspiration-stained shirt, open at the throat and without a tie. His trousers were of some dark material and his feet were shod in a pair of white summer shoes, somewhat soiled. The reporters jotted down additional statistics: the prisoner was five feet eight inches in height and weighed 147 pounds. He had emigrated from Bohemia at the age of sixteen. At the time of his arrest he was working as a bricklayer but he had previously been employed in a Cleveland slaughter house. At this, some of the reporters exchanged glances.

Sheriff O'Donnell now revealed details of the questioning which led to the signed confession. O'Donnell himself had conducted the questioning on Friday morning. Shortly before lunch he obtained admission from Dolezal that the prisoner had known and had gotten drunk on occasion with both Andrassy and Mrs Wallace. The prisoner also admitted to having had a quarrel with Mrs Polillo in his apartment just two nights previous to the discovery of parts of her body. This fitted with Coroner Samuel Gerber's findings at the time Mrs Polillo's remains were discovered. Coroner Gerber had said that condition of the body indicated that Mrs Polillo had been dead for approximately two days.

'We were in my room drinking Friday night,' the sheriff quoted Dolezal as telling him. 'She had two drinks. I had two drinks. She was all dressed up and wanted to go out. She wanted some money. She grabbed for ten dollars I had in my pocket. I argued with her because she had tried to take some money from me before. But I didn't kill her. I didn't kill anybody.' He would say nothing further.

As it was lunch time the sheriff called a recess in the questioning and Dolezal was given a meal. Shortly after lunch the questioning was resumed but this time by County Detective Brown instead of Sheriff O'Donnell.

'She did hit you, didn't she?' Brown asked, his steady stare revited on the pale-eyed man before him. Dolezal's reply, as reported by the sheriff, revealed to the county detective that a break might be near.

'She came at me with a butcher knife.'

'And you hit her, too,' Brown said, not so much as a question as a statement of fact. In response a torrent of words flowed from the prisoner.

'Yes, I hit her with my fist,' Dolezal answered, according to the sheriff. 'She fell into the bathroom and hit her head against the bathtub. I thought she was dead. I put her in the bathrub. Then I took a knife—the small one—and cut off her head. Then I cut off her legs. then her arms.'

The confession then told of the disposal of the dissected body. Dolezal said he put parts of the body at the rear of the Hart Manufacturing Company at 2315 East Twentieth Street. The woman's coat and shoes, the confession said, were also placed at the rear of the Hart establishment, the remainder of her clothes being burned. The rest of the body—head, lower legs, and left arm—were stuffed into two baskets which he carried some three miles to Lake Erie at about four o'clock in the morning. The quarrel and fatal fall were described as having taken place sometime between two and four o'clock.

Dolezal's statement told of crossing ice until he reached the breakwater in the lake, then of throwing the contents of the two baskets into the open water beyond. The statement said he returned several times to the place from which the head, lower legs and left arm had been thrown into the lake, in order to see if they had possibly been washed back ashore. But they had vanished from sight.

The United States Weather Bureau office at Cleveland, in a checkup, revealed that the temperature during the night of January 25th – 26th was near zero, and that considerable ice had formed between the shore proper and the breakwater, while there was some open water beyond the breakwater, due to an offshore breeze. This substantiated Dolezal's account.

In making public the confession the sheriff's office pointed out what appeared to be a number of significant facts. Dolezal's apartment was, by actual measurement, only 235 yards from the spot where the first parts of Mrs Polillo's body were found, in the rear of 2315 East Twentieth Street. The quilt which was found with the torso and bones of the eleventh and twelfth victims was traced to the Scoville Rag and Paper Company warehouse at 2276 Scoville Avenue, from which place it was believed to have been stolen. The skeleton of Mrs Wallace was found under the Lorain-Central Bridge in the Cuyahoga River basin, only a few blocks from Dolezal's apartment. Mrs Wallace had lived at 2027 Scoville Avenue just a block from Dolezal's residence. Dolezal had abandoned the Central Avenue apartment in August, 1938, at which time the police, spurred by the finding of the remains of the eleventh and twelfth victims, were making a concentrated search of the area in the vicinity of the Central Avenue house.

The Dolezal confession caused a tremendous sensation in Cleveland. If the police were chagrined because it had resulted from the efforts of the sheriff's office instead of their own department, the first public reaction of the department was a sporting one. As soon as he was notified of the sheriff's announcement of the Dolezal confession, Safety Director Eliot Ness declared: 'The sheriff is to be commended for his investigation. The leads he has uncovered will, of course, be followed up to see what possible connection the Polillo case may have with any other.' Ness then pledged the cooperation of the police department with the sheriff's office.

Those Clevelanders who, eager for a solution of the torso murders case and a final removal of the fear which had stalked the city for four years and who, at first blush, misread the sheriff's announcement regarding Dolezal as indicating arrest of the Head Hunter, were soon disillusioned. Sheriff O'Donnell himself was quick to announce that he was not fully satisfied with the Dolezal confession.

'There are some things,' the sheriff said, 'we want him to tell us.'

Certain discrepancies between the Dolezal statement and known facts were pointed out. The statement told of throwing Mrs Polillo's head, lower legs, and left arm into Lake Erie beyond the breakwater, yet all of these parts of the woman's body, save the head, were found in the rear of a vacant building on Orange Avenue, S. E., near East Fourteenth Street. If Dolezal was telling the truth, how did they get there? The statement also mentioned the placing of Mrs Polillo's coat and shoes in the rear of the Hart Manufacturing Company's building. These were never found.

On Wednesday, July 12th, Attorney Fred P. Soukup, who had been retained as Dolezal's counsel, declared that Dolezal had denied the Polillo killing and that he had said he was 'in a daze' when he made the confession. Suspicion that Dolezal had been under pressure before making his statement dimmed when Monsignor Oldrich Zlamal, of Our Lady of Lourdes Catholic church, visited Dolezal and was told by the prisoner that he had not been abused in Cuyahoga County jail.

The strongest blow so far in the case against the confession came the next day with the announcement by Dr. E. E. Ecker, a pathologist at Cleveland's Western Reserve University, that he had tested the stains on the wood scrapings which had been earlier identified as blood. The marks, said Dr Ecker emphatically, were not bloodstains!

At a preliminary hearing on July 17th before Justice of the Peace Myron J. Penty the charge of murder against Dolezal was reduced to one of manslaughter. 'The murder charge was placed against Dolezal after his oral confession,' the sheriff later said. 'However, Dolezal's own statement that he had killed Mrs Polillo in self-defense during a drunken argument resulted in the charge being reduced to manslaughter at the preliminary hearing.'

With the reduction of the charge against him newspaper and public interest in Dolezal rapidly waned. The figure of the bleary-eyed, unkempt man who sat in a Cuyahoga County jail cell faded from the public eye in the welter of news events that crowded the front page and radio newscasts. Bombs exploded in a Jerusalem broadcasting station and in King's Cross and Victoria railway stations in London. Another bomb blocked the Leeds-Liverpool canal in England. Japanese troops were occupying all of Shanghai save the International Settlement. An explosion in a coal mine near Providence, Kentucky, brought death to twenty-eight entombed miners. And scientists at Baldwin, Long Island, were sending a radio signal to Mars, thirty-six million miles away – and waiting in vain for an answer.

The German-Soviet non-aggression pact, announced by Germany on August 21st, and which seemed to make war a certainty, was still the number one topic of conversation when, on Thursday, August 24th, Frank Dolezal once more made the top headlines and in a startling fashion. He had killed himself.

At forty-eight minutes past one o'clock that afternoon Deputy Sheriff Hugh Crawford, who with Deputy Sheriff Adolph Schuster had been assigned the duty of keeping watch on Dolezal, returned to find Dolezal had strangled himself with a noose made of strips of cleaning rags which had been wound around his neck and a hook in the cell. Crawford later stated he had left Dolezal alone for three minutes in order to notify a visitor in another cell that visiting time was up. The other deputy sheriff and Dolezal guard, Schuster, had left shortly before in order to escort some visitors downstairs.

'Dolezal, after placing the rope of rags around his neck threw his body forward, thus throwing his full weight on his neck,' Sheriff O'Donnell declared in explaining how the prisoner, who was five feet eight inches in height, managed to hang himself from a hook which was placed only five feet seven inches above the cell floor. 'Dolezal,' the sheriff continued, 'had not only fashioned the rope with which he hung himself from strips of cleaning rags but he also had, for some unknown purpose, additional strips of the same kind of cloth wound around his waist and concealed beneath his trousers.

'We found Dolezal hanging limply against the wall. My own knife was used to cut him down, which was done by Assistant Chief Jailer Archie Burns while Deputy Sheriff Crawford held Dolezal's body. We called for a male nurse and the fire rescue squad, meanwhile trying to revive the prisoner.'

But neither the Rescue Squad's oxygen nor the jail physician's insulin could revive Dolezal.

When Coroner Samuel Gerber announced there would be no autopsy because no criminality was involved, William E. Edwards of the Cleveland Crime Commission came forward with a demand that an autopsy be performed. Edwards' action was partly inspired by the finding of discrepancies in statements concerning the length of time in which Dolezal had allegedly been left alone. Edwards said he also had an affidavit from Charles Dolezal, forty-four-year-old brother of the dead man, requesting an autopsy.

'In view of all the street corner rumours and other reports of brutal treatment of Dolezal,' Edwards said in insisting on an autopsy, 'I think it only fair to the sheriff and the public to make as thorough an investigation as possible to ascertain the truth or falsity of these reports.'

Dolezal's defense counsel, Attorney Soukup, came forward with a complaint that he had not been notified until three o'clock, more than an hour after his client's death, of what had transpired. Soukup said he had seen Dolezal on the Tuesday prior to the suicide and that the prisoner was at that time depressed by his treatment in jail.

'I'm convinced there was no physical mistreatment of Dolezal after I came into the case,' said the attorney, 'but he complained other prisoners taunted him and deputy sheriffs called him "names." I had a hunch something like this would happen before Dolezal ever came to trial. What kind of a jail are you running, anyway? I thought you were keeping a twenty-four hour watch on him!'

'We were,' Chief Deputy Sheriff Clarence M. Tylicki is quoted as replying. 'We tried to watch him all the time.'

'Oh,' was the attorney's rejoinder, 'I suppose you gave him all the protection you could.'

An autopsy was conducted on Friday, the day after Dolezal's death, by Coroner Gerber, County Pathologist Reuben Strauss and Doctor Harry Goldblatt, assistant professor of pathology in Western Reserve University's School of Medicine. The autopsy, it was announced, disclosed that six of Dolexal's ribs had suffered fracture. This report brought another angry statement from Attorney Soukup.

'It is absurd,' he said, 'to imagine Dolezal could have done the work he did if he had received the fractures to his ribs before he went to jail. Dolezal worked at his job as bricklayer continuously until he was arrested July fifth.'

At the inquest, conducted on Saturday, the day after the autopsy, by Coroner Gerber, Sheriff O'Donnell and other officials of his office testified.

'Dolezal was never subjected to any violence,' Sheriff O'Donnell insisted. O'Donnell told of possessing a paper purported to have been signed by Dolezal which told of two previous attempts at suicide by the prisoner.

'Dolezal said he hurt himself when the noose slipped and he fell to the floor, striking a bench. He promised me, after the second attempt, never to try suicide again. We did all we could to keep him from committing suicide.'

In referring to accusations of mistreatment, Sheriff O'Donnell retorted: 'We treated the man too well. We have nothing to hide. Any and all investigations in the past on alleged beatings in the jail, have led to no findings whatever by the investigating body.

'Dolezal must have been afraid to face the grand jury,' the sheriff insisted. 'I'm sure we had the right man. We did all we could in the case. We got a confession from from and we were close to tying him up with another of the torso murders. We did everything we could to prevent him from committing suicide. He was in good spirits. We never bothered him at all.'

The death of Frank Dolezal solved nothing. It only added one more puzzle to the greater mystery which was the Torso Murders Case. Was he the cause of the death of Mrs Polillo when a blow from his fist in a drunken brawl caused her to fall and strike her head against the bathtub, as the confession declares? Or was he a man so overcome with terror at his predicament that his statements were only the babblings of a benumbed mind? Or was he not only guilty of Mrs Polillo's death but also of another of the torso murders as the sheriff declared? We will probably never know.

Some months before the arrest of Dolezal, in January of 1939, the *Cleveland Plain Dealer* published a letter which had been received by Chief George Matowitz of the Cleveland Police Department. The letter purported to be from the elusive Head Hunter himself and was mailed from Los Angeles. As it could be the actual swan song of the perpetrator of the revolting series of torso murders, the letter is of more than passing interest. It read as follows:

> Chief of Police Matowitz:
> You can rest easy now, as I have come out to sunny California for the winter. I felt bad operating on those people, but science must advance. I shall astound the medical profession, a man with only a D. C.
> What did their lives mean in comparison to hundreds of sick and disease-twisted bodies? Just laboratory guinea pigs found on any public street. No one missed them when I failed. My last case was successful. I know now the feeling of Pasteur, Thoreau and other pioneers.
> Right now I have a volunteer who will absolutely prove my theory. They call me mad and a butcher, but the truth will out.
> I have failed but once here. The body has not been found and never will be, but the head, minus the features, is buried on Century Boulevard, between Western and Crenshaw. I feel it my duty to dispose of the bodies as I do. It is God's will not to let them suffer.
> (signed) 'X'

The letter of a thrill-seeking crank, a madman, or the Head Hunter of Kingsbury Run? Police could not locate the remains mentioned in the message. The letter reads like the work of a person with some education which lends credence to the belief held by many at the time of the killings that the murderer was an insane surgeon. Just as many held that the criminal was a chripractor or a chiropodist gone mad. The killer might even have been a crazed medical student or a butcher who had fallen into a nightmare of insanity, a mind bereft of reason yet retaining knowledge of the skill with the knife he had learned earlier in life.

In closing the file on the Cleveland Torso Murders Case—it is with regret that we must stamp it 'Unsolved'—one is struck with wonder by the vast ramifications of the affair and the march of events, touching so many lives, which the Head Hunter set in motion that grim September night of 1935 when he killed and dismembered his first victim and hid the pitiful remains in the underbrush of Jackass Hill in Kingsbury Run. With the skillful strokes of his knife, the torso murderer ushered in three years of fear in which at least eleven other of his victims were to be uncovered, most of them drab figures, ignored by the world in life and doomed to remain nameless in death.

As the curtain falls on the drama of the Cleveland Torso Murders Case—a strange play in which the star of the show never appears but dominates the moves of the visible players—one must come to the conclusion that the Head Hunter stands unique among the more sinister figures in all the annals of crime. Shrouded in what has proved an impenetrable mystery, a faceless, invisibly entity as unreal as a nightmare, he was in truth a terribly real monster whose shadow lay for three years across a great city.

There is no evidence to show conclusively that the Head Hunter was a single individual and not several persons. Nor does ther exist absolute proof that 'he' was not a woman. However, in the absence of proof of the last two contentions and in face of the striking similarities of the killings—such as the skilled manner of dissection—it is but natural to assume that the Head Hunter of Kingsbury Run was, indeed, a single killer, sadistic and diabolically clever; insane but a genius in his chosen blood-stained field.

ANTHONY BERKELEY

Who Killed Madame X?

The case of Madame 'X' might have come almost unchanged out of the pages of any modern detective novel.

All the stock ingredients of the mystery story are present— the mysterious woman, with a mysterious past; the mysterious attack by an unknown assailant; the anonymous letters of threats beforehand; the suspicion on the wrong person; the disappearance of the weapon (in this case probably not a blunt but a sharp instrument); and a dozen other details which the detective-novelist looks on as part of his stock-in-trade. Instead of fiction copying fact, fact here definitely copies fiction.

On the night of February 4, 1929, a Mrs Jackson was returning with a friend, Mrs Dimick, from a cinema to her bungalow at Limeslade Way, about six miles from Swansea in Wales. The time was ten o'clock and the night was a dark one.

Mrs Jackson and Mrs Dimick were next-door neighbours. The two women parted at the latter's bungalow, and Mrs Dimick went indoors.

She had been inside only a few seconds and was still taking off her coat when she heard screams. Recognising Mrs Jackson's voice, she hurried out, towards the back door of the bungalow occupied by Mr and Mrs Jackson, 'Kenilworth.'

About eight feet outside the back door Mrs Jackson was lying on the ground in a heap. Her husband was bending over her when Mrs Dimick arrived, and Mrs Dimick thought he was trying to help her up. He said: 'Help me to pick her up, Dimmy. I don't know what has happened.'

Between them they pulled Mrs Jackson into the scullery. Mrs Dimick attended to her, and after a time Mrs Jackson recovered

113

enough to stand up and walk into the sitting-room. It is doubtful whether she was ever entirely unconscious.

At about midnight Jackson called in a doctor, who took Mrs Jackson at once to hospital. She lingered there for six days in a semi-conscious condition, and then died. Although asked whenever opprtunity seemed to offer, she was unable to tell the police or the doctors who had attacked her. It is most probable that she did not know. A fortnight later Jackson was arrested and charged with her murder.

That is the straightforward story of Mrs Jackson's death. Behind that story there is another one, anything but straightforward.

The first suggestion of this mysterious background is in a remark made by Jackson to the doctor shortly after the three of them arrived at the hospital. He said: 'I have been married to her for nearly ten years, and I still do not know who she is.'

Jackson was not alone in looking on his wife as a woman of mystery. Her neighbours and friends found her equally baffling. By them she had been considered at one time a woman of considerable means. The move to the little bungalow 'Kenilworth' had been made only a couple of years before her death.

Before that the Jacksons had lived in a much larger house, which Mrs Jackson, by lavish expenditure, had made into a 'miniature palace.' Jackson himself was a fish hawker, with a steady but small business, so clearly little of the money thus spent came from him.

Mrs Jackson had extravagant tastes, and at that time the means to indulge them. She would spend several pounds on flowers for the decoration of her table on a single day; her clothes were of the smartest and most expensive; she would dispense £1 notes as tips with regal generosity; if any extravagant whim took her, such as hiring a car or a motor-launch for the day, she gratified it instantly.

And the cash? That came to her by post regularly every Wednesday morning—sometimes 'a whole bundle of notes,' sometimes only two or three pounds.

Mrs Jackson's own explanation to her friends was that she was a novelist and a journalist. None of them, not even her husband, had any idea of the real truth. For Mrs Jackson was not a novelist or a journalist, though she certainly conducted a large and lucrative correspondence. She was an unusually successful blackmailer.

It was mentioned during the hearing a few years previously of a charge of misappropriation that the accused man had parted with a large sum of money to a harpy referred to as Madame 'X'. The suppression of the woman's name was requested by the police in the hope that some restitution would be made by her in return. It is hardly necessary to say that the police were too optimistic, and the only result was that the woman whose name they so carefully shielded was able to escape the public disclosure she so richly deserved.

Madame 'X' was Mrs Jackson.

Mr Jackson, apparently, had believed all his wife had told him when they first met, in 1919, and accepted the idea that she was a wealthy woman who did a little journalism and so on just for fun.

There was a curious touch about their marriage; for Mrs Jackson, objecting to the name of her husband as too ordinary, persuaded him to be married in the name of 'Captain Ingram.' In 1932, however, Jackson, who had never been very happy about this quite innocent but unnecessary deception, insisted upon being married again in his own name.

Mrs Jackson was fond of little mysteries connected with names. She made a great secret of her own birth, occasionally letting out as if by accident that she was the daughter of the Duke of Abercorn.

Actually, as the police were able to establish later by the interesting proof of a deformed finger-nail, she was the daughter of an agricultural labourer in the North of England called Atkinson.

There were, in fact, few points on which Mrs Jackson ever told the truth, even when it was possible; and there were many points on which it was impossible for her to be truthful.

When Jackson at last came up for trial, it was obvious that the case against him was of the flimsiest description. Indeed, the prosecution in a trial for murder can seldom have offered a flimsier one. There was, literally, no actual evidence against him at all. The prosecution's whole case amounted really to nothing more than a mild suspicion, and to bolster it up, suggestions were put forward which were quite unwarrantable. The police depended upon these points:

1. The dead woman was not actually wearing her coat at the time of the attack. From the position of the bloodstains, near the hem, it had apparently been over her head with the lining next to the head. The inference drawn by the prosecution was that Mrs Jackson had entered the house and taken off her coat, and was then attacked by Jackson, who threw her coat over her head to smother her cries and shield him from becoming blood-stained. She then ran out, and fell down outside.

2. Jackson had said on the way to the hospital that he would inform the police, but did not do so.

3. Jackson did not inform two neighbours, who called at the bungalow shortly after the attack, of what had happened.

4. A tyre-lever was found by the police under a cushion in the bungalow.

That, really, was all the evidence of fact put forward against Jackson. To support it, the police suggested:

(A) That Jackson might have been glad to get rid of a wife who, once a source of income, had now become a liability.

(B) That Jackson had staged a quarrel with his wife immediately on her return, as a prelude to attacking her.

(C) That Jackson had always made a great mystery about his wife, when there was, in fact, no mystery about her at all.

(D) That certain anonymous and threatening letters recently received by Mrs Jackson had actually been written by her husband to divert subsequent suspicion from himself.

It will be seen that the evidence of fact, with the exception of the curious circumstance about the coat, amounts to just nothing at all. As for the tyre-lever, if Jackson had used this he would hardly have kept it for some time afterwards under a cushion; moreover, it had to be admitted that there was no trace of blood on it, as, indeed, there was not on Jackson himself; and rebutting evidence was called to prove that Mrs Jackson had been seen shortly before using a tyre-lever for some small domestic job.

In proof of the four suggestions, no evidence was offered at all. They were just thrown out, and left at that. Yet one of them is plainly impossible, for there was simply no time for Jackson to have staged a quarrel; Mrs Dimick was only a few seconds inside her own house, and certainly not more than a couple of minutes between parting from Mrs Jackson and seeing her on her hands and knees outside her own back door. As for the mystery there is overwhelming evidence that everyone who ever came in contact with her knew there was mystery surrounding Mrs Jackson, and the mystery was none of her husband's making; in view of this evidence it is difficult to understand how the prosecution could make this assertion.

Counsel for the defence had little trouble in demolishing this empty case; but the judge (Mr Justice Wright) summed up definitely against the prisoner. He pronounced that it was 'impossible to conceive that the attack could have been made in any other way' than that suggested by the police; he made light of the anonymous letters; he repeated that there was no mystery attached to Mrs Jackson; he considered the circumstantial evidence against Jackson to be 'very strong'; and he concluded with these words:

'If any stranger did murder this woman, it must have been done as the result of a deliberate scheme and of set purpose. I have heard no evidence at all which would indicate in any way that Mrs Jackson had any enemies likely to do her harm. . . . There is no evidence of any secret enemy. That is merely a surmise or possibility, and against that there is all the evidence which the prosecution has produced.'

In view of the anonymous letters, and the evidence given in plenty that Mrs Jackson had appeared actually to fear an attack for at least the past two years, these observations would appear a little surprising. So, at any rate, the jury appeared to think, for, in spite of the plain lead thus given them, they acquitted Jackson.

Who, then, did kill Mrs Jackson?

If this case resembles a detective novel in most respects, in one important particular it differs, for there are no clues at all. Whoever killed Mrs Jackson succeeded in achieving that very difficult feat, the clueless murder. Clueless, that is to say, so far as identity is concerned; for it is not difficult to reconstruct the crime.

Obviously the assailant was waiting for Mrs Jackson in the shadow of the house. He attacked her as soon as she had put the bulk of the house between herself and the road.

I think possibly he grasped her by the coat collar, that the coat came off in the struggle, and that the murderer than flung it over her head exactly as the police suggested. It does not take long to deliver a dozen frenzied blows. By the time Jackson, who was in bed, had got down to the back door and Mrs Dimick had arrived a moment later, the assailant had made off into the surrounding darkness, taking his weapon with him. The whole thing was soundly planned, and flawlessly executed.

Suppose we press the resemblance to a detective story and consider how the detective of fiction would have gone about the job.

As soon as the fact of Mrs Jackson's profession as a blackmailer became known to him he would have assumed (knowing the rules of fiction) that he had no further to look. Somewhere in that circle, or among the friends or relatives of Mrs Jackson's victims, the murderer would be found. Perhaps the circle may have been a wide one; but, wide or narrow, to it he would confine his inquiries.

Side by side with this he would puzzle over the murderer's get-away. Was it made by car, by motorcycle, by cycle, or on foot? A car was seen by one witness standing not far from the bungalow with its lights out—so that it had probably nothing to do with the crime.

This murderer was a clever fellow, and he would not make such an obvious blunder as that. Probably he got away by the safest method, on foot for a mile or two first, however he progressed after that. In any case we may assume that the police made all possible inquiries under this heading.

Then there is the weapon. It inflicted wounds of a peculiar character. Two of them might have been made by a blunt instrument, seven were cuts, and the cuts in the coat were of a triangular nature. Surely this is interesting evidence. The police pinned their faith on the tyre-lever, so we do not know if they considered any other kind of weapon, and, if so, what?

In any case, I am sure of one thing: our detective of fiction would not have let this case go up for trial with such meagre evidence of fact. He would have unearthed some more somehow—and he would certainly have put up a better case.

For on his main point I think we may agree with him without hesitation. Mrs Jackson was killed by someone, whether victim or friend of victim, connected with her blackmailing activities. And though murder is never justified, can we be altogether sorry that the case of Madame 'X' will now remain a mystery for ever?

FREDERIC BOUTET

Pierre Torture

This is a story about Pierre Torture, the headsman of the town of Colmar. His surname doubtless was bestowed on one of his ancestors by reason of his function, for the post of executioner had passed down from father to son for many generations.

His house, in accordance with the feeling of abhorrence associated with his sinister calling, was situated outside of the town, some way from its outer suburbs.

One winter's evening in 1780, while he was enjoying his rest by a corner of his fireplace, Pierre Torture heard a violent knocking at his door.

He opened it.

Three men, wrapped in heavy cloacks and with their hats pulled so deep down over their faces so as almost to disguise them, stood before him.

'You are the headsman?' one of them asked roughly.

'Yes.'

'You are alone?'

'Yes.'

He had no sooner answered than the three men threw themselves on him, and in spite of his exeptional strength overcame him. They then gagged and bound him.

They now bundled him into a roomy closed carriage which was waiting for them hard by, in the misty darkness, and got into it themselves.

They drove off at a quick pace, and it was not until they were already far from the town that the man who had already spoken to Pierre Torture addressed him again.

'You need not be alarmed,' he said. 'No one will harm you.

120

We are taking you to carry out a sentence which has to be carried out. When you have accomplished this task, you will be taken back to your home safe and sound, and you shall receive two hundred louis as reward. But do not attempt to find out where you are going or who we are, and do not cry out for help or try to escape or we shall kill you.'

They then unbound him, showing him, however, threateningly at the same time a naked dagger; and the conveyance rolled on in the silence of the night.

At daybreak next morning they put a band round his eyes. The windows of the carriage were carefully darkened with blinds.

The journey continued all that day and throughout the following night and one more day, horses being changed several times and fresh starts made at a quickened rate. The three men and their prisoner ate in the carriage and slept in it. Pierre Torture, whose every movement was closely watched, could not tell in what direction they were travelling. It seemed to him, however, that they had crossed the Rhine.

On the evening of the second day the prisoner, his eyes still bandaged, was able to tell by the sounds made by the wheels that they were crossing a bridge: a drawbridge, apparently, for he could hear heavy chains rattling also. In a few seconds the horses were brought to a standstill.

A gate opened and Pierre Torture, guided by the men, got out of the carriage and advanced some yards. Presently they went up some stairs, and then through a succession of long halls, their footsteps resounding beneath the lofty vaults. The cold was icy.

At last they stopped and the bandage was taken from his eyes.

He found himself in a sort of huge crypt, hung with funereal black draperies and dimly illuminated by the light of torches. In front of him, against the wall, stood a row of stone stalls in which a number of men, garbed like judges, sat motionless. They were not masked, but Torture, owing to the nature of the lighting and to the distance, could not make out their features.

In the middle of the crypt, in the glare of the torches held up by attendants garbed in hooded gowns, a young woman was standing dressed in a long dark robe and covered by a thick veil. At her feet was a block of wood, and leaning against it a sword, which Torture recognized as similar to those used by executioners in Switzerland.

Then one of the members of the singular tribunal began to speak in German. He occupied the central seat, and seemed to be the president of the court. He said to Torture:

'You are here to fulfil your function. This woman is condemned to death, and you will behead her.'

Torture, who had been bewildered until this point by all he had been witnessing, how recovered his senses a little and protested. He declared he could not act as headsman in this way without the prescribed order from the authorities over him. He was an official executioner and not an assassin.

The president merely repeated his commands.

On Torture persisting in his refusal, the president—the while a great clock struck eleven—went on:

'You have a quarter of an hour in which to obey. If you have not accomplished your task within that period of time, it is you who will be the first to die. We shall find a more compliant executioner. . . .'

The great clock ticked off the seconds. . . .

'You have only two more minutes,' the judge said presently.

And an attendant handed Torture the sword.

The woman knelt down, turning back her veil as she did so.

Torture lifted the sword with a convulsive movement. . . .

An instant later the woman's head rolled upon the floor.

Torture's nerve deserted him and he fell, fainting.

He was lifted to his feet, and with his eyes again bandaged, he was taken back into the carriage. . . .

Two days later he was left at the door of his own house.

ELIZABETH VILLIERS

The Mystery of the Village Beauty

The prettiest girl in Peasenhall village was Rose Harsent, whose father was employed at one of the farms to deliver milk for his master. With his family he lived in one of the picturesque cottages in the village, and thought himself fortunate when Rosie was picked out for praise at the Sunday School belonging to the little place of worship, which for some reason was called 'The Doctor's Chapel.'

So well did Rosie behave at Sunday school that Mr Crisp, the deacon, and his wife were interested in her, and when she was old enough to go to service they offered her 'a place' in their house.

An old-fashioned building was Providence House, where Mr and Mrs Crisp lived, and though it was of considerable size only one maid was kept. Thus Rosie was left a good deal alone, and, in a sense, it may be said that instead of really living in the house with her master and mistress she was shut away in a cottage to herself. That is not actually true, but it is practically. As is the case with many old buildings, Providence House had been altered and added to time and again till it was rambling and ramshackle inside. The kitchen communicated with the rest of the house by a door, but when that door was shut it might be said to be quite 'on its own.' The servant's bedroom was over the kitchen, and reached by a separate flight of stairs that led from the kitchen itself, so that room did not communicate with the rest of the house.

Thus kitchen and bedroom may be said to have formed a two-roomed cottage apart from the rest of the house, and in that two-roomed cottage Rosie lived alone.

123

That Mr and Mrs Crisp were good, kind, deeply-religious people there is no doubt; they may have relatives alive now, and it would be cruel to write a word that could harrow their feelings or give them a pang of remorse, but it is impossible not to feel that they were wrong in leaving so pretty, and so sprightly a girl as poor Rosie alone thus. Scandal began to get busy, as scandal so often does in country villages, and two young men named Wright and Skinner had a particularly ugly story to tell.

They declared that one day when Rosie was cleaning the Doctor's Chapel they saw a handsome man, with singularly black hair and black eyes, come down the street and stop to speak to her. She replied to him, giggling, jesting, then he went into the chapel with her and closed the door.

The two young men knew that man with black hair well. He was William Gardiner, the master carpenter at the works of Messrs. J. & J. Smith, agricultural implement makers, in Saxmundham, and a teacher at the Primitive Methodist Sunday school—he was not connected with the Doctor's Chapel.

The father of six bonnie children, he was happily married, living in a double-fronted cottage in Peasenhall, only a little way down the hill from Providence House where Rosie was in service. Of course, she knew him and his wife well—everyone knows everyone else in a village like Peasenhall—and Mrs Gardiner had shown her many kindnesses. Once, when the girl had had a bad cold, the good woman had given her a little bottle of camphorated oil with which to rub her chest.

Everyone liked Mrs Gardiner—it would have been difficult to do anything else in view of all that is known about her—and Gardiner was a good and conscientious workman, and an earnest member of the Primitive Methodists. Still, these two men saw him enter the chapel with Rosie, and as they must have had very little to do, and very unpleasant minds, they crept to an open window to listen to and watch what was going on inside.

According to their own account they heard the man and the girl talking in a very shameful, not to say blasphemous, way— she was uttering jokes no girl with any self-respect would have spoken. Being what they were, these two young men repeated what they had overheard and described what they said they had seen, and soon the whole village was blazing with the story.

Then came two other men, who told that they had seen something in the conduct of Rosie and William Gardiner at a Sunday School outing which shocked them considerably, and a good deal was made of all this, though, later on, most of it was proved untrue or greatly exaggerated. It was a case in which 'nothing is lost in the telling'; everyone who repeated the story added something to it.

Of course the authorities at the chapel where Gardiner was so highly thought of heard the tales, and in the end the superintendent of the circuit held an inquiry into the matter. Gardiner attended, and told his story with a straightforwardness that impressed all. He absolutely denied what had been said, declared there was not a word of truth in the accusations, and spoke in so candid and earnest a way that the officials—all men of the world, remember, and ready to vindicate a wronged girl— fully believed him.

They advised him to be particularly careful in his conduct in the future, but there had never been anything except vague suspicion against him, and the inquiry ended in his being told his friends were sure he was innocent, and his being allowed to hold his church offices.

Mrs Crisp seems to have spoken to Rosie on the subject, but she denied the story too, her mistress believed her, and it might have been thought the scandal would have been forgotten. But whenever mud is thrown some of it is sure to stick, and in spite of the fact that he had been cleared by the inquiry, William Gardiner found many people looking at him doubtfully. He squared his shoulders and flung back his head. The thing was a lie, he said; he meant to live it down, and went on about his work quietly as if nothing had happened.

Perhaps the one living soul who took the least notice of the ugly story was William Gardiner's wife. This murder mystery, with its surrounding atmosphere of vice and scandal, would make very unpleasant reading save for one bright spot which lightens its sordid gloom; that brightness comes from a wife's most beautiful devotion.

Nothing which happened, nothing which could happen, shook

Mrs Gardiner's faith in, and devotion for, her husband. She deserves to go down to history as a real heroine, a noble woman, whose love was as near perfection as mortal love can be. When the village seethed with these scandals concerning William Gardiner and Rose Harsent, Mrs Gardiner took pride in showing herself by her husband's side at chapel or elsewhere.

'I have a good husband,' she said again and again. 'All this talk about him and Rosie does not trouble me because I know it's not true.' And seeing her so splendid in her faith, many who had been ready to believe the worst felt ashamed of their thoughts.

Presently the village folk became tired of talking scandal about Gardiner, and found another lover for Rosie.

There was a young shop assistant in the village, who must have been a very romantic young man. Probably he was no worse than most other people, and the fact that he was so young would excuse everything. He fell very desperately in love with Rosie, and used to write her letters so full of extravagent admiration that her head was turned still further. Here are some extracts from these love-letters, they will give a good idea of the young man's state of mind:

> My innermost yearnings have made me write down on paper a few lines about her who has enraptured my heart, a rose among the many thorns that reside in our midst. . . .

> Her shapely form and wavy hair make her the idol that I worship, she means to me my very existence. . . .

> A glimpse of her will cheer me at any time through the day. . . .

> The time may come when she will leave me to woo some other man, then life will not be worth living, but should I win her heart for my own it will be like heaven on earth.

> Like the old song, she's a lily of the valley and the bright and morning star.

Many of his letters were not nearly so poetical as these, indeed some were very unpleasant, and reading them, it is clear that poor, foolish Rosie had forgotten all self-respect, and taken the downward path in ugly earnest. As is the case with so many foolish girls, she had thought it clever to be improper, she allowed jokes to be made in her presence that no decent woman will hear; she believed she was showing her brilliance by frivolity and sin.

A year had gone by since that scandal about her and William

Gardiner in the Doctor's Chapel, and as she took a foolish delight in shocking some of the good folks round, the only wonder is she had been allowed to stay in her situation so long. The Crisps were kind folk, they were slow to believe evil of anyone, least of all this girl they had watched grow from childhood to early womanhood, and so poor Rosie drifted on from careless folly to sin and then to tragic death.

On a Saturday afternoon, May 31st, 1902, the village postman, a man named Brewer, called at Providence House and delivered a letter in a yellow envelope—such an envelope as was used in the offices attached to the works where Gardiner was employed, but a common sort of envelope which could have been bought anywhere. The postmark showed the letter had been posted that same day at a neighbouring village.

Mrs Crisp took the letter from the postman, and saw it was addressed:

> MISS HARSENT,
> Providence House,
> Peasenhall,
> Saxmundham.

The handwriting was fairly good, quite easy to read, but rather what is called of the 'round hand' type, not the writing of a person who used his pen very much. On reading the address Mrs Crisp went into the kitchen, carrying the letter, and put it on the table—Rosie was out for the moment, and her mistress left it lying there waiting for her.

When the girl came back she saw that letter on the table, and caught it up eagerly. There and then she read the few words it contained:

> *Dear R., —I will try to see you to-night at twelve o'clock at your place. If you put a light in your window at ten for about ten minutes then you can put it out again. Do not have a light in your room at twelve, as I will come round the back way.*

In the view of what was to happen in the brief darkness of that summer night, that letter, with its shameful request, is important.

In such places as Peasenhall few people are out of doors after nine o'clock, then who was the man who was going to watch for that signal at ten o'clock? Was he going to lurk in the village street in the darkness watching, or did he live in some cottage so placed that he could see the window of Rose's room from his own?

Many people asked these questions during the first weeks of that June, and always the answer was that William Gardiner's house, though some distance down the lane, stood in such a position that from its front upper window he would be able to watch the light shining amid the trees.

That night at ten o'clock, a light lamp shone in the window of Rose Harsent's bedroom for a few minutes. It was the signal for which her lover waited, whoever he might have been.

A dreadful thunderstorm broke over the village, the rain fell in torrents, the roads were thick with mud. Mrs Crisp was awakened by the tumult, and thought of Rosie sleeping in that bedroom shut away from the rest of the house.

'I think I'd better get up and see if Rose is frightened,' she said to her husband, but he retorted that the girl would be all right – she was not the sort to be frightened of thunder, his wife had better stay where she was. Mrs Crisp obeyed, but the storm—or was it some occult power?—made her nervous.

She could not sleep, she lay watching the flash of the lightning, listening to the voice of the thunder, and, just before the church clock struck twelve, there came other sounds. She heard nothing plainly—how should she when the rain was rattling down?—but it seemed to her that the noise was that of a fall, of breaking glass, of a muffled scream.

The thunder died, the darkness of a cloudy night in June settled about the lonely house—all was very still.

On the Sunday morning Rose's father, Mr Harsent, came round to Providence House with the milk as usual, and knocked at the kitchen door.

There was no reply, and thinking his daughter had been kept awake by the storm and was over-sleeping herself in the morning, he knocked more loudly. Still there was no reply. He was going away when something made him glance through the window into the kitchen.

At the foot of the stairs leading to her bedroom, Rose Harsent was lying.

William Harsent ran round to the front door of the house, and hammering upon it, brought Mr Crisp down. The two men made their way through the house to the kitchen, and there saw that what the father had feared when he had caught that glimpse through the window was only too true. Rose Harsent was lying dead in the kitchen at the foot of that flight of stairs which led to her bedroom—the room above the kitchen and away from the rest of the house.

The girl was dressed in her night clothes; she seemed to have been carrying a lamp in her hand, and to have dropped it, for it lay shattered near, and the oil from it was running on the floor. A candlestick was overturned beside her, and a little distance away was a broken medicine bottle bearing a label which told it had once contained medicine for 'Mrs Gardiner's child.' Also on the floor was a newspaper—a similar copy had been delivered at William Gardiner's house the day before by Rose's little brother, who helped a newsagent with his rounds.

A doctor and the police were sent for, but it did not need a medical man to decide the cause of death. The girl's throat was most terribly cut, and there was in addition a queerly-shaped jagged wound on the breast. She had been dead for many hours.

The whole village was seething with excitement that quiet Sabbath morning, when the sun was shining after the midnight storm, and on the lips of everyone in the place was the question:

'Who has killed Rose Harsent?'

It is a question which has never been satisfactorily answered from that time to this.

An inquest was held, but all inquiries made the mystery grow deeper. It was plain the girl had more than one lover in the crudest sense of the word—at least two young men came forward to confess to the association—and there were those scandals about Gardiner and her. In addition there was the shop assistant, who had written so many eloquent letters, and he might have been suspected, but he was able to prove an alibi that was beyond dispute. He could account for every minute of his time, and was not in Peasenhall at all on the night she met her death.

The other young men were in the same position; the police had ample evidence that neither could know anything of the matter.

When these were cleared of any connection with the mystery, the police – not unnaturally – turned their thoughts to William Gardiner, whose name had been linked with hers a year or so before, and in the end William Gardiner was openly charged with the murder.

Public opinion ran high against him in little Peasenhall itself, as well as in the old-world neighbouring town of Saxmundham. In the streets and the market-place, in farm and in homestead, in villa and cottages the crime was discussed, and practically every voice declared that William Gardiner was guilty. Not that anyone had any special proof to offer, this was the harvest of the seed laid by that scandal of a year before.

It was the memory of those nasty stories with which the place had rung twelve months earlier that prejudiced all now, and made the world believe in William Gardiner's guilt.

Not that the opinions of those who had been his friends and neighbours should have been taken as evidence against him. Those who know country villages understand how fierce of prejudices, how narrow of mind the general outlook is. If a man is accused, nine times out of ten he is condemned, be the proofs against him never so slight, and it was so in this Peasenhall case.

Amid all the turmoil and indignation that assailed the unhappy man in these dark days, there was one splendid exception—his wife's devotion shone as a golden ray amid the gloom. Mrs Gardiner was sure of her husband's innocence, though all the world besides might condemn him. He was a good, deeply religious man, a kind father, a devoted husband, she said, not all the evidence the world could bring would make her believe him guilty.

There came the dreadful day when he was taken from the little home where he had been happy, from the wife who trusted him, from the children he loved, to the county gaol, the shadow of the gallows over his head.

In due time the assizes came, and William Gardiner stood his trial.

It was in November, 1902, that Mr Justice Grantham sat to try the case. Mr Dickens, K. C.—son of the celebrated novelist, Charles Dickens—was leader for the Crown, and the prisoner was defended by Mr. E. E. Wild. So hot was public opinion against Gardiner it was feared that it was quite possible he would not have a fair trial, yet that fear was vain, English justice triumphed, and, as events proved, his counsel made one of the most brilliant defences in the whole annals of criminal cases. Mr. E. E. Wild later became Sir Ernest Wild, K. C., and it was at what was called the Peasenhall trial he first leaped into fame.

Terribly against the prisoner was the story of the prosecution. All that scandal of the previous twelve months was told first, and then they came to the night of the murder. Witness after witness was called, and all gave their evidence against Gardiner with a curious spite and intensity of vengeance for which it is difficult to account.

A man named Burgess, a bricklayer, told how on the night of May 31st, at about ten o'clock, he had met Gardiner outside the latter's cottage, and while they stood talking together Burgess happened to glance in the direction of Providence House, and distinctly saw the signal light gleaming in Rose Harsent's window; plainly Gardiner could have seen it also if he had watched for it. Then came a gamekeeper named Morris, who said when the storm of the night had passed, he had come past Providence House, and had noticed footprints in the damp earth—footprints which seemed to lead from the kitchen door of the house to the road which ran past Gardiner's cottage. They were footprints made by a man who wore shoes with india-rubber soles, those soles which have lines across them, and Gardiner possessed such shoes. Also, when his house was searched, a knife was found in it which was stained with blood, and finally, as has been said, that letter which made the appointment with poor Rosie was enclosed in a yellow envelope exactly resembling those used in the office of the works where Gardiner was employed. The handwriting was not definitely identified as his, but more than one expert was convinced that he, and he alone, had written that letter.

This was the story the prosecution told, the theory on which they built their case.

The man was desperate; he had become entangled with the girl, and knew that before long she would have to leave her situation owing to her condition, and then there would be more scandal. At all costs he dreaded the disgrace which would come to him if it were known that he had been her lover, and with cold-blooded deliberation he had planned her murder. He had sent that letter, and in the evening had sharpened the knife, determined to do the deadly deed by slipping out of the cottage while his wife and children slept. With eloquence the counsel for the prosecution pictured the girl receiving the letter with many mingled emotions—how on going to bed in the evening she had taken the lamp upstairs, though then it was unlighted, and she had used the candle instead. Presently as ten o'clock approached she had lighted that lamp and set it in the window—while its beams had shone out into the night Gardiner and his bricklayer friend, standing at the former's door, had seen its rays. In due time the lamp was turned out, the girl had undressed, and sitting up in bed, had waited while the two hours crept away—waited for the coming of her secret lover.

The storm broke, the thunder crashed across the sky, the lightning lit the little whitewashed room with blue flame, and thus, her heart torn with excitement and dread, Rose Harsent remained till midnight struck, when she heard the faint tapping at the kitchen door, which told her her lover had come.

Carrying the lamp, because she had to return it to the kitchen, and with the lighted candle in her hand as well, she crept down that wooden staircase which lay between her room and the kitchen. She opened the door, and out of the storm came the desperate man who had repented his wicked love and wanted her out of his way for ever.

Only a few words could have been said, the blow was struck, and, with her dreadful scream, Rose fell at the foot of the stairs. Perhaps it was the sight of the lamp with oil which gave him the dreadful idea of setting fire to the house and burning the body, but the prosecution said he had brought paraffin in that medicine bottle which bore the name of Mrs Gardiner, that as the girl lay dead he poured the oil over her body and set it on fire, then, without waiting to see how his evil work prospered, he fled out into the stormy night again.

Certainly paraffin had been set on fire, the poor girl's nightdress was burnt, but no very great damage had been done. Still, if the bottle had held paraffin, if the newspaper had been carried there to start the fire, what stronger proof of William Gardiner's guilt could be found? When Mr Dickens took his seat after his opening speech, almost everyone in the court felt the story fitted together as perfectly as the pieces of a jig-saw puzzle when placed in their right position.

The discovery of the blood-stained knife at his house seemed the crowning point, while the people of the cottage next door to the Gardiners said they had heard sounds as if he were walking about in the night, and he and his wife were seen in the wash-house early on the Sunday morning. Witness after witness appeared for the prosecution, all letting their prejudice against the man in the dock be seen. Probably there was never a case in which so much local spite was shown against a prisoner.

When the case for the prosecution had ended Mr Dickens must have taken his seat quite convinced that he had put the rope about the neck of the man who had been guilty of a very brutal murder.

But—

The case for the defence opened, and slowly the whole affair was seen in a different light.

The chief witness for the defence was William Gardiner's wife.

None of us, looking back in these days, can grasp faintly the greatness of the martyrdom the woman had borne in the weeks and months which had followed that tragic 1st of June to the November when the trial came on. If she had denounced her husband probably many friends would have rallied round her, she would have had monetary and all other help. 'Poor, wronged, innocent woman,' people would have said. 'Let us help her and her children; it is no fault of hers that her husband is a murderer.' And if she had talked about those other scandals, and how she had suffered from the wickedness of a bad man, she would have had a thousand sympathizers. She would have gone with the tide of public opinion.

This was what this heroic woman did not do. The whole world, so far as she knew it, believed her husband guilty, but she was sure of his innocence. She and her children were hooted in the village streets, her neighbours, who had been her friends, drew their skirts aside as they passed her.

'She is a murderer's wife,' they said, taking no heed of the fact that in English law a man is innocent till he is proved guilty. 'She must be as bad as he is if she believes in him.'

It was cruel—cruel. Those people did not realize the added suffering their hasty judgment gave the aching heart of that woman whose soul was on the rack. She had monetary troubles to face, she had practically to beg for the means to pay for her husband's defence, she had to support her children and herself—the eldest of the family was only thirteen—and, above all else, there was the knowledge that the husband she loved was in prison, with the shadow of death creeping near and ever nearer to him.

This was the sorrow she bore alone, scorned by her neighbours because of her love.

Is it possible to believe that the man who has inspired such devotion was unworthy of it? She proved a sensible, clear-sighted woman of resource and courage as well as of loyalty and love, and would she, can any reasonable person believe, have fought for the husband she loved—would have loved the husband for whom she fought—if he had been the mean murderer the prosecution described?

She went into the witness-box, and her evidence cleared away the most important points. She said that the medicine bottle had been given to her with a draught for one of the children, but that had been long ago, and afterwards she had used it to buy two pennyworth of camphorated oil. Later on Rosie Harsent had complained of a cold on her chest, and in her kindness Mrs Gardiner had given the girl the oil; that accounted for the presence of the bottle in the kitchen of Providence House. The newspaper also was not the copy which had been delivered at her home—she could not find that copy, it had been destroyed, but she was sure she had seen her husband reading it on the Sunday morning, according to his custom.

The knife with the bloodstains had no sinister meaning. It was what they always used when 'hulking' rabbits—the Suffolk word for disembowelling—and the Gardiners had stewed rabbit for dinner that Sunday. Further, she produced the shoes with the barred rubber soles. They did not look as if they had been worn for some considerable time; certainly there was no trace of bloodstains on them, or on any garment Gardiner had worn.

She told the story of the night of the crime. Gardiner had gone to the cottage door about ten o'clock, she said—the time for the signal lamp to be placed in the window—but his only object had been to watch the storm clouds that were gathering. Later they went to bed, but the children were frightened of the storm, so they had little sleep—it was her steps the neighbours heard moving about the house. Her husband remained in the bedroom, nursing one of the little children who was fractious with teething. He comforted it during the storm.

'That is my alibi,' said Mr Wild in his speech for the defence when he came to that picture of the father nursing the little one amid the roar of the thunder.

Mrs Gardiner went on to explain that because she had been kept awake by the storm it would have been quite impossible for her husband to leave the house without her knowledge. Thus she swore most positively that she knew he was innocent.

Gardiner gave evidence in his own defence. He swore he had never been Rose Harsent's lover—that he had never been in the Doctor's Chapel with her, excepting once when he had happened to be passing, and she had called him in to help her to shut a heavy door—that the scandal started by the young men had been absolutely false—that he knew nothing of any light put as a signal in the windows of Providence House—that he had been ignorant of the murder till he heard of it during the morning.

Evidence followed which confirmed his story. For instance, two local gentlemen declared that the scandal which those busybodies had started must be false, as if they had stood where they had said they did it was impossible they could hear or see what was going on inside the chapel; while an egg-merchant of very high standing in the neighbourhood told how he had been

kept out late by the storm, and returning home in the early hours
of the Sunday morning, had passed along the road without seeing
the footprints the gamekeeper had described. Then came a
maltster, who wore such shoes in the course of his work, and
he told the court that he had passed along the road on many
occasions, though not on that particular night. It was suggested
the gamekeeper had made a mistake in the date.

All that was strong in the prisoner's favour, but the judge
summed up against him, and the jury retired to consider their
verdict. Presently they returned to say there was no chance of
their agreeing—later it became known that eleven were in favour
of a verdict of guilty, but that one alone stood out, firm in his
belief in Gardiner's innocence. That juror was a brave man,
for he had a good deal of badgering to put up with; the judge
even had him into the court to ask if he did not think he would
change his mind if time were given him.

He answered straight and plain: 'No, my Lord, I have heard
nothing to convince me that the prisoner is guilty.'

At that there was applause in court.

That meant there would have to be a new trial. Gardiner was
taken back to prison, and his devoted wife had the nerve-racking
misery to go through again. Fortunately the story of her heroic
trust had rung through the land, and mercifully a public
subscription was started to help her in her dreadful need.

Months later, in the early part of 1903, the second trial came
on before Mr Justice Lawrance, Gardiner being again defended
by Mr Wild, whose eloquence had done so much for him. Once
more the evidence was given, the dreary case dragged out its
length, the jury retired, and—again they disagreed.

Queerly enough, it was said that in this case eleven were in
favour of a verdict of not guilty and one stood out on the other
side.

By this time the opinion of the world had changed. Peasenhall
might keep its opinion of his guilt, but larger cities were
convinced of his innocence; his own manner in the witness-box
had told in his favour, while his wife's words had gone to every
heart. When it was known that there was a second disagreement,
Ipswich, the scene of the trial, gave itself up to public rejoicing,

which was intensified later when the Home Secretary decided there should be no third trial. William Gardiner came out into the world a free man, that world where his wife was waiting to welcome him.

The case made a great excitement, and many used it as an argument in favour of England's adopting the very sensible Scottish law which allows a verdict of 'Not proven' to be returned, while south of the Tweed the jury are obliged to say definitely 'Guilty' or 'Not Guilty.'

William Gardiner's trial was ended. With his wife and children he left the neighbourhood where he had suffered, and began life afresh elsewhere, while it seemed as if the mystery of Rose Harsent's death would never be solved.

Some time afterwards a clergyman, who had given great thought to the case, came forward with a theory which seems to explain everything, and the more it is examined, the more convincing it becomes.

According to him the death was not murder but accident. The girl had had that letter from the lover making the midnight appointment—the man who had written it had been in the habit of visiting her, and there was no thought of murder in his mind. She had taken the lamp upstairs and placed it in the window as usual, then had waited, perhaps reading the newspaper to while away the time and help her to forget the storm.

As midnight approached she rose from her bed, and with the newspaper under her arm, and the lighted lamp in her hand, was going downstairs when her eye happened to light on the camphorated oil bottle, and for some reason she took that in her other hand to carry it downstairs.

At that time nightdresses were very long and voluminous garments, the flimsy magyars of today were not heard of, so Rose Harsent had trailing folds of calico about her. There was an extra loud clap of thunder as she reached the stairs, she started, her foot became entangled in her nightdress, and she fell headlong, unable to save herself.

Her scream was what Mrs Crisp had heard. In her fall the girl flung the unlighted lamp from her, it crashed to the stone floor, the paraffin was spilt and caught alight from the candle, but Rose knew nothing of that danger. The medicine bottle had remained in her hand as she fell, she crashed upon it—and her injuries were inflicted by the broken glass.

The fact that the injury to her throat and breast were jagged is the strongest proof of this theory. Had a knife been used the cut and the stab would have been deep and clean. Broken glass would have accounted for the injury, and the bottle was broken in a rather unusual way, which maes this theory more probable.

The pity is that at the time of the examination the doctors did not think of searching the wounds for broken glass.

BENJAMIN BENNETT

Who Shot the
Earl of Errol?

The course of our lives is governed by the basic twin emotions of love and hate. They are present in the highborn and the low, the rich and the poor. For basically we are moulded in the same crucible, now stirred to good, now goaded to evil by strivings and frustrations in matters of love.

So from the bottom of the social scale and the ill-starred actors in the tragedies of a school hostel in Windhock, a boarding house in Dundee and a rondavel on a Natal sugar estate, we ascend to a stage on an upper level where the roles were played by an earl, a wealthy baronet and women of the aristocracy—and a love problem was likewise solved with a bullet.

But here was no open and impetuous killing with the murderer making no attempt to cloak his identity or escape from the scene. This was the crime of a master mind, ingeniously conceived and boldly executed, which was to rank as one of the great African mysteries of all time.

The story opens in October, 1940, on a voyage from England to South Africa. Sea travel was a hazardous undertaking. The submarine menace was at it height and brought with it a succession of anxious days and blacked-out nights. there was always a conscious fear that disaster and possibly death would follow the ripples of a speeding, silent torpedo.

Yet after a while danger and death were accepted by most of the passengers with fatalistic resignation. It was war and in times of war the inevitable becomes part of the daily routine.

For Sir Henry John Delves Broughton and Diana Caldwell, however, the voyage was anything but dull or a waiting for something that never happened. Begun as a wartime necessity, it developed into close friendship that bloomed into courtship.

It was, though, no fleeting shipboard romance but rather an attraction of opposites. Sir Delves Broughton, divorcee and father of two children, was 56; Miss Caldwell, 26, young enough to be his daughter.

He was a striking, rather ascetic-looking, personality whose manner and bearing made you forget his crippled drag-foot and arthritic wrist. Though he was obviously more than middle-aged, with evidence of poor health and good living, he had a natural, easy charm and ready wit.

His background and upbringing were typical of his family tradition and class: Eton-educated, law studies, war service with the Irish Guards in World War I until he was boarded out medically unfit; a great, inherited, fortune, a landed estate of 15,000 acres, racing stables . . .

For 28 years he had been a county magistrate. On the outbreak of World War II he was appointed High Sheriff at Chester but his military duties prevented him taking office. These, however, did not last long.

Now he was on his way to Kenya where he had rented a house on the Karen estate of more than 6,000 acres. His object was a quiet life and the recapture of his health. He would occasionally go big game hunting and (if they were wanted) offer his services for the war effort in East Africa.

Diana Caldwell fitted into a different section of the scale. Her means were more modest and her attainments, perhaps, were unnoticed. But she was gay and attractive, lively and intelligent and physically desirable. Broughton was charmed.

Their fellow-passengers at first looked on them as perhaps a widower and ward or uncle and niece; the man, wordly-wise, reserved and cultured; the girl, friendly, vibrant, bubbling with life.

But there was nothing paternal about Broughton's feelings. He was completely under her spell. He wanted to marry her and told her so. Yet shrewd and cynical as he was, he did not allow himself to be blinded to the year-gap that separated them. He knew the risks but he was resolved to meet them more than halfway.

He suggested that side by side with a marriage contract there should be an extra-marital arrangement or pact. If, after a while, they found they were not well suited and wanted a divorce, neither would stand in the way of the other. They would part without recrimination or regret; there would be no bonds.

In the event of Miss Caldwell falling in love with someone else and wanting her freedom, she would forfeit the marriage settlement of £5,000 a year.

But this was the gloomy side of the picture. It was like a healthy young couple drawing a joint will. Neither thought of death but a will was one of the necessities of life. Sir Delves and Diana Caldwell looked forward, not to separation or divorce, but to a pleasant life together.

They landed at Cape Town and travelled by train to Durban. There, on November 5, 1940, they were married by antenuptial contract. Honeymooners now, they sailed for Mombasa where they disembarked and journeyed to Nairobi. Karen estate, their new home, was 14 miles away. To reach it they motored by way of the Ngong Road, a main thoroughfare leading out of Nairobi, and a two-mile branch road. The double-storied, luxuriously furnished house stood in tropical gardens and acres of wooded land.

Broughton and his young bride settled down to the carefree existence still possible for wealthy English settlers in the ever-green serenity of the East African countryside. War-torn Europe was far away and danger seemed remote. Only the sandbagged streets in Nairobi and the uniforms of tall, bronzed South Africans and stocky, fair-skinned Englishmen, brought an awareness that in the Abyssinnian highlands, in Eritrea and Somaliland were Mussolini's soldiers and airplanes.

In Nairobi the cry was, as elsewhere, 'if a short life, then a gay one.' Immorality, vice and marital infidelity were flaunted and accepted with a shrug of tolerance or an amused indifference.

There was in Nairobi at this time a man they called the 'Great Lover' – 39-year-old Jocelyn Victor Hay, Earl of Errol and Baron Kilmarnock, Military Secretary and Assistant Director of Manpower in Kenya. He was handsome and polished as a film star. He knew it and made full use of his looks and charm;

there was keen competition among Kenya's social set for his attentions and affections.

Like Sir Delves Broughton, whom he had met in 1927, he came of an ancient family. The earldom was created in 1453 and Errol was hereditary Lord High Constable of Scotland with a seat in the House of Lords. He had been married twice, the first time at the age of 22, and twice divorced, the second time in 1930.

In his impressionable days he had been attracted to Sir Oswald Mosley and joined the British Union of Fascists. He took out a membership card and found some spurious excitement in the black-shirted parades in the East End of London. But it was a passing phase and he had little association with Fascists or Fascism in the immediate pre-war years.

Unlike Sir Delves, Errol's family ties had brought him no great wealth or estates and he was more or less dependent on his Government appointment and allowances as a captain in the British Army. But he did own some of the family heirlooms including a set of pearls said to be worth, in normal times, between £10,000 and £30,000 and insured at the higher figure.

As might be expected, he moved in the best circles in Nairobi. He soon renewed acquaintance with Sir Delves and was introduced to the new Lady Broughton. The two men quickly became close friends. Broughton admired, as he said, the younger man's 'bain, humour and kindness,' though not his way with women.

For his part Errol had the well-bred Briton's respect for another well-bred and wealthy Briton. They knew each other by friendly nicknames. Broughton was 'Jock' and Errol 'Josh.'

It was not long before the handsome young earl became a frequent visitor to Karen House; and perhaps his falling in love with Lady Diana was inevitable. She likewise was infatuated with him. They were a striking couple. The 13-year age difference was neither apparent nor an obstacle. Errol had behind him the ripe wisdom of full living yet his zest for life did not wane. Lady Diana was young but she knew her mind.

At first Broughton was uneasy; but he saw no cause for alarm in the friendship between his wife and Errol. In a way he was

Lord Errol

flattered by the attention men paid his lovely wife and determined not to become a butt as a jealous or ageing husband. He readily sanctioned her attendance at dances and other functions without him.

'One must keep a young wife amused,' he once said philosophically, and there is no reason to doubt that, at the outset at any rate, he meant it. At all times he was conscious of the pact he had made and he believed that a broadminded approach would succeed in making the marriage work and keep his wife happy.

Sir Delves and Lady Broughton entertained lavishly and in turn were received by Kenya's leading personalities and socialites. Among the invitations they accepted was one from Lieutenant Commander J. B. Soames to spend a few days on his farm at Nanyuki.

Sir Delves and Soames had been friends since boyhood and both looked forward to a reunion.

Nanyuki is a scenic gem on the equator nestling at the foot of snow-capped Mount Kenya. Its glacier-seamed slopes fall away into vast, sprawling forests of cedar, camphor and yellowwood. There, elephant and other wild beasts live and die. Along the road encircling the mountain's base are country inns and hotels and treetop cottages that are the tourist's big game spotting hideways.

Time in these idyllic surroundings passed pleasantly for the Broughtons. Some of their leisure they spent in revolver practice. Broughton used a Colt but for a big game hunter accustomed to firearms he was in poor form. Lady Diana was gun-shy at first but she learned to shoot well.

Their visit to the range was to assume a vital importance in the months ahead.

Then poison began to flow. Within a short time three anonymous typewritten letters reached Sir Delves. The first, left in the notice rack at the Muthaiga Country Club in Nairobi, read:

> You seemed like a cat on hot bricks at the club last night. What about the eternal triangle? What are you going to do about it?

Another said:

There is no fool like an old fool. What are you going to do about it?

The third was in similar terms.

When they heard about them, the police tried unsuccessfully to trace the author (for they seemed to have been composed by the same person) and identify the typewriter.

Was the writer one of Errol's discarded mistresses who, perhaps, hoped in this way to warn Broughton and, at the same time, recapture Errol's affections? Or was it a man who believed Broughton was unaware of the ripening friendship between Errol and his wife? A man, moreover, whose wife had been seduced by Errol?

Or were the letters part of a long-range plot that was even then being hatched for Errol's elimination and the laying of a false trail?

The second Christmas of the war arrived and Nairobi prepared to celebrate. The world situation was grim but Kenya's only inconvenience was the blackout. Time did not lag; enjoyment was not scarce.

During the rounds of parties and dances Errol and Lady Diana fell more deeply in love.

It was not, however, until early in the New Year that Sir Delves was convinced of a change in his wife's affections. The solemn pact he had made now became a grim reality, jeopardising his happiness. He was still in love with his wife. He had believed her infatuation for Errol would pass when she got to know him better and learned of his amours. But disillusionment was near.

At a dinner party at Karen on the night of January 12, 1941, Errol and Lady Diana danced to the music of gramophone records. They seemed unaware of the other dancers and the guests who watched them.

Gladys Helen, Lady Delamere, Mayor of Nairobi, sat beside Sir Delves.

'Have you heard the talk that Josh is wildly in love with your wife?' she murmured.

Broughton's eyes blazed. His reply was inaudible. He ignored or did not hear Lady Delamere's other conversation. According to her, his face registered the emotions of 'anger, misery, rage, agitation and restlessness.'

The seeds of jealousy had taken root. He had resolved to allow Diana full freedom and give her everything she wanted to make her happy; but she had fallen in love with a twice-divorced philanderer whose private life was notorious and who had little, if anything, to offer in worldly possessions.

Later that night Errol called Lady Delamere into the lounge.

'I have a confession to make, Gladys,' he said. 'I want your advice.'

She was fond of Errol and wanted to see him happy. She knew his previous marriages had been failures. His wives had been too old for him (just as Broughton was now, apparently, too old for his wife).

'What,' she asked, 'do you want me to advise you about?'

'I am in love with Diana. She is wonderful. I'll do anything for her. I am going to marry her, come what may. What do you think I should do?'

'I guessed you were in love with her,' Lady Delamere said. 'The only honourable thing to do is to make a clean breast of it to Sir Delves.'

'You are right, Gladys, as you usually are,' Errol said. 'I will—as soon as possible.'

Afterwards Lady Delamere spoke to Lady Diana alone. 'Do you know Josh is very much in love with you?'

'Yes,' she said. 'And I am with him, too.'

'What are you going to do about it?' Lady Delamere asked. 'Does he want to marry you? Are you thinking of a divorce?'

'There are various factors I have to take into account,' Lady Diana said. She wanted to be fair to her husband even though they had foreseen such a situation when they made their pact.

'Take your happiness where you can find it,' Lady Delamere counselled. 'There's a war on. But you are perfectly right when you say you should be fair to your husband and tell him the position. If you and Josh are in love, as you say you are, it is the only proper thing to do.'

Both Errol and Lady Diana agreed to seek a suitable opportunity.

Meanwhile, Broughton went to consult his old friend, Soames, to whom he could speak frankly and get equally frank advice. During the few days he stayed at Nanyuki he helped himself liberally to whisky and gin. One night he drank three whiskies and showed the effects.

'Ever since this trouble,' he said shamefacedly next day, 'I've been drinking whisky and gin. They help to send me to sleep. I never used to take spirits, but you know how it is . . .'

He told Soames about his marriage to Diana Caldwell; that, although at first he had not objected to her friendship with Errol, he had recently become upset at their frequent outings together. He did not want to curb Diana's natural desire to enjoy herself . . . but there was a limit.

'I feel the limit has been reached,' he said. '*Now.*' He was silent for some moments.

'I am wondering,' he said eventually, 'whether the two are in love with each other.'

By this time he was virtually certain this was the case. Lady Delamere had remarked that Errol was 'wildly in love' with his wife. He may, however, have sought the benefit of Soames' advice without wanting to admit the full extent of Diana's infatuation.

'My advice,' Soames said, 'is that you ask Errol direct whether he is in love with your wife. If he says "no," tell him to leave her alone. If he says "yes," I suggest you ask her whether she is in love with him. If she says "yes," I think you should return to England.'

The advice was sound. Sir Delves followed it. He asked Diana if she was in love with Errol.

'Yes,' she said frankly, 'I am. It is something I just cannot help. It has happened; there is no use blinking facts . . .'

Broughton tried to temporise. Maybe, he thought, she was not as deeply in love as she believed.

'Let us go away together for three months,' he urged. 'You will then know whether this really is a serious affair and not merely an infatuation. If, after three months of not seeing him, you still feel the same way, well, it will be time to honour our pact. I promise you I will stand by it. But let us give our marriage a longer trial.'

But Diana was sure of herself and of Errol. A three months' absence, or even three years, would make no difference. She was in love with Errol and did not want to be separated from him.

Broughton called on Errol at his home in Nairobi. He wasted no time on preliminaries.

'You know, Josh,' he said, 'I do not take notice of gossip but it has been clear to me for some time that you are in love with Diana. I have spoken to her and she tells me she is in love with you too.'

'Did she?' Errol said eagerly. 'Well, she hasn't told me that yet. But I can tell you quite frankly, Jock, that I'm frightfully in love with her.'

'You probably know,' Broughton said, 'of the conditions under which we married. We made a pact not to oppose each other's divorce if our marriage did not work out. But I'm not convinced Diana *is* seriously in love with you. I've suggested to her that she and I go away together for three months, say, to Ceylon. In that time she will be able to make up her mind and be sure of herself. If she then still believes she is in love with you and wants a divorce so that she can marry you, I'll make no objection.'

Broughton paused.

'But Diana says she doesn't want to go away with me,' he said. 'Won't you persuade her? I'm sure it will be for the best.'

'No, Jock,' Errol said. 'I think that is a poor idea. Once you were to leave the country with Diana what is there to prevent you from making every effort to stop her coming back to me, even if she wants to? Shipping is scarce these days. It might be months, even years, before she could return.' He shook his head.

'I don't like it. I'm afraid you can't count on me to help you in that plan, Jock.'

'Listen,' Broughton said urgently, almost despairingly. 'Diana is so young. She has been so happy in Kenya with me. Please

Diana Seymour-Caldwell, 1937

give me a chance to make something of our marriage! Won't you arrange to leave Nairobi! Perhaps, if you apply to do service elsewhere, they will let you go.'

'It's no use, Jock,' Errol said. 'Please don't ask me. I am as much in love with Diana as she is with me. I couldn't think of deliberately going away from her. I would be running away from the very thing and the very person I want more than anything in the world. I'm sorry it has worked out like this for you, Jock, but I suppose it was fated to be . . .'

'But have you thought of your financial position?' Broughton asked, clutching at any straw. 'You can't afford to keep Diana in the luxury she has been used to as my wife. She has her own means now. I am allowing her £5,000 a year. You've got practically nothing apart from your pay and allowances.

'It might be sufficient for you, but not for you and Diana together. I know Diana would not take a penny of the money I've settled on her if you two were to be married. She is the straightest person I know where money is concerned.'

Errol said placatingly: 'Of course; I would not expect her to take it nor would I deign to live on her money. But we'll manage somehow. We'll have enough for our needs. And we're in love, Jock. Don't forget that. You can put up with a lot when you're in love.'

The arrival of Lady Broughton and her friend, Lady June Carberry, halted the conversation.

Sir Delves told his wife briefly he had been unable to win Errol over to his views nor would he fall in with any of his compromise suggestions. There was nothing to do but implement the pact. He would see his lawyer and arrange for a divorce.

'I'll wait a lifetime for Josh,' Diana said (according to her husband) 'if you can't arrange for a divorce soon.'

Sir Delves now realised his wife was virtually lost to him but he still saw a faint gleam of hope.

'I made up my mind to bow to the inevitable,' he explained later when he spoke of his interview with Errol. 'The only thing for me to do was to cut my losses and go, say, to Ceylon. Perhaps I would return to Kenya in a few months. She might then no longer be in love with Errol. It was possible, I thought, that she did not know her own mind and was being dazzled by Errol's good looks and charm with women.

'I loved her, in spite of everything, and I hoped that all might still come right in the end.'

In what tone and atmosphere had Sir Delves spoken to Errol? According to him, the conversation was calm and dignified. He was trying his best, by persuasion and reasoned argument, to save his marriage from the rocks, pleading with someone who did not seem to care whether it foundered. If Errol gave a different version or description to his friends it was not divulged.

It may be that Sir Delves mastered his feelings and masked his emotions like the suave and polished English gentleman everyone said he was. On the other hand, he may have shown the reaction of the average husband in his position.

There was one eye-witness present, Waweru, Errol's head boy for 14 years. He knew no English but he could gauge the nature and tenor of the conversation by the facial expressions and gesticulations of the two men. Errol may have been no hero to Waweru but, like a trusted valet, he betrayed none of his master's secrets or affairs until he had to in court.

This is how he described the scene:

'Sir Delves Broughton did not show any pleasure in his look when he arrived at my master's home. He waited for half-an-hour before my master arrived. Then he looked very angry and began to strike the table with his fist. My master, he looked grieved. He spoke in a low voice but Sir Delves, he talked loudly. It seemed to me something was wrong. They were not laughing and joking as they usually did.'

Perhaps Sir Delves did not realise he was as angry as he appeared to be to Waweru when he argued, pleaded and banged the table. There can be little doubt he was resentful. That he had genuinely agreed to 'cut his losses' was later to be called into question, but in fact he did address a letter to Soames in confirmation of this intention. He wrote:

I have taken your advice. I put the position to Errol and Diana. They say they are in love with each other and mean to get married. It is a hopeless position and I'm going to cut my losses. I intend getting out. I think I'll go to Ceylon . . . There's nothing for me to live in Kenya for.

It was scarcely surprising that Broughton was in no mood to attend the dinner party Errol gave at his home on the night of this interview. He had been invited, with Lady Diana and other guests, some time before. His absence caused no concern nor the reason for it much comment. All the guests knew it heralded the end of his marriage.

Errol, however, attended a luncheon party at Karen the following day, January 19. Few of the guests would have thought that only a few hours before Sir Delves Broughton had admitted defeat. He greeted Errol with a friendly smile and was, as usual, a charming and amiable host. It was English sportsmanship at its best and most poignant.

'The old boy seems to have taken it on the chin,' one of those in the know remarked after lunch. 'You've got to hand it to him. He's still in love with Diana but he's stepping out of the picture for Josh.'

On the surface this was exactly what it appeared to be. Broughton was placing his wife's and Errol's happiness before his own.

But was he?

Was there resignation only on his face? Was he masking his true deep feelings?

On January 21 Broughton telephoned the police to report a theft at Karen House. Two Colt revolvers, a .45 and a .32, some money, ammunition and other odds and ends were missing from his study.

One of the Colts he had used for target practice at Soames' farm.

The police called. There appered to have been no attempt to force the drawers in which the articles were kept, nor was there any sign of a burglary.

Broughton was asked when he missed the revolvers and ammunition.

When he was looking through the drawers for something, he said. He had heard nothing either by day or night to indicate that anyone was rifling his study.

Did he suspect any of the servants? There were a number of Natives employed on the estate.

No—but it might have been a Native. Firearms and ammunition fascinated them.

The police questioned the servants and searched their quarters and possessions. They found nothing. They promised to be on the alert for Natives in unauthorised possession of Colt revolvers and ammunition.

'It is lucky I still have my hunting guns,' Broughton laughed. 'But I liked a revolver handy too. Now I have got none. I do hope you are able to recover them. It is almost impossible to get others to replace them these days.'

He mentioned the loss of his revolvers when he wrote to Soames. He knew Soames would be interested as he had seen the firearms used on his shooting range a few weeks before.

On the morning of January 23 Sir Delves implemented his promise to honour the pact. He consulted a lawyer in Nairobi and instructed him to begin proceedings for a divorce as soon as possible. He met his wife at the Muthaiga Country Club for lunch and told her what he had done.

'She was terribly upset,' he said afterwards, 'and could scarcely sit still. I assured her there was no longer anything to worry about or to be upset over. I repeated I realised I had to cut my losses and there was nothing to be done except for me to go away.

'I said I intended leaving for Ceylon at the end of the following week but I asked her to stay on at Karen House till I had gone— for the sake of appearances.'

Errol was in happy frame of mind that afternoon. Broughton was acting sportingly, not to say magnanimously, and he looked forward with pleasurable anticipation to the evening in Lady Diana's company.

'I'm dining tonight at the Muthaiga Club with Lady Broughton and Lady Carberry,' he told a friend. 'The old boy will also be there. But after dinner Diana and I are going to dance at the Claremont Roadhouse. We're going to leave the old boy and Lady Carberry behind.

'He insists that I bring Diana home by 3 a.m. as she is very tired. Anyhow, that suits me, too. I'm also fagged and have to be at office early in the morning.'

Broughton seemed anxious to make dinner that night a happier affair than lunch. He wanted to show his guests that his word was his bond. He would make his exit graciously.

'How is Diana?' he asked Errol as they chatted in the club lounge before the women joined them. 'She was in a dreadful state at lunch. But I spoke to her afterwards and got her all right.'

'She's grand now, Jock,' said Errol. (Diana arrived as he spoke.) 'Here she is . . . Isn't she beautiful?'

They drank champagne cocktails before dinner. A bottle of the best champagne nestled on ice in a silver bucket beside the table. With it Sir Delves intended to propose as strange and melodramatic a toast as can ever have been honoured outside Hollywood.

Others dining at the club that night had no inkling of the dramatic undertones to the gay conversation at Broughton's table. He appeared to have drunk a little too freely. He was voluble and uninhibited. Lady Diana was radiant, Errol smiling and happy at the prospect of being alone with her later in the evening.

Suddenly Sir Delves pushed back his chair and rose to his feet. In his hand he held a glass of champagne.

'I want . . .' he said gesturing towards his wife and Errol . . . 'I want to propose a toast.' There was a momentary silence. Broughton smiled wryly. Then he raised his glass.

To Diana and Josh. I want to wish them ever happiness in the future. And may their union be blessed with an heir . . . To Diana and Josh and the future heir.

For a moment the diners sat uncomfortably still. Then they picked up their glasses and laughingly pledged the toast.

Let us picture the scene at the Muthaiga Country Club and at Karen House some hours later in the words of witnesses who testified at the trial.

'After dinner,' Lady Carberry said, 'Errol and Lady Diana went to the Claremont Roadhouse to dance and Sir Delves and I remained talking in the lounge. He had some brandies. Suddenly he became peevish and said he was not going to allow his wife £5,000 a year and a house at Karen . . . and she could . . . well go and live with Josh.

' "We have been married only three months," he said, "and look how it is for me now." He appeared to me to be drunk.

'At 11.30 p.m. we had supper and Sir Delves said he was very tired and sleepy. We chatted a bit longer and left the club at 1.30 a.m. for Karen House. We arrived there half-an-hour later.

'I was not feeling well and went to my room. I waited for ten minutes for Wilks, the maid, to bring me my quinine. Sir Delves, wearing a dressing gown, put his head round the door and asked whether I was all right. I said I was and he said goodnight a second time.

'Wilks was talking to me when a car drew up and I heard Errol and Lady Broughton come into the house. I heard nothing more till a car drove away about ten minutes later. Lady Broughton and I walked for 30 minutes and then she went to her room. About 20 minutes or so later Sir Delves again came to my door and inquired whether I was all right. I assured him once more that I was and, as far as I know, he went back to his room.'

Mrs Phyllis Barkas, who saw Broughton and Lady Carberry talking in the club lounge, said: 'I heard him remark, "To think a woman would treat me like this after we had been married only a couple of months." He sounded upset. He looked very tired too.'

'The dinner party,' Broughton said, 'was a most cheerful affair. Mine was an attitude of complete resignation in view of the circumstances I had encountered. There was nothing else to be done. I realised it.

'After dinner my wife and Errol went to the roadhouse to dance. I made no objection to the arrangement but I asked him to have her home by 3 a.m. I thought that was late enough for a woman who had been upset all day and had recently been out frequently at night.

'Lady Carberry and I left the club at 1.30 a.m. I'm afraid I had a lot to drink during the course of the evening which had been very festive. I hardly ever drink spirits as they make me rather more than depressed.'

'Lady Carberry says you were peevish,' he was asked, 'and

you said you refused to give your wife £5,000 a year and a house?'

'I am sure I said all that Lady Carberry says I did,' Sir Delves agreed. 'I was very naughty, I admit, having had a lot to drink and I was very tired too. When I got out of the club into the fresh air I fear I did rather pass out . . . We got back to Karen House at 2 a.m.

'I went to my room and Lady Carberry to hers. I heard my wife and Errol arrive about 15 minutes later. Then a car drove off. I undressed and went to bed.'

So there were Sir Delves, Lady Diana and Lady Carberry all in Karen House and, according to them, Errol had driven back to Nairobi—alone.

At 5.30 a.m. on January 24 the telephone rang in the office of Chief Inspector Herbert Lanham, in charge of Crime Records, Nairobi.

'There has been an accident,' the caller said. 'A car is overhanging a gravel pit on the Ngong Road about 250 yards on the Nairobi side of the Karen turn-off. It looks as though the driver has been killed.'

On the floor beside the front seat was the body of a man in captain's uniform. He was in a kneeling position, the top of his head an inch from the floor. It appeared as though the body had been tucked up after falling from the seat.

Dr. F. W. Vint, Senior Government Pathologist, performed a post-mortem and established that the death of the Earl of Errol (for he was soon identified) had not been caused in a car accident but by a murderer's bullet. It had entered below the left ear and was found lodged in the medulla of the brain.

Assistant Superintendent A. J. Poppy, of the Kenya Police, examined the car for clues. He found traces of blood on the windscreen and round the driver's seat. In addition to the bullet extracted from Errol's brain, another had buried itself in the hood of the car.

How and where had the killer stood when the shots were fired?

In Dr. Vint's opinion he had most probably been outside the car, poked the firearm inside and fired at close range—from not

The car in the gravel pit

more than nine inches, and even as near as three to six inches. Under the microscope unburnt powder grains removed from the skin surrounding the wound were found to be black. The cartridges had obviously contained black powder.

But how had the car come to overhang the gravel pit? Errol could not have been at the wheel at the time. The theory was that after firing the fatal shot the killer had entered the car, tipped the body on to the floor in case someone should arrive unexpectedly, then started the engine and headed for the pit at slow speed. Just before impact he had leaped out and made a getaway.

No fingerprints of value were discovered on the car and no casts were taken of footprints in the vicinity of the 'accident.' Murder clues had to be sought elsewhere and in other directions.

A friend broke the news to Lady Diana by telephone. Errol, he said, had been killed in a car mishap shortly after he left Karen House. Shocked and unnerved, she staggered to Lady Carberry's room. For a while she could not speak. Then hysterically she sobbed that Josh was dead. Sir Delves, hearing something was amiss, hurried in.

'What is the matter?' he cried seeing his wife's ashen face. She was near collapse.

'Josh has been killed in a car accident . . .'

Broughton seemed to be stunned. 'Good God,' he gasped as he sank on to the bed.

He suggested that Lady Carberry should take Diana to her home at Nyeri, about 100 miles from Nairobi, between the Aberdare Range and Mount Kenya. She was prostrate with grief and, he believed, unlikely to recover in surroundings where she would be constantly reminded of Errol. Lady Carberry agreed and made arrangements for the journey.

Broughton arrived at the Nairobi police station at 10 a.m. and asked Inspector J. R. May, of the crime branch, where Errol's body was.

'I have a handkerchief here belonging to my wife,' he said. 'Will you permit me to place it on his breast before he is buried? It is a last request of my wife. You know, she was very much in love with him.'

'I don't suppose there will be any objection to that,' May said. He looked curiously at Broughton and noticed he was agitated and nervous. His hands shook and his body quivered as he spoke.

Later in the day Broughton telephoned Lady Delamere.

'Isn't it tragic about Josh's death!' he said.

By then the news had spread throughout the town and was the chief topic of conversation.

'Do you know,' Broughton went on, 'my wife, Lady Carberry and I dined with him at the Muthaiga Club last night. He left Karen House at about 2 a.m. after bringing Diana home. He must have been killed in the accident shortly afterwards. He always drove very fast. He might have missed the road in the blackout and crashed into the gravel pit.'

'Yes, I suppose something like that must have happened,' Lady Delamere said. 'He was probably killed outright.'

Broughton telephoned her again in the afternoon to tell her more of the party at the club.

'It was such a happy affair,' he said. 'Who would have dreamed that poor Josh would have met his death so soon afterwards? I proposed a toast to him and Diana. I gave them both my blessing . . . and then this terrible thing had to happen.'

From his words and tone Lady Delamere gained the impression that he was overwhelmed by events and still could not grasp their significance. Only a few hours after he had offered to sacrifice himself, his matrimonial problem had been solved by the death of the man who had caused it.

That evening Sir Delves spoke to her again.

'I am going to ask you to do me a favour,' he said. 'Will you please drop a letter Diana has written into Josh's grave?'

'I am afraid I cannot do that,' she replied. 'You will have to do it yourself if Diana is not in a fit state to attend the burial.'

She met Broughton the next day as she walked away from the funeral.

'I am sorry I am late,' he murmured. 'I intended to be here on time but my car broke down. What shall I do with this now?' He pulled out the letter he had spoken of the previous night.

'Take it there yourself,' she said pointing to the grave. Sir

Delves went to the graveside, stood motionless for a moment beside it, and dropped the envelope.

Shortly afterwards he invited her to lunch at the Muthaiga Club. Once again he harped on the shock of the tragedy and how fond Errol and Diana had been of each other. As before, he reverted to the dinner party and the toast he had proposed. He seemed to lose no opportunity of emphasising his goodwill and decision to stand aside for the young couple.

Then his tone changed. He became scornful and harsh.

He said he never wanted to see his wife again. If he was able to leave Kenya he hoped she would not accompany him then—or any time.

'He talked at length,' Lady Delamere recalled, 'about his first wife and his daughter. He referred to them in terms of great affection and expressed regret that he was no longer married to his first wife. I do not think his behaviour was quite normal. He was nervy and jumpy and wanted company; he did not want to be left alone.'

Inspector C. G. Fentum took a statement from Sir Delves detailing his movements on the night before the crime. It repeated what he had already told Lady Delamere and others.

'I was in my room at Karen House,' he said, 'when my wife and Errol arrived after 2 a.m. I do not know who was driving the car as I did not go out. Errol stayed probably about ten minutes and drove off alone.

'I cannot say whether or not he was normal when he left as I was upstairs. But I do know he was his usual cheerful self at the club and there was nothing abnormal about him then.'

Next day Poppy arrived at Karen House to continue investigations. As he spoke to Broughton he smelt something burning.

'What is that?' he asked.

'We are burning some rubbish in a pit,' Broughton said. 'Wilks told me the other day there was a lot of stuff lying round so I decided to burn it. I set it alight myself. I love bonfires. I have been a gardener all my life and that is one of the jobs I like most.'

Poppy did not place a guard over the pit for a day or two and the charred mass was not examined until January 30 when Chief Inspector W. R. Elliott, of the C.I.D., visited Karen House.

By then the police suspected that Broughton knew more about Errol's death than he cared to admit. Though he repeated that he had irrevocably made up his mind to 'leave a clear field for Josh,' the tragedy had undoubtedly provided him with a timely way out of his dilemma.

Without hesitation Broughton led Elliott to the pit. 'Here is where I burned the rubbish,' he said. 'You are at liberty to take it all away for analysis if you like.'

The detective poked about and found a piece of sacking and a remnant of woollen material that appeared to have once been the top of a golf stocking. Neither Broughton nor anyone else at Karen played golf or wore this type of stocking. It was later examined by Mr. M. H. Fox, Government Chemist, who established that the stains on it were human blood; it was impossible, however, to tell to which group it belonged.

The heat of the pit grass fire would have been about 1,200 deg. F. In a laboratory test even at 360 deg. F., a piece of bloodstained woollen material gave no positive result for pigment and protein constituents. The stocking, whether it had belonged to Broughton or Errol or whether the blood had come from either of them, was valueless as a clue.

The police realised that the solution of the mystery depended entirely on examination of the firearm used and the bullets it had ejected. They had two in their possession, one from Errol's brain and the other from the hood of the car. But there was still no sign of the revolver. Karen House and the grounds were searched in vain.

'I don't think you will find any revolvers here,' Broughton told Elliott. 'My two Colts were stolen on January 21. They were the only two I had in the place. And,' he added wryly, 'civilians cannot get firearms these days.'

'Tell me,' he said later, 'I don't think that will be necessary.'

No fingerprints had been found on Errol's car and to take Broughton's at that stage would have been pointless.

Sir Delves' next question must have surprised, perhaps even embarrassed, the detective.

'Tell me,' he said lightly, 'what is it like in prison in Nairobi?'
Elliot shrugged.

'Just like most other prisons. No home comforts. Hardly a
place to go for pleasure!'

'Are Europeans hanged for murder in Kenya?' Sir Delves
asked next.

Again Elliott parried the question.

As elsewhere in British possessions and colonies, he said, the
law did not discriminate between white and black when it came
to punishment for murder. Any man condemned to death would
be hanged unless there was a recommendation to mercy or
commutation of sentence.

Broughton listened gravely.

'Suppose,' he mused, 'you were to come home one day and
found your wife with another man. If you shot him dead and
reported to the nearest police station would you be hanged for
murder?'

'It is doubtful,' Elliott said. 'A lot would, of course, depend
on circumstances.'

'What punishment them would he receive in such
circumstances?'

'It might be as little as three or six months in prison.'

The conversation passed to other more conventional subjects
and Elliott left.

The mystery was as baffling as ever or, rather, there was hardly
a shred of proof on which to effect an arrest. The killer had left
no identifiable fingerprints or footprints. The death weapon had
vanished.

Then the police learned of Broughton's shooting practice on
Soames' farm some weeks before he reported the theft of his
Colts. On the range they picked up four bullets. They were rather
weatherbeaten and corroded but they were unmistakably .32
calibre slugs.

They appeared to be identical with the bullet that had killed
Errol and the one in the car roof.

Assistant Superintendent A. E. Harwich, of the Uganda
Police, and Fox, the Government Chemist both ballistics experts,
were asked to compare the so-called 'crime bullets' with the

'Nanyuki bullets.' Under the comparison microscope they matched the markings on all the bullets and reported they had been fired from the same weapon with five right-hand rifling grooves.

The markings on test bullets ejected from the weapon would, if identical with the others, have been conclusive, unanswerable proof. But even without these the experts believed there was no possibility of the two sets of bullets having been fired from different firearms.

Furthermore, the live cartridges found on Soames' range were proved to contain black powder. Grains of powder extracted from Errol's ear were likewise black. This, in Fox's opinion, confirmed the link between the 'crime' and the 'Nanyuki' bullets.

Poppy and Elliott returned to Karen House on February 6 in another bid to find the revolver and clinch the case against Broughton.

As before, Sir Delves received the officers courteously and showed interst in their investigations. He seemed as anxious as anyone to help solve the crime and remove suspicion from himself.

'Have you found the revolver yet?' he asked.

'No, not yet, but we still hope to.'

'You will have some difficulty if it has been buried somewhere in Africa,' Broughton said.

'Yes, Africa is a big place. But maybe it is hidden nearer than we think.'

Broughton also wanted to know about the technique used to prove that bullets were ejected from one particular weapon. But the detectives had no time to instruct him in the art of scientific deduction. They did, however, assure him there were ways and means of establishing this point.

In spite of their suspicions and theories the police hesitated to arrest Broughton on a murder charge. The evidence had to be strong enough to link him with the crime. They knew there was a motive—Errol's action in stealing his wife. But against this was his firmly expressed intention to 'cut his losses' and the steps he had already taken to carry out his undertaking.

Even though all the bullets appeared to have been fired from the same revolver how would a jury react if it could not be produced for their inspection?

Jurymen are notoriously reluctant to convict a man of murder purely on expert opinion of tiny marks that can be examined only under a microscope. They want something more convincing than scratch marks and lectures on them.

The police decided to test a theory on the assumption that Sir Delves had been the killer. No one in the house had heard him leave his room before Errol drove away or re-enter it later. Had he done so, he would almost certainly have been heard going down the creaking staircase.

Then how could he have slipped out of his room on the first floor and gained Errol's car without being seen? Could he have climbed down the drainpipe outside his window or lowered himself stealthily from the balcony?

Darkness would have cloaked his movements but he would have run the risk of injury had he lost his foothold. Assuming he had succeeded and crept to the car to await Errol's return from the house. If he had shot him there or a few hundred yards further on the gunfire would have been heard. Sound tests with a .32 revolver, two minutes walk from the house, proved this. On the fatal night no one would have been expecting shots. They might be mistaken for the backfiring of a car.

On the other hand, Broughton might have met Errol at the car and suggested a drive back to Nairobi during which they could have a further discussion about Lady Diana and the future. If the shooting had taken place a mile or more from Karen House, or near the gravel pit, nothing would have been heard.

The police believed they had the answer to the murder weapon question too, even though they could not lay hands on it. Sir Delves' report of the theft of the Colts might well have been part of a pre-determined murder plan. He might have hidden them in a secret place in or outside Karen House. After the detectives' visit to investigate the burglary he had recovered one of the Colts and kept it ready for use.

After the murder he had ascended the drainpipe, or tempted fate by entering through the front door, and subsequently disposed of the revolver as successfully as before. Or he might have concealed it on his way back to the house.

Even this theory posed some awkward questions: Had a man of Broughton's age and physical disabilities the strength and agility to clamber in and out of his bedroom window? Could he, on some pretext, have alighted from the car near the gravel pit, shot Errol and then, after bundling the body on to the floor, have started and leaped from the car a moment before it crashed? If so, could he have returned on foot to Karen House, a distance of little more than two miles in the blackout, and been able to knock at Lady Carberry's door 50 minutes after his first inquiry about her health?

Motive was easier. Who but Broughton had reason for Errol's death? Who else possessed a firearm that could discharge apparently identical bullets at Errol and at the target on Soames' shooting range?

The police decided on March 14 to arrest Sir Delves Broughton.

Two months later he appeared for trial before the Chief Justice of Kenya, Sir Joseph Sheridan, and a jury. The proceedings were to last almost six weeks.

The galleries were crowded daily with women who might have stepped out of *Vogue*. Their names were to be found in *Debrett*, *Who's Who* and the London illustrated magazines. And besides aristocracy were ordinary folk, housewives, businessmen, and soldiers on leave.

Mr. (later Sir) Walter Harrigan, K.C., Attorney-General for Kenya, prosecuted and Mr. H. H. Morris, K.C., then at the height of his fame as a criminal advocate in South Africa, was invited to lead Mr Lazarus Kaplan (now Q.C.) for the defence.

Many of Mr Morris's triumphs had been won by his wide knowledge of ballistics and Sir Delves Broughton's legal advisers had realised that here the issue would turn on the identification of the 'crime' and the 'Nanyuki' bullets and the calibre of the murder weapon.

'In a case of this nature,' the Attorney-General said in his opening address to the jury, 'it is not necessarily the duty of the Crown to establish motive. If it can, then so much easier is it for you, gentlemen, to find that a crime has, in fact, been committed and to arrive at a just and proper verdict. If, of course, motive is not proved the reverse is the case. But here, I suggest, motive will guide your judgment to a great extent.

'The Crown will submit that it *is* supplied by the fact that the Earl of Errol had taken Sir Delves Broughton's wife away from him and broken up his marriage. On the night of January 23, you will hear in evidence, a dinner party was held at the Muthaiga Country Club at which Broughton actually toasted the health of his wife and Errol and expressed the hope that they would have offspring of their union.

'Nevertheless and in spite of that, the Crown will allege that Broughton was incensed by jealousy, or perhaps his pride was hurt, and he was determined to take the law into his own hands. It will be suggested that the toast was merely acting; that Sir Delves never had the intention, as he expressed it, of 'cutting his losses.' This was part of his plan, a plan to murder, carefully thought out, probably between January 18 (when he had a stormy interview with Errol) and January 21 (when he reported the theft of his revolvers).

'And, gentlemen, as this was a planned murder, it eliminates the possibility of a lesser verdict of manslaughter being returned.

'We shall try to establish that Errol died from a bullet in the brain fired from a revolver which, at any rate, three days before had been in Broughton's possession. The Crown will, moreover, try to prove there was no theft of the Colt revolvers and that one of them was used in the killing . . .'

Mr. Morris was at his most forceful and brilliant in cross-examination. He realised the vital duel would be with the small-arms experts of the Crown but from other witnesses he gained a host of facts that would, in advance, substantiate the assertions Broughton was to make and destroy as well the police theory that he had clambered down the drainpipe. If it could be shown it was virtually impossible for Broughton to have performed these acrobatics and that he did not leave the house before Errol drove away, it would (apart from the ballistics evidence) be the end of the Crown case.

'There will be evidence,' Mr Morris said early in the trial, 'that Sir Delves consumed a quantity of liquor at the Muthaiga Club on the night of January 23 and was under its influence by the time he returned to Karen House. He was also extremely tired and suffered from night blindness which prevented him driving a car at night, much less in a wartime blackout. Also, he had a broken wrist, the result of a car accident some years ago.'

Mr Morris had medical support for his statements. An X-ray plate showed that portions of the two principal bones of Broughton's right wrist had been removed causing displacement of other bones. The wrist had osteo-arthritis which meant a weakness of the arm (how, therefore, could he swing over the balcony or shin down the drainpipe in a blackout—much less climb back again?).

Broughton had sunstroke during the early days of World War I, Mr Morris said, and had since been afflicted with night blindness, a condition that worsened with the years. For corroboration he questioned Dr. R. J. Harley-Mason, an ophthalmic specialist, who had examined Broughton shortly before the trial.

Dr Harley-Mason said he had found no organic changes indicating Broughton's condition, but he agreed it frequently existed without organic changes being visible. In any case, Broughton's vision was not quite normal because of a slight degree of shortsightedness and astigmatism in both eyes.

'Would you say he is *not* suffering from night blindness?' Mr Morris demanded an unequivocal answer.

'He might be,' Dr Harley-Mason said. 'I cannot say he is not. Other things being equal, I should say a person suffering from this condition might more easily lose the road than one with normal vision.'

'Is this,' the Attorney-General asked, 'an advanced case of night blindness? According to the defence, Sir Delves Broughton appears to have been suffering from it for something like 25 years?'

'No,' the doctor said. 'It is not advanced and he would be inconvenienced only in the lower degrees of illumination, whether natural or artificial.'

Another eye specialist, Dr. A. Philip, set traps to test whether Broughton was shamming but found the condition genuine. He suffered from night blindness 'to some extent.'

But Mr Morris was unable to remove so easily the hurdle placed in his path by a professional big game hunter who had accompanied Broughton and others on an expedition to the Southern Masai Reserve, Kenya's popular hunting ground. This was only a short time before Broughton's arrest when presumably he was still afflicted by his disabilities.

'I formed a good opinion of Sir Delves as a big game hunter,' this expert said. 'He is no weakling by any manner of means. He carried and used an elephant gun. In the face of danger I would say he is a brave man. His walking? He seemed able to walk as well as I can and I am 56, the same age as he is.'

This offered a somewhat different picture of the man Mr Morris wished to portray to the jury as a limping, arthritic and ageing man, handicapped by night blindness and a useless wrist, unable, even if he had wanted to take the risk of descending a drainpipe, to go after the man who had stolen his happiness.

Yet Mr Morris seemed to have raised a doubt in the minds of the jury whether Broughton was as nimble and skilful as a commando on rough terrain, capable of committing a murder and being back in his room in less than an hour so cool and collected that Lady Carberry had noticed nothing unusual in his voice.

Witness after witness agreed with Mr Morris that Sir Delves was, or gave every appearance of being, the very last person who would do murder.

'It would be a correct estimate,' said Second Lieutenant H. T. Dickinson, 'to say Sir Delves is an English sportsman and a gentleman. On a number of occasions Lady Broughton went out with me. I never knew Sir Delves to be jealous, nor did I find any disposition on his part to curb her pleasures. In all my association with him I never heard him utter one word of disparagement of Lord Errol.'

Was Broughton able to drive a car at night?

'He had a chauffeur,' Dickinson said, 'and he very rarely drove after dark. Two years ago in England, when he drove at night, the car landed in a hedge. I did not consider it safe to let him continue driving.'

'Do you,' the jury foreman asked, 'regard Sir Delves Broughton as a man who could plot a crime such as he is now charged with?'

'No; certainly not,' Dickinson said firmly.

Then came Broughton's lifelong friend Soames, the man to whom he had turned for guidance and counsel.

'I do not,' he said quietly, 'consider him quick-tempered or passionate, or the type of man to commit a crime of this nature.'

Lady Carberry, to whom Broughton had seemed 'peevish' after his wife went with Errol to dance at the roadhouse, said she had seen Sir Delves on many occasions 'courteous, considerate and most cheerful, with a sense of humour, and not at all jealous.' Invariably he allowed Lady Diana to go to any party she wished without him. Nor had she heard him voice any objection to her dining or dancing with his friends with or without him.

She had not heard him utter one word of bitterness or resentment against Errol before or after his death. It was clear to her that he was prepared to agree to a divorce and that Errol would thereafter marry Lady Diana.

The Attorney-General would not agree that these glowing tributes made it impossible for Broughton to have committed murder. His behaviour and good-natured acquiescence in the divorce arrangements was very likely a 'facade and a sham.' In public he might have acted the perfect English gentleman, willing to honour his pact and allow Errol to steal his wife, as it were, under his very nose. But silently and implacably he was plotting to remove his rival and divert suspicion—or exculpate himself should he ever be linked with the crime.

Mr Morris invited the jury to accompany him along another intriguing trail. He recalled the anonymous letters Broughton had recieved and suggested they were from Errol's enemies; the cuckolded husbands of women who had fallen for Errol's charm; or women who had been brushed off for later conquests. Any of these evilly-disposed persons, Mr Morris suggested in his questioning, might have lay in wait for Errol at the crossroads and shot him.

Again, what of his membership of the British Union of Fascists? Might he not have been the victim of a political assassination?

Poppy said he had found Mosley's book 'U.F.' in Errol's home as well as a British Union of Fascists membership card. According to this the monthly subscriptions had been paid in May, 1934. Poppy knew, too, that Errol had assisted the Fascist movement in England and had addressed meetings on Fascism.

In his re-examination and later cross-examination, the Attorney-General showed that Errol had no part in the internment of enemy aliens. Nor had he any association with Fascism as Britain drifted to war. Who then did Mr Morris suggest the jury regard as guilty of a 'political murder?' Was it some patriotic Englishman who considered the time ripe, early on the morning of January 24, for revenge on a man who had admired Mosley and bought his book six years before? Or was the assassin an English Fascist? Or an Italian spy working in Kenya who had carried out a coldblooded execution on instructions from Rome?

Mr Morris smiled as the Attorney-General poured ridicule on his hints and suggestions but refused to remove them from the defence picture.

But all this was to prove preliminary sparring. The main clash had yet to come.

The experts produced the 'crime' and 'Nanyuki' bullets as well as scores of photographs to illustrate that the markings on all were identical. They showed the grains of black powder from Errol's skin and compared them with similar specks from live cartridges found at Nanyuki.

'All the bullets were fired from the same .32 revolver,' Harwich said definitely. 'This is not an opinion but a statement of fact.'

'Have you any doubt whatever?' the Attorney-General asked.

'No,' Harwich said. 'There can be no doubt at all. I say that with full realisation of responsibility regarding the prisoner in the dock.'

His opinion was as emphatically endorsed by Fox.

There was, however, a small but vital point to which no one, save Mr Morris, had yet paid attention. In the end, the life of Sir Delves Broughton was to depend on it.

Both Harwich and Fox agreed with Mr Morris that the bullets were fired from a weapon with five right-hand rifling grooves. The markings showed that clearly.

From experience and long study of firearms, Mr Morris knew that the Colt is a six-grooved gun. If, therefore, the Crown case was that Broughton had committed the murder with one of the missing Colts, it must fail. The murder weapon was five-grooved; it could not, therefore, have been a Colt.

'Mr Harwich,' Mr Morris said, and his eyes gleamed behind his spectacles as they always did when he was about to deliver a knock-out blow, 'will you agree with me that a Colt is a six-grooved gun?'

'Yes,' Harwich said.

'Then it stands to reason,' Mr Morris said triumphantly, 'that you cannot get a five-grooved bullet out of a six-grooved gun?'

There could be no argument with that.

For hour after hour Mr Morris aimed his broadsides at Harwich based on the assertions and findings of world famous authorities on ballistics and the axiom: 'No matter how carefully projectiles and cartridge cases are examined, the facts are useless unless, and until, a weapon is found to correspond with them.'

Though Harwich and Fox persisted that the bullets were the same, and that their photographs and the comparison microscope showed it, Mr Morris invariably countered with the absence of the weapon.

'Until you produce it,' he challenged, 'and until you fire test bullets from it, your assertions cannot be accepted as proved.'

A cable was sent from the office of the Attorney-General to the manufacturers of Colts in the United States. Were their revolvers always six-grooved? Back came the reply: Yes.

And the Crown abandoned its line that Broughton faked the theft of his Colts and committed the crime with one of them.

Yet the vital question remained: With what weapon *had* Errol been shot? Could it, perhaps, have been a Smith and Wesson, a five-grooved firearm, of the same calibre as the Colt? (No one had ever seen Broughton in possession of one.)

Soames, who had watched Broughton at practice on the shooting range at Nanyuki, was recalled by the Attorney-General to describe the type of revolver used. It was, to the best of his recollection, a .32 Colt which, he thought, 'broke,' with a Colt, a six-grooved one, that did not 'break?'

Mr Morris had a knack of getting the reply he wanted to strengthen his case. His question was simple but perfectly phrased.

'You say,' he said to Soames and the jury hung on each word for this was the Crux of the trial, 'that the gun Sir Delves used on the range broke? What would you say if he were to deny that? If he were to say the weapon he used did *not* break?'

'I would believe him if he said so,' Soames said unhesitatingly.

Once again the Crown case was shaken.

According to its own experts, the fatal bullet came from a five-grooved weapon. It could not then have been a Colt. Yet the 'Nanyuki' bullets, according to Broughton now supported by Soames, had been fired from a Colt.

'Tell me,' Mr Morris asked Soames as though in afterthought, 'how long has the shooting range on your farm been used?'

'It has been a hunting camp since 1920,' Soames said. 'There has been a good deal of revolver practice there though I do not recollect a .32 being used before.'

Mr Morris had reason to be well satisfied when the Crown case closed. Against the suggestion that jealousy had caused Broughton to commit the crime, was pitted the fact that he had been willing to grant his wife a divorce when he realized it was useless to compete with Errol. Doubt had been cast on the alleged plot to hide the Colts and then to commit murder with one of them. Mr Morris had questioned Broughton's ability, when he was the worse for liquor, to climb up and down a drainpipe. The pit had yielded no clue and there were no incriminating fingerprints or footprints.

There seemed to be nothing sinister in the talk about the accommodation in the Nairobi jail and the penalty for murder in Kenya. It was unusual but that was all.

The police had agreed it would be surprising if, after so many visits by detectives, Broughton had not thought he was suspected.

He had been in the colony only a couple of months and was strange to its laws and customs.

Sir Delves Broughton, dignified, suave and unruffled, was the first witness in his defence. Watching him, some must have felt the mere allegation of murder against such a man was a ghastly mistake; that no jury could but accept the word of this Englishman who had sportingly given up his wife only to find his act bring him within shadow of the gallows.

Mr Morris's first question was direct: 'Sir Delves, did you have anything to do directly or indirectly, with the death of the Earl of Errol?'

'Certainly not.' The suggestion to Broughton seemed quite preposterous. He was almost defiant.

First he told of his infirmities which, in turn, would have made it 'impossible' for him to have been responsible for Errol's death.

As a young Irish Guards officer at the outbreak of World War I he had gone to France and suffered sunstroke. He was boarded out of the army with a 40 per cent disability. That was not the end of his misfortune. A year later his right wrist was badly fractured and he was permanently disabled in a car crash.

Since then he had been unable to play games requiring the use of his right wrist. His eyesight too had blurred since the sunstroke. For the past two years he had been unable to see the sides of the road. He no longer drove a car.

He spoke of his divorce, his shipboard romance, the pact he had made with Diana Caldwell and their marriage; then of the discovery that his wife was in love with Errol.

'Lady Delamere says,' Mr Morris recalled, 'that when you watched Errol dancing with your wife that night after dinner at Karen, your face registered about five different emotions, anger, misery, agitation and so on. What have you to say to that?'

Sir Delves smiled. 'No, I do not think so,' he said courteously. 'I am a very placid man. But what she said to me on that occasion did confirm my worst suspicions and I was very absent-minded afterwards.'

Coolly and precisely, as though he were reading a part about another man in a play, he told of the events that led to the climax of the drama, the dinner party at the Muthaiga Club and his return to Karen House with Lady Carberry at 2 a.m.

Mr Morris put another vital question: 'Sir Delves, did you leave Karen House again that night?'

'No. Certainly not.' The answer was emphatic.

'You see,' Mr Morris said, 'the suggestion is that you climbed down to the ground by the guttering to avoid being seen leaving the house by the staircase; that you overtook Errol before he drove away; that you were responsible for his death?'

Sir Delves shrugged. 'It would have been quite impossible for me to have climbed out of my room in that manner,' he said. 'It would have been sheer agony because my right wrist is full of arthritis. My physical condition, in addition, was against my doing anything like that. As I have already confessed, I imbibed rather freely that night and I was feeling and, no doubt, showing the effects as well?'

'When did you hear of Errol's death?'

'Next morning. My wife told me. Someone had telephoned her. I was flabbergasted and she was distraught. So much so that she could not give a statement to the police. She refused to believe he was dead. She said to me: 'You go and see whether it is really he.' Unfortunately there was no doubt about it.'

'I asked her,' he went on, 'whether she wanted anything of hers placed on the body. She gave me a handkerchief which I took to the police. Later, at the funeral, I dropped a note in Errol's grave at her request.'

The allegation that he had criticised his wife to Lady Delamere?

He sounded injured. 'I have never done such a thing in my life,' he said.

The fire in the garden pit?

'We burnt an accumulation of rubbish in it. It had been lying about for some days.'

The piece of bloodstained stocking?

He knew nothing about it. 'To the best of my recollection,' he said, 'I have never worn a stocking in Kenya.'

His remarks to the police about fingerprints and conditions in the Nairobi jail?

'It was perfectly obvious to me, judging by the frequent visits the police paid to my home, that I was suspected. I offered them my fingerprints and suggested they go over Errol's car and compare any they found with mine. They did not do so. I wanted to clear myself of these accusations.'

For hours the Attorney-General cross-examined Broughton. He was never in difficulty, at a loss for a word or stumped for an explanation. Nor did he deny his distress that Errol had ousted him.

'Did you ever quarrel with Errol or your wife?'

'No,' he said. 'Never.' And the evidence supported him.

Then what about the Native Waweru's interpretation of the interview between the two men?

'Waweru lied when he said I was not my normal self on that occasion,' Broughton said. 'There was no heat in our conversation though I do not suppose Errol or I looked pleased.'

When and how did he first suspect there was an affair between Errol and his wife?

'Partly through the anonymous letters I received and partly by observation. I do not mind how many men fall in love with my wife as long as she does not reciprocate. She never gave me the slightest cause for jealousy till she started going out with Errol. This, I admit, came as a bit of a shock and I did my best to persuade her to come to Ceylon with me. But she did not want to.'

Had he always implicit faith in is wife?

'Yes. I did not discover, till after Errol's death, that he had been with her at Malindi early in January.'

(Malindi is a coastal resort and old-fashioned fishing village about 80 miles north of Mombasa.)

Did he know that Lady Diana had been seen in Nairobi from January 19 to 23 when she was supposed to have been at Nyeri with the Carberrys?

'No. I had no idea.'

To the suggestion that his wife left on January 19 because he was 'impossible to live with,' he replied firmly: 'Not in the least. I never reproached her once after she told me she loved Errol. But I do admit I was very upset.'

Broughton had claimed to have told Errol he would be unable to support Lady Diana in the comfort she was used to and that his means were insufficient for her.

'Did you not know that Errol had some very valuable possessions?'

'I realised it for the first time on January 19 when I saw my wife wearing three ropes of pearls,' Broughton said. 'I asked her where she got them. She told me Errol had given them to her as a gift. She handed them back to the family immediately after the murder.'

Had he heard the pearls were insured for about £30,000?

'I believe they were insured for £10,000 a few years ago. But because of the war I suppose they could be bought today for £800. In addition to the pearls there were two or three cigarette boxes my wife wanted to own after Errol's death. She bought them from the estate. She also gave a home to two of Errol's dogs no one else wanted.'

What of his conversation and 'peevishness' when he sat with Lady Carberry after his wife and Errol had gone to dance at the roadhouse?

'Perhaps I began to feel sorry for myself over recent events. I am ashamed to say I drank too much. I remember very little of the conversation.'

'When you heard of Errol's death on the morning of January 24,' the Attorney-General challenged, 'you say you were flabbergasted?'

'Yes. I was,' Broughton said frankly. 'I was dumbfounded.'

'But was it not a very satisfactory solution to your domestic problems?'

'I do not think,' Sir Delves said frigidly, 'that an average man would relish resuming married life with one who had been madly in love, and still is, with another man.'

The Chief Justice took up the questioning.

'This toast that you proposed to your wife and Errol at the Muthaiga Club. It was rather unusual was it not? To toast them and their future heir too? Was it a genuine toast?'

'It was perfectly genuine, my lord,' Broughton said. 'I had resigned myself to the situation by then and the toast was the most extreme gesture I could make.'

'Was the dinner party a cheerful affair?' the Chief Justice asked.

'Yes, very cheerful. Everyone was in top form.'

Broughton's evidence and cross-examination lasted 22 hours and was spread over six days. Mr Morris could not have wished for a better witness. There was never a misplaced word or an unnecessary one.

Next most important defence witness was Captain T. W. Overton, Assistant Inspector of Armourers in the East African Services. He had completed a four-year course at the Royal Arsenal, Woolwich, as well as three long refresher courses at the Military College of Science. During a 29-year military career he had studied small arms and given expert testimony in 11 cases on small arms and ammunition.

Mr Morris handed him the 'crime' bullets and the corroded ones from the Nanyuki shooting range.

'The Crown experts,' he said, 'have stated that all were fired from the same weapon. They have pointed to what they say are numerous identical marks. What is your comment?'

'I have examined all the bullets very carefully,' Captain Overton said, 'and I have come to the conclusion that those found in Errol's brain and in the hood of his car were fired from the same weapon. Those found on the range were fired from a different one. The first two have a distinct characteristic, the longitudinal engraving which is identical in each bullet and must be peculiar to the weapon from which they were fired.

'I did not find a longitudinal engraving corresponding to this on any of the other four bullets. If they had been fired from the same weapon as the other two they would also have had the same longitudinal engraving.

'On the four I found a common distinctive characteristic, a series of engravings in one groove on each bullet. These characteristics, however, were not present in the ''crime'' bullets.'

The Attorney-General recalled Fox to comment on these findings. In spite of what Overton said, Fox declared he had counted more than 50 points of agreement between the 'crime'

bullets and one of those picked up on the Nanyuki range. He
was satisfied with a sequence of only ten which the jury could
see for themselves on the large number of photographs he had
prepared. The chance of a sequence of ten identical characteristics
recurring was one in 3,500,000.

The other defence evidence was called mainly to underline
the admissions of the Crown witnesses that violence was
obnoxious to Broughton and he was most unlikely to have
resorted to murder through jealousy.

Major R. B. Pembroke said he had been out at night with
Lady Broughton with Sir Delves' approval. He had not found
Broughton at all jealous nor had he seen him irritable or morose
though he sometimes seemed depressed.

Mr J. D. Hopcraft, a farmer, who had known Broughton for
21 years, described him as a 'good sportsman, a very good loser
and very good company.'

Lieutenant V. de V. Allen, Assistent Superintendent of the
Nairobi prison, found Broughton even-tempered while he was
awaiting trial. Almost daily he strolled with him over the veld.
His walking was not good. On one occasion he walked 2-3/10
miles in 40 minutes and was distressed though the sand road
was good.

The prison doctor, Dr J. C. Carruthers, said Broughton made
no attempt to exaggerate his ailments. Considering the life of
luxury to which he had been accustomed, he might have been
expected to show some irritability in prison. Yet he was always
cheerful save for the first few days of his confinement.

As the prisoner had elected to give evidence Mr Morris was
called upon to address the jury before the Attorney-General. (The
procedure is different in the Union where the prosecutor
invariably addresses the jury first and is followed by counsel for
the defence whether the prisoner testifies or not.)

He contended the murder was committed between 2.30 a.m.
and 3 a.m. within 100 yards of the gravel pit where Errol's car
was found. A suggestion that it had taken place within the
precincts of Karen House was unlikely. The place was occupied
and there were servants about. The risk of the shots being heard
was too great for the killer to take.

In any event, he suggested, at least two persons and probably three had participated in the crime. Had there been only one assailant he would have had to be very powerful—he would have had to jump on the running board of the car as it turned from the branch road into the Ngong Road. And to do so he would have had to be agile, sure of hand, foot and eye. Broughton had none of these physical attributes.

Who were the murderers?

It was not for the defence to suggest or prove their identity. The onus was on the Crown to establish, beyond reasonable doubt, that it was the prisoner.

Mr Morris nevertheless harked back to his Phillips Oppenheim solution to the mystery—Errol, one-time Fascist, disciple of Mosley, might have been the victim of a Fascist plot. Alternatively, there was the fact that he had had many love affairs. It would be surprising if he had not incurred the enmity of some individuals in the colony.

Hinting that a woman might have been one of a trio involved in the crime he said pointedly: 'Hell hath no fury like a woman scorned.'

He knew the strongest single factor in Broughton's favour was the absence of the murder weapon. In his opening address the Attorney-General had said the theft of the Colts was stage-managed, that the crime was committed with a gun that Sir Delves had in his possession three days before.

'We have shown conclusively, gentlemen, that the fatal bullet was not fire from a Colt which is a six-grooved gun. It came from a five-grooved gun. And there is not a shred of proof that one was ever in Broughton's possession. For the Crown to convince you, or to link him with the crime, it must prove not only that the 'crime' and 'Nanyuki' bullets were fired from a five-grooved gun, but that Broughton possessed one on the night of Errol's death and, with it, shot him dead.

'The Crown has failed utterly to do this. It was the cross-examination of the Crown's own experts that brought out the fact that the 'crime' bullets were sped from a five grooved weapon and that, therefore, a Colt could not have been used. What then is left of its case?'

Threats?

'Broughton is a man of placid disposition. There is no proof that he uttered a single threat against Errol's life at any time.'

Departure from his room?

'There is nothing to show he left Karen House after his arrival with Lady Carberry. The evidence is rather the other way. Not a single garment he wore was specked with blood.'

Vengeance?

'Sir Delves is a man of vast wealth, much travelled and accustomed to entertaining on a lavish scale. He is a game loser. That he made a pact before the marriage shows he had taken into account the disparity in the ages between his wife and himself. When she fell in love with Errol he accepted the situation with good grace and arranged for a divorce.

'It is incredible that a man with murder in his heart could dine with his victim and even toast him a few hours before killing him in accordance with a diabolical and carefully thoughtout plan.

'Are we to believe that in an instant Broughton was able to overcome intoxication and considerable physical disabilities, take the risk of leaving the house in which people were still about, assume the strength and vigour of a young man, shoot his victim, drive the car to the gravel pit in the pitch darkness of a blackout and with defective vision—and then hasten back across rough country to the house, all in the space of a short time?

'Evidence has shown that Broughton has not driven a car at night for years. Are we to believe that a man whose whole conduct has been shown to be inconsistent with guilt, transformmed himself instantly into the shape of a human fiend?

'You cannot, gentlemen. You cannot find the prisoner guilty of this crime.'

The Attorney-General agreed, in his address, that the vital part of the Crown case was the expert evidence that the bullets fired at Nanyuki and to kill Errol had come from the same weapon. It was no part of the case that the bullets were fired from a 'Colt revolver' but from the 'same gun.'

Three live cartridges had been found at Nanyuki containing black powder. Black powder had also been embedded in the skin on Errol's neck where a bullet had entered. This suggested that all the cartridges came from a box of 50 used by Sir Delves and Lady Broughton at Soames' shooting range.

The Attorney-General admitted that but for the testimony of Harwich and Fox, there would be no case for Broughton to meet. He asked the jury to accept the findings of the experts. Fox had taken three months to compile his evidence using a comparison microscope. preparing and comparing many photographs. Neither he nor Harwich had been shaken 'one iota under the most severe and remorseless cross-examination.' Against this Mr. Morris had pitted the evidence of Captain Overton whose examination of the bullets with dividers, a magnifying glass and a pair of calipers had occupied two hours.

The Attorney-General ridiculed the political murder theory.

'With all due deference to counsel for the defence,' he said, 'I suggest his claim that Errol was the victim of a political murder is absurd. Surely he cannot be serious in urging you to find he was shot because he paid one month's subscription to the British Union of Fascists in 1934 and addressed a meeting or two in Kenya long before the war.

'It would, indeed, be most remarkable if the supposed Fascist assassin had known that Errol would be driving down the Karen branch road early on that morning, recognised him in the blackout, jumped on the running board and shot him dead. I do not think, gentlemen, you will for a moment consider this possibility or that the murderer was the writer of the anonymous letters.

'I submit that during his interview with Broughton on January 18, Errol sealed his fate. On the morning of January 21, I suggest that as Errol was to die from a revolver bullet, Broughton considered it time to get rid of his own revolvers. Accordingly he reported their theft to the police. Burglaries, you have heard it stated in evidence, are hardly known at Karen.

'Yet, on the night of January 20 there is, apparently, this burglary without any sign of forcible entry and, of all things, Broughton's two Colts are stolen. I have already suggested, and I repeat, that this was a faked burglary.

'What can be more exasperating than to see one's wife taken

away by another man? Even though Sir Delves says he was prepared to ''cut his losses'' it is doubtful, to say the least, that he was willing to give her up and allow Errol to get away with it.

'There was a great change in his attitude after he toasted his wife and Errol at the Muthaiga Club. The Crown submits that this was not a genuine toast. Though he wished them happiness and drank to their future heir, his true feelings were very different. He took liquor before, during and after dinner to muster courage, to work up his mind to the requisite pitch for murder. He was also peevish, as you have heard, and swore about his wife.

'If you analyse his reactions and conduct throughout the police investigations you will come to the conclusion that he was acting a part and, if I may say so, acting it magnificently. And his interpretation of that part was helped by his experience as a magistrate.

'Mr Morris declares he was physically incapable of murder. But was he? He is a big game hunter. He has stalked lion. He uses an elephant gun. There was nothing wrong with his walking or powers of endurance on the hunting expedition to the Southern Masai Reserve.

'As for his night blindness, of which you have heard much here, I submit it never worried or crossed Broughton's mind until this case when he believed that mention of it might help his story that he could not have driven the car or returned to Karen House over a rough road in the blackout.'

The Chief Justice also seemed sceptical of the theory that a Fascist had committed the murder for political reasons.

'Counsel for the defence,' he summed-up, 'has suggested to you that Errol might have been the victim of a political murder, that he was shot either as a traitor or because he was for a short while a member of the British Union of Fascists. It is for you to decide the possibility of either of these submissions. You will remember, however, that it was as long ago as 1934 that he had some connection with the Union of Fascists or addressed meetings on Fascism. And you will ask yourselves whether his death, six years later, might be the result of a Fascist intrigue or plot.'

Broughton, Sir Joseph Sheridan said, had known intimately

Errol's movements on the night of the crime—that his wife had gone dancing with him and that she could be expected back at Karen House about 2 a.m. or 3 a.m. Would the alleged Fascist assassin, or the author of the anonymous letters, have known his movements in such or more intimate detail?

'The Crown has put forward jealousy as the principal motive for this crime. The defence has countered with evidence and statements by various witnesses that Broughton never, at any time, showed jealousy or uttered a threat against Errol.

'I have, however, yet to learn that even though a person is of good breeding and high traditions he is immune to the ordinary frailties of human nature. Sir Delves had been done a very great wrong by Errol. In your deliberations, gentlemen, you will consider human nature. None are exempt from temptation, no matter what their station in life and affairs.

'You will have to decide too whether Broughton was playing a part on the night of the crime. Was his toast to Errol and his wife at the Muthaiga Club sincere or not? It might have been sincere. He might genuinely have intended to 'cut his losses,' as he says, give his wife a divorce and go away.

'On the otgher hand, you will consider whether it was not an "unnatural" toast, as the Crown alleges. Similarly, you will have to decide whether the burglary at Karen House a few days earlier was genuine or a bogus one for the purpose of furthering some long-term scheme.'

The Chief Justice endorsed the argument of both counsel that the strength and weakness of the case rested on the evidence of the ballistics experts.

Fox was a scientist who had given his evidence with great precision. He had stated definitely, and remained unshaken under cross-examination, that all the bullets were fired from the same revolver, one that had been used at the Nanyuki practice range and again in Errol's car. He was supported in his findings by Harwich.

Captain Overton, the small arms expert called for the defence, on the other hand, had not the time, opportunity or the facilities Harwich and Fox enjoyed. Here, again, it was the task of the jury to weigh the contradictory evidence and decide whose to accept or reject, remembering always that the Crown had to prove its case beyond reasonable doubt—that any reasonable doubt must be given to the prisoner.

The Chief Justice glanced at his watch. It was 5.40 on the afternoon of July 1, 1941.

'Gentlemen,' he said quietly as he put aside his notes, 'night is falling but let not the question of time influence you in any way. Take all the time you want for there is a consideration of the gravest import in the balance.'

The jury was away for more than three-and-a-half hours. When the fateful knock on the door of the juryroom was heard, conversation stopped. The final act in six weeks of drama was at hand.

Sir Delves Broughton had been lounging in the dock. He showed little sign of the strain of the trial or the last suspense-filled hours of waiting. Now he straightened and looked at the men who were to say whether he would live or die.

'Not guilty,' the foreman said.

'Sir Delves Broughton,' the Chief Justice said curtly, 'you are acquitted.'

'Thank you, my lord,' Broughton said as though he had expected no other verdict. 'I would like, through you, to thank the police and prison officials and all the others connected with this case for the courtesy and consideration I have had from them at all times.'

The Chief Justice nodded and left the court ignoring the hubbub and congratulations showered on the man who, a few moments before, had stood at the crossroads between life and death.

Mr Morris was not in court to witness the climax to one of the great cases of his career. He had to leave Nairobi after making his address to the jury. Reports that later reached him disclosed that the jury foreman had called on each of his colleagues in turn to state his views. One, evidently puzzled or unimpressed by the volumes of expert evidence, held the opinion that when bullets were exposed to the air or the ground, as at Nanyuki, they eventually lost weight!

Eleven of the jury wanted to return a verdict of 'Not Guilty and Innocent.' The 12th would agree only to the conventional 'Not Guilty.' This was the form at last agreed on.

Broughton himself wrote to Mr Morris describing how he paced up and down while the jury deliberated. When they announced their verdict in a 'still, crowded court,' there came 'a sob of relief from all sides and some clapping.'

'But,' Sir Delves added, 'the judge looked furious. His summing-up was dead against me though I must admit he did instruct the jury that if they were not satisfied all the bullets were fired from the same gun, the Crown case fell to the ground . . . The jury took him at his word . . .'

It was also whispered that what weighed considerably with the jury was Fox's statement that he had spent hours, even days, studying his photographs of the bullets. Instead of his painstaking task convincing the jury more than the two-hour analysis of Captain Overton, they believed that if he had been so certain, from a comparison of the markings, that all the bullets had come from the same revolver, he would not have had to devote so much time to the study of his photographs!

Several days after the trial Mr Morris was invited to a Rotary Club lunch in Joannesburg. As he entered the dining hall a fellow-advocate tried to catch him off-guard.

'Tell me, Harry,' he whispered, 'who shot Errol?'

'My God,' Mr Morris whispered back, 'I quite forgot to ask.'

Sir Delves Broughton left Nairobi soon after his acquittal and returned to England. On December 5, 1942, exactly two years and a month after his marriage to Diana Caldwell, he committed suicide in a hotel room in Liverpool by swallowing an overdose of medinal, a drug of the barbitone group.

His estate, valued at £75,000, he left to Lady Vera Broughton, his first wife, whom he had married in 1913.

Will the death of the Earl of Errol ever be solved and the murderer brought to justice?

Was Broughton fortunate to have escaped conviction? Or had fate enmeshed him in a web of circumstances that might have cost him his life but for the brilliance of Morris and his knowledge of firearms?

There can be no quibble with the jury's verdict. They had a reasonable doubt and rightly acquitted. Juries are always reluctant to condemn a man on technical evidence. Science and scientists are forever making advances, rejecting old theories and firmly held beliefs for new ones in the light of further knowledge and experience.

The missing clue, which influenced the decision here, was the weapon that killed Errol. Unless test bullets could be fired from it the jury believed absolute proof was lacking. For who could say, without risk of making an error, that it would have imprinted identical markings on bullets? The jury were not prepared to take that risk.

Who then did murder Errol?

As he indicated in his address, Mr Morris believed that a woman might well have been involved in the crime with one or two men as accomplices. While he was in Nairobi he received an anonymous letter naming a prominent socialite who had allegedly lost Errol's affections. She, it was said, would have had the dual motives of jealousy and desire for revenge that the Crown attributed to Broughton.

The known facts and circumstances of the case could, of course, have made this a possibility. Errol had let it be known that he intended to go dancing with Lady Diana after dinner on the night of January 23 and that the 'old boy' insisted on her returning to Karen House by 3 a.m. Even if he had not spoken of his arrangements, there would have been little difficulty in keeping him under observation.

'The Woman' and her accomplices, perhaps men whose homes had been ruined by Errol, could have ascertained his movements that night as readily as Broughton himself. They might, without arousing suspicion, have watched the Muthaiga Club, followed Errol and Lady Diana to the Claremont roadhouse and then decided to intercept him at the intersection of the Ngong Road and the turn-off on his return from Karen to Nairobi. They might have taken up a position well off the road hours beforehand. The blackout would have been in their favour.

If one of them possessed a Smith and Wesson revolver it would at once explain the calibre of the 'crime' bullets and bear out Mr Morris's contention that the 'Nanyuki' bullets fired by Broughton from a Colt, differed from them.

'The Woman' might have stopped Errol by waving a torch and on the pretext of asking for a lift, approached and shot him. Her accomplices could have stage-managed the accident and all would have returned to Nairobi hours before the crime was discovered.'

It would have been as simple as that. The murderers also had the inestimable advantage that suspicion was almost immediately directed at Broughton and they were afforded ample opportunity of disposing of the murder weapon.

This theory would have meant, as a corollary, that Broughton's report of the theft of his Colt revolvers was genuine and it was pure coincidence that they vanished without trace only a few days before Errol's death; that he had not left his room after returning from the Muthaiga Club with Lady Carberry.

It implied also that his second inquiry about Lady Carberry's health was not to impress on her his *continued* presence in Karen House at a vital hour but simply to extend to her the normal courtesies of a thoughtful host—even though he was the worse for liquor!

How would a fiction writer have solved the mystery?

Everything seemed to point to Sir Delves Broughton as the most likely person to have committed the crime. He had the motive, the time, knowledge of Errol's movements and, above all, the opportunity. He was a man with a clear and lucid brain; a wide experience of the law, the stagecraft of the courtroom; and a knowledge of firearms.

Suppose he had concealed the Colt revolvers in some inaccessible spot, known only to himself, then reported their loss so that after Errol's death he could prove, *with the aid of the police*, that he had no smallarms at the time. Unknown to anyone else he might have owned a Smith and Wesson, or some other .32 calibre firearm, with which he intended to kill Errol.

He deduced correctly that the police would conclude that the theft of the Colts was faked and that, therefore, the murder had been committed with one of them. It was a master stroke. He knew it would be possible to prove that the fatal bullets could not have been fired from a Colt. And he had ensured that his Smith and Wesson was as effectively hidden from the police as the Colts.

The liquor he had drunk on the night of January 23 did not dull his senses but rather sharpened them and strengthened him in his resolve to dispose of the man who had robbed him of his wife and his happiness. He deceived Lady Carberry and Mrs Barkas by feigning tiredness and passing out. The toast to Errol and his wife was pre-arranged as a further counter to any suggestion of ill-will.

Back at Karen House at 2 a.m. he knew he would not have long to wait. He had told Errol and Diana to be home no later than 3 a.m.

He changed from his dress suit into everyday clothing, slipped on a dressing gown and showed himself to Lady Carberry soon after 2 a.m.—to impress on her his presence in the house. She heard him again at her door about 50 minutes later inquiring how she felt. She would not guess he had been out in the interval.

How did he manage to leave his room and reach Errol's car before he drove away?

He might have decided to risk walking downstairs and out of the front door after his wife and Errol had entered. On the other hand, it was more likely he shinned down the drainpipe. His infirmities made this difficult but not impossible. A man with murder in his heart, thirsting for revenge, would not think of difficulties but only of carrying out his plan in spite of them.

When Errol returned to his car he found Broughton who suggested they drive back to Nairobi and discuss on the way the plans for the divorce and the future. The unsuspecting Errol would have had no objection.

As they approached the Ngong Road Broughton, on some pretext, asked Errol to stop. He alighted, walked round to the driver's seat and then, before Errol was aware of what was happening, shot him. Quickly re-entering the car, he pushed the body to the floor, started the engine, steered for the gravel pit and jumped clear.

He returned to Karen House on foot. On the way he buried the revolver at a spot he had previously selected or he may have decided to attend to this at a later stage. He regained his room by way of the front door or the balcony and established his alibi by talking a second time to Lady Carberry. She, feeling unwell, would scarcely have bothered to notice whether he was nervous or agitated.

But Broughton's master stroke was the choice of a weapon for the murder. Having sent the police on a false trail in search of the missing Colts, he could safely commit the crime with another revolver no one knew he possessed and which he would ensure was never found after it had served its purpose.

In a mystery story Sir Delves Broughton would have achieved a unique formula for murder.

ELLIOTT O'DONNELL

The Corpse Box
of Hell Gate

One morning in June, 1859, a small fishing boat was leisurely ploughing the waves near Hell's Gate. It was a typical American summer morning—a dazzling blue sky above, a dazzling blue sea beneath, and sunbeams, the brightest of laughing, golden sunbeams, everywhere. Being early, there was an absence of that intense heat which strikes newcomers from across the Atlantic as so appalling, and the air was still comparatively cool and fresh. Everything, indeed, suggested life, young, vigorous, joyous life; and one could not imagine a cheerier scene. Doubtless with some such appreciation of this surroundings the sole occupant of the fishing boat sat with one hand grasping the tiller and the other holding, for awhile, his freshly filled pipe. Then, suddenly, he leaned forward, with his eyes fixed upon some object floating on the water. Tacking, so as to come close up against it, he discovered, to his astonishment, that it was an enormous oak chest. Now, although the weather for some considerable time past had been fine, this did not preclude the possibility of a marine catastrophe of some sort, and the fisherman supposing that the chest came from some vessel that had, perhaps, struck an iceberg, or gone down in a collison off the perennially fog-girt coast of Newfoundland, resolved to tow it ashore and see what it contained.

Accordingly, attaching it by means of a rope to his craft, he tacked about again, and made, as nearly as possible in a bee line, for Port Morris. Having lost no time in arriving there, he towed the chest up alongside the quay, and called to some of the men he knew to give him a hand in hauling it up the steps. The men complied, but the task proved by no means an easy one, as the steps were steep and slippery and the chest tremendously heavy.

At last, however, it was safely landed, and then the work of opening it commenced. As knot after knot of the rope bound round the chest was undone, many and varied were the speculations as to what was inside. Some suggested clothes, others books, while others, again, hinted at money—piles of glinting, gleaming gold, maybe Californian ingots or bright and sparkling Spanish doubloons. The fisherman was almost beside himself with joyful expectations; he had found it, he kept on remarking, and whatever it contained, no matter what it was, would be his.

After much coaxing and pulling, the rope around the box at length slackened and fell off, the lock, in response to a vicious jab from an improvised jemmy, abruptly yielded, and the lid, amid the most tense silence and excitement, was raised. It was then that the fisherman and his mates experienced the shock of their lives. Instead of gold, the inside of the chest revealed a row of white, distorted corpse faces and a confused mass of human remains, bodies, arms, legs, hands and feet, all packed promiscuously into the smallest possible space. Never had a morning sun looked down on a more blood-curdling and revolting spectacle. For some seconds those present were too appalled and terrified to speak; but when reason and the power to act returned to them, they immediately made off, helter skelter, in search of the police, broadcasting the news all along the quay as they went. It was thus that the affair was brought to the notice of the Portal Authorities, who immediately ordered a medical examination, with the result that the remains found in the chest, and partially covered with lime and shavings, were proved to be those of an elderly man and woman, a young man and young woman, a little girl of about six years of age, a boy of about four, and a negro. All were in night attire, which, with the exception of the negro's, was of the finest texture, the woman's being ornamented with the most costly lace, and marked with initials that were either C.W., or G.W. On the stocking of one of the children was an unmistakable M.A. Beyond these marks there were no clues to identity, the faces of all the bodies being rendered absolutely unrecognizable through the action of lime and water. The inspecting doctor declared that the bodies had been in the chest and sea for at least seventy hours. The negro had been decapitated, and possibly to make room for him, his body, like that of the elderly man, had been doubled up, and his head placed, as if in bitter mockery, close beside his feet. The rest of the corpses were whole, and saving for a wound, probably caused by a dagger, on one of them, entirely free from any indications of violence. Indeed, it was impossible to say exactly, presuming they had been killed, how they had been killed.

This is the gist of the case as actually reported in the Press, but as it was not followed up, at least so far as I can discover, one can only conclude that the matter was for some peculiar reason, perhaps best known to the American police of that date, abruptly dropped, and the affair left a mystery. Among those who read this solitary report of the case speculation would seem to have been rife; some suggested the whole affair was simply a very gruesome jest on the part of New York medical students, others that the bodies were those of a party of foreigners murdered on some foreign yacht or other vessel, either in New York harbour itself or in its immediate vicinity.

A solution to the mystery, which is somewhat different from either of these, has occurred to me, but before I give it, I must remind my readers that it is merely a suggested solution, that it must therefore be taken on that understanding, and simply for as much as it is worth. Here it is.

At the time of the finding of the 'Corpse Chest' the United States was being terrorized by various singularly daring and sinister gangs of desperadoes. One of them, mainly composed of Italians, confined itself to robbery with violence in big cities, while another included among other specialities that of train wrecking, accompanied by wholesale plunder and murder. An article in reference to the latter appeared in the Foreign News column of the *News of the World* for June, 1895.

Here is a short extract from it:

A man called M'Laughlin has been tried at Chicago (Illinois) on the accusation of causing trains of cars on the Galena and Chicago railroad to be thrown from the tracks. From what has been disclosed it is apparent there is a league of villains in the West, banded together for the purpose of murder, theft, and arson. Women as well as men belong to the gang, which has branches in Chicago, Cleveland, Buffalo, and all the Lake cities. Causing railroad accidents is one of their favourite deeds.

Now, since it is a fact that there was a gang of this description at work at the time the 'Corpse Chest' was found, in my opinion, it is not at all unlikely that this said gang was responsible for the butchery of the seven unidentified people whose remains were found in the chest. It requires no very great strain of the imagination to conjure up some such circumstances as the following (cases, more or less similar to the one I am about to portray, were, at that period, constantly occurring):—To begin with, we will suppose that a planter named Garcia Williams, prior to the finding of the chest, was living with his family, some distance up country, possibly on the borders of Mexico. As his name implies, he was of mixed origin, and the hot southern blood in him revealed itself in his swarthy complexion and extremely arbitrary and passionate disposition. His wife, a full-blooded Spaniard, was still beautiful, despite her fifty odd years, and even more haughty and despotic than Garcia himself. They only had one child, Leopold, to whom they were very devoted, and in the summer of 1857, Leopold, his wife and two children, a boy and girl, were staying with them.

The plantation was a large one, and among the hundreds of slaves employed on it was a young and rather handsome, though sinister looking, half-caste called Fernando. His mother, undoubtedly, was Anna, the negress, but the identity of his father was by no means so apparent. Only a few of the older slaves remembered that 'the boss' once had a sneaking regard for the slim and by no means ill-favoured Anna, but this recollection, of course, was only hinted at in the strictest secrecy. Now, whether it was simply on account of these suppressed rumours, or whether it was because she had acquired some perfectly authentic information on the subject, it was only too evident that Garcia's wife cordially detested the young half-caste.

On one occasion she had caused him to be soundly whipped for not being what she was pleased to term 'sufficiently respectful', while for another small offence she had ordered him to be placed all day in the pillory. He had tried to run away once, but the punishment he received made him think twice before repeating the offence.

In the spring of 1857 Garcia Williams bought several new slaves, and among them a young woman called Tady. Now it so happened that Tady was quite beautiful, and, as a consequence, she soon had a band of admirers. Johnson, the black foreman, was one, Caesar, a very puny middle-aged nigger, another, and the handsome Fernando a third; but it soon became apparent that she favoured the half-caste most of all.

Had Fernando's disposition been different all might yet have gone tolerably well, but he was vain as well as ill-natured, and nothing, apparently, delighted him more than taunting and deriding his less fortunate rival, Johnson. The two frequently had high words, and on one occasion they came to blows. Johnson got the worst of it, and after being knocked down in the presence of Tady, he went off vowing immediate vengeance.

A day or two later, a commotion was caused among the negroes, owing to several of them having lost things. These losses, trivial enough to the majority of people, meant a lot to coloured slaves, who possessed little beyond what they stood in; and their lamentations were loud and bitter. But something much more serious was to follow. Mrs Williams, junior, on going into her room one night to dress for dinner, missed her purse, and it was then discovered that a valuable pearl necklace had disappeared too. A hullaballoo was, of course, raised, and presently Johnson, the foreman, informed Mrs Garcia Williams, senior, he had found a clue.

Leading her to the flower-bed immediately beneath the window of her daughter-in-law's bedroom he pointed triumphantly to a knife. It was lying in full view, with one open blade a mass of sparkles in the brilliant sunshine. 'Der missus, see dat,' Johnson cried, pointing excitedly to it, 'de villen who stole de purse and de jewels drop dat in his hurry.'

'Do any of the slaves possess a knife?' Mrs Williams exclaimed, eyeing it as if it were a rattler or some kind of reptile.

'Mebbe some of 'em do, missus,' Johnson said, 'any rate I ken find out.'

Some hours later Johnson came to the house accompanied by a whole troop of blacks, who, on seeing the knife, swore it belonged to Fernanado. He was the only nigger on the plantation, they avowed, who owned one. The order was then given for Fernanado's quarters to be searched. It did not take long to look through the young half-caste's possessions, as they consisted, only, of a small tin box with a few ounces of tobacco in it, a tawdry frame without any picture, an old dilapidated wide-awake hat, a ditto pair of store shoes, reserved for very rare occasions, and a few articles of the coarsest and cheapest clothing; and Caesar, the middle-aged nigger who conducted the search, was turning away, satisfied, but obviously disappointed that the necklace was not there, when, at Johnson's suggestion, he examined the bunk itself, and under a loose piece of boarding he discovered not only what he was looking for but all the other missing articles as well.

It was in vain that Fernando protested; his indignant denial of the charge availed him nothing. Loaded with chains and pursued for some distance by an angry mob, he was led triumphantly into the presence of Mrs Garcia Williams, who in the temporary absence of her husband only too willingly undertook the task of dispensing justice.

Upon hearing the sentence, namely, that he should be strapped to the pump, in the usual way, for an indefinte period, Fernanado promptly fell on his knees before his tormentor and grovelled. She was inexorable, however, and to the pump he went. Strapped so tightly to the iron upright that the rope, in places, literally cut into his flesh, he was placed in such a position that drops of water from the pump invariably and constantly fell on exactly the same spot on his bare head, which was, at the same time, exposed to the fierce rays of a pitiless sun.

At first, of course, the water felt cool and refreshing, but it was not long before a slight tenderness was felt in the affected spot, and after that a dull aching, that speedily became more and more acute. At length the torture was so great that Fernando shrieked, and when he could shriek no longer, he lost consciousness.

In this condition he was liberated and tossed carelessly aside, to lie huddled up and bleeding on a pile of refuse, till his benumbed faculties and muscles had recovered sufficiently to enable him to move.

A day or two later, he was whipped back again to work. He bore it for a week, and then one night, when the snores of all around him assured him that, at all events, the bulk of the nigger population was asleep, he made another dash for freedom.

This time luck favoured him. Stealing down to the river unobserved, he secured a raft without any difficulty and made off on it down stream. He landed at dawn, and footing it at a rapid pace all day, without ceasing, he arrived at sunset in a big city.

Not knowing what to do and desperate with hunger and exhaustion, he was contemplating breaking into a store and running the risk of being caught, when he was suddenly accosted by a stranger, who, expressing sympathy with him in his plight, took him to a restaurant and stood him to a meal. As one might imagine, this led to an exchange of confidences. Fernanado told the stranger about the cruel and unjust treatment he had been subjected to on the plantation, and the stranger, in return, informed Fernando that he belonged to a gang of train wreckers and robbers who happened just then to be in urgent need of recruits.

Finally, after some discussion as to terms of service, obligations and risks, Fernanado was prevailed upon to join the gang. He had his own reasons for doing so. Needless to say, perhaps, revenge was his one absorbing passion. In order to satisfy it he worked night and day, and so successful was he that he was soon able, with the money he had acquired, to establish a system of espionage on his late employer's plantation, by which all the movements of the family were periodically reported to him.

And at last he reaped his reward. The news came through that Mr and Mrs Garcia Williams, their son and his wife and children, accompanied by Johnson, were about to depart by boat from Matamoras to New Orleans, whence they were going by rail to New York City. Fernando had a naturally quick brain, and never did it work more rapidly than now.

The family sailed as was announced from Matamoras, and, in due course, reached New orleans.

On landing there, they found a couple of four-wheelers standing on the quay, and commandeering them at once they got in, telling the drivers to make direct for the best hotel in the town. The drivers of the vehicles, however, being members of Fernanado's gang, instead of taking them to the leading hotel, drove them to a lonely spot, some little distance outside the confines of the town. The rest was singularly easy. Fernando and his colleagues pounced out upon the vehicles, the drivers of which, instead of urging on their horses, immediately pulled up. The passengers, shrieking and protesting, were then, none too delicately, dragged out and made to enter a sinister looking house on the wayside, a house which Fernando had chosen and carefully prepared for their reception. In the centre of the room into which they were roughly hustled was an enormous oak chest, and into this chest the victims, with one exception were thrust alive. The one exception was Johnson, who, being considerably over six feet in height, could not be got in whole, and so, luckily for him, had to be decaptitated.

Then after the contents had been plentifully sprinkled with lime, the chest was shut, locked and corded, after which it was taken back to New Orleans by cab, placed on board a tramp steamer, and finally dropped into the sea—somewhere about latitude 40°N and logitude 73° W.

But that is not all. The train that left New Orleans later on that evening was wrecked and set on fire by other members of Fernando's gang. Hence, of course, it was not unnaturally suppposed that Garcia Williams and his family, who, it was known, intended to travel by this train, were included among the unfortunate passengers whose hopelessly charred and mulitated remains could not possibly be identified; and, consequently, no one ever thought of associating the Garcia Williams family with the reamins subsequently found in the oak chest near Hell's Gate. I repeat this theory is merely a theory; but I might add that it is not altogether groundless, since it is founded on co-incidental happenings, namely, train wrecking and the gross ill-treatment of slaves.

The fact that the remains were sprinkled with lime—a sometimes powerful preservative—easily accounts for the fact that the doctor who examined them said they had only been in the water about seventy hours.

COLIN WILSON

Who was Harry Whitecliffe?

According to a book published in France in 1978, one of England's most extraordinary mass murderers committed suicide in a Berlin gaol in the middle of the jazz era. His name was Harry Whitecliffe, and he murdered at least forty women. Then why is his name not more widely known—at least to student of crime? Because when he was arrested he was masquerading under the name Lovach Blume, and his suicide concealed his true identity from the authorities.

The full story can be found in a volume called *Nouvelles Histoires Magiques – New Tales of Magic –* by Louis Pauwels and Guy Breton, published by Editions J'ai Lu. In spite of the title—which sounds like fiction—it is in fact a series of studies in the paranormal and bizarre; there are chapters on Nostradamus, Rasputin and Eusapia Palladino, and accounts of such well-known mysteries as the devil's footprints in Devon.

According to the chapter 'The Two Faces of Harry Whitecliffe', there appeared in London in the early twenties a collection of essays so promising that it sold out in a few days; it consisted of a series of marvellous pastiches of Oscar Wilde. But its author, Harry Whitecliffe, apparently preferred to shun publicity; he remained obstinately hidden. Would-be interviewers returned empty-handed. Then, just as people were beginning to suggest that Whitecliffe was a pseudonym for some well-known writer—Bernard Shaw, perhaps, or the young T.S. Eliot—Whitecliffe finally consented to appear. He was a handsome young man of twenty-three, likeable, eccentric and fond of sport. He was also generous; he was said to have ended one convivial evening by casually giving a pretty female beggar five hundred pounds. He professed to adore flowers, but only provided their stems were not more than twenty centimetres long. He was the kind of person the English love, and was soon a celebrity.

Meanwhile he continued to write: essays, poetry and plays. One of his comedies, *Similia*, had four hundred consecutive performances in London before touring England. It made him a fortune, which he quickly scattered among his friends. By the beginning of 1923 he was one of the 'kings of London society'.

Then, in September of that year, he vanished. He sold all his possessions, and gave his publisher carte blanche to handle his work. But before the end of the year he reappeared in Dresden. The theatre there presented *Similia* with enormous success, the author himself translating it from English into German. It went on to appear in many theatres along the Rhine. He founded a press for publishing modern poetry, and works on modern painting—Dorian Verlag—whose editions are now worth a fortune.

But he was still something of a man of mystery. Every morning he galloped along the banks of the river Elbe until nine o'clock; at ten he went to his office, eating lunch there. At six in the evening, he went to art exhibitions or literary salons, and met friends. At nine, he returned home and no one knew what he did for the rest of the evening. And no one liked to ask him.

One reason for this regular life was that he was in love—the girl was called Wally von Hammerstein, the daughter of aristocratic parents, who were favourably impressed with the young writer. Their engagement was to be announced on 4 October 1924.

But on the previous day Whitecliffe disappeared again. He failed to arrive at his office, and vanished from his flat. The frantic Wally searched Dresden, without success. The police were alerted—discreetly—and pursued diligent inquiries. Their theory was that he had committed suicide. Wally believed he had either met with an accident or been the victim of a crime—he often carried large sums of money. As the weeks dragged by her desperation turned to misery; she talked about entering a convent.

Then she received a letter. It had been found in the cell of a condemned man who had committed suicide in Berlin—he had succeeded in opening his veins with the buckle of his belt. The inscription on the envelope said: 'I beg you, monsieur le procureur of the Reich, to forward this letter to its destination without opening it.' It was signed: Lovach Blume.

Blume was apparently one of the most horrible of murderers, worse than Jack the Ripper or Peter Kürsten, the Düsseldorf sadist. He had admitted to the court that tried him: 'Every ten days I have to kill. I am driven by an irresistable urge, so that until I have killed, I suffer atrociously. But as I disembowel my victims I feel an indescribable pleasure.' Asked about his past, he declared: 'I am a corpse. Why bother about the past of a corpse?'

Blume's victims were prositilutes and homeless girls picked up on the Berlin streets. He would take them to a hotel, and kill them as soon as they were undressed. Then, with a knife like a Malaysian 'kriss', with an ivory handle, he would perform horrible mituliations, so awful that even doctors found the sight unbearable. These murders continued over a period of six months, during which the slum quarters of Berlin lived in fear.

Blume was finally arrested by accident, in September 1924. The police thought he was engaged in drug trafficking, and knocked on the door of a hotel room minutes after Blume had entered with a prostitute. Blume had just committed his thirty-first murder in Berlin; he was standing naked by the window, and the woman's body lay at his feet.

He made no resistance, and admitted freely to his crimes—he could only recall twenty-seven. He declared that he had no fear of death—particularly the way executions were performed in Germany (by decapitation), which he greatly preferred to the English custom of hanging.

This was the man who had committed suicide in his prison cell, and who addressed a long letter to his fiancée, Wally von Hammerstein. He told her that he was certain the devil existed, because he had met him. He was, he explained, a kind of Jekyll and Hyde, an intelligent, talented man who suddenly became cruel and bloodthirsty. He had left London after committing nine murders, when he suspected that Scotland Yard was on his trail.

His love for Wally was genuine, he told her, and had caused him to 'die a little'. He had hoped once that she might be able to save him from his demons, but it had proved a vain hope.

Wally fainted as she read the letter. And in 1925 she entered a nunnery and took the name Marie de Douleurs. There she prays for the salvation of a tortured soul . . .

This is the story, as told by Louis Pauwels—a writer who became famous for his collaboration with Jacques Bergier on a book called *The Morning of the Magicians*. Critics pointed out that the book was full of factual errors, and a number of these can also be found in his article on Whitecliffe. For example, if the date of Blume's arrest is correct—25 September 1924—then it took place before Whitecliffe vanished from Dresden, on 3 October 1924 . . . But this, presumably, is a slip of the pen.

But who was Harry Whitecliffe? According to Pauwels, he told the Berlin court that his father was German, his mother Danish, and that he was brought up in Australia by an uncle who was a butcher. His uncle lived in Sydney. But in a 'conversation' between Pauwels and his fellow-author at the end of one chapter, Pauwels states that Whitecliffe was the son of a great English family. But apart from the three magistrates who opened the suicide letter—ignoring Blume's last wishes—only Wally and her parents knew Whitecliffe's true identity. The judges are dead, so are Wally's parents. Wally is a 75-year-old nun who until now has never told anyone of this drama of her youth. We are left to assume that she has now told the story to Pauwels.

This extraordinary tale aroused the curiosity of a well-known French authoress, Francoise d'Eaubonne, who felt that Whitecliffe deserved a book to himself. But her letters to the two authors—Pauwels and Breton—went unanswered. She therefore contacted the British Society of Theatre Research, and so entered into a correspondence with the theatre historian John Kennedy Melling. Melling had never heard of Whitecliffe, or of a play called *Similia*. He decided to begin his researches by contacting Scotland Yard, to ask whether they have any record of an unknown sex killer of the early 1920s. Their reply was negative; there was no series of Ripper-type murders of prostitutes in the

early 1920s. He next applied to J.H.H. Gaute, the possessor
of the largest crime library in the British Isles; Gaute could also
find no trace of such a series of sex crimes in the 1920s.
Theratrical reference books contained no mention of Harry
Whitecliffe, or of his successful comedy *Similia*. It began to
look—as incredible as it sounds—as if Pauwels had simply
invented the whole story.

Thelma Holland, Oscar Wilde's daughter-in-law, could find
no trace of a volume of parodies of Wilde among the
comprehensive collection of her late husband, Vyvyan Holland.
But she had a suggestion to make—to address inquiries to the
Mitchell Library in Sydney. As an Australian, she felt it was
probably Melling's best chance of tracking down Harry
Whitecliffe.

Incredibly, this long shot brought positive results: not about
Harry Whitecliffe, but about a German murderer called
Blume—not Lovach, but Wilhelm Blume. The *Argus* newspaper
for 8 August 1922 contained a story headed 'Cultured Murderer',
and sub-titles: 'Literary Man's Series of Crimes'. It was datelined
Berlin, 7 August.

> Wilhelm Blume, a man of wide culture and considerable literary gifts,
> whose translations of English plays have been produced in Dresden with
> great success, has confessed to a series of cold-blooded murders, one of which
> was perpetrated at the Hotel Adlon, the best known Berlin hotel.

The most significant item in the newspaper report is that
Blume had founded a publishing house called Dorian Press
(Verlag) in Dresden. This is obviously the same Blume who—
according to Pauwels—committed suicide in Berlin.

But Wilhelm Blume was not a sex killer. His victims had been
postmen, and the motive had been robbery. In Germany postal
orders were paid to consignees in their own homes, so postmen
often carried fairly large sums of money. Blume had sent himself
postal orders, then killed the postmen and robbed them—the
exact number is not stated in the *Argus* article. The first time
he did this he was interrupted by his landlady while he was
strangling the postman with a noose; and he cut her throat. Then
he moved on to Dresden, where in due course he attempted to

rob another postman. Armed with two revolvers, he waited for
the postman in the porch of a house. But the tenant of the house
arrived so promptly that he had to flee, shooting one of the
policemen. Then his revolvers both misfired, and he was caught.
Apparently he attempted to commit suicide in prison, but failed.
He confessed—as the *Argus* states—to several murders, and was
presumably executed later in 1922 (although the *Argus* carries
no further record).

It seems plain, then, that the question 'Who was Harry
Whitecliffe?' should be reworded 'Who was Wilhelm Blume?'
For Blume and Whitecliffe were obviously the same person.

From the information we possess, we can make a tentative
reconstruction of the story of Blume-Whitecliffe. He sounds like
a typical example of a certain type of killer who is also a
confidence man—other examples are Landru, Petiot, the 'acid
bath murderer' Haigh, and the sex killer Neville Heath. It is
an essential part of such a man's personality tht he is a fantasist,
and that he likes to pose as a success, and to talk casually about
past triumphs. (Neville Heath called himself 'Group Captain
Rupert Brooke'.) They usually start off as petty swindlers, then
gradually become more ambitious, and graduate to murder. This
is what Blume seems to have done. In the chaos of postwar Berlin
he made a quick fortune by murdering and robbing postmen.
Perhaps his last coup made him a fortune beyond his
expectations, or perhaps the Berlin postal authorities were now
on the alert for the killer. Blume decided it was time to make
an attempt to live a respectable life, and to put his literary
fantasies into operation. He moved to Dresden, called himself
Harry Whitecliffe and set up Dorian Verlag. He became a
successful translator of English plays, and may have helped to
finance their production in Dresden and in theatres along the
Rhine. Since he was posing as an upper-class Englishmen, and
must have occasionally run into other Englishmen in Dresden,
we may assume that his English was perfect, and that his story
of being brought up in Australia was probably true. Since he
also spoke perfect German, it is also a fair assumption that he
was, as he told the court, the son of a German father and a Danish
mother.

He fell in love with an upper-class girl, and told her a romantic story that is typical of the inveterate daydreamer: that he was the son of a 'great English family', that he had become an overnight literary success in London as a result of his pastiches of Oscar Wilde, but had at first preferred to shun the limelight (this is the true Walter Mitty touch) until increasing success made this impossible. His wealth is the result of a successful play, *Similia*. (The similarity of the title to *Salome* is obvious, and we may infer that Blume was an ardent admirer of Wilde.) But in order to avoid too much publicity—after all, victims of previous swindles might expose him—he lives the quiet, regular life of a crook in hiding.

And just as all seems to be going so well—just as success, respectability, a happy marriage, seem so close—he once again runs out of money. There is only one solution: a brief return to a life of crime. One or two robberies of postmen can replenish his bank account and secure his future . . . But this time it goes disastrously wrong. Harry Whitecliffe is exposed as the swindler and murderer Wilhelm Blume. He makes no attempt to deny it, and confesses to his previous murders; his world has now collapsed in ruins. He is sent back to Berlin, where the murders were committed, and he attempts suicide in his cell. Soon after, he dies by the guillotine. And in Dresden the true story of Wilhelm Blume is soon embroidered into a horrifying tale of a Jekyll-and-Hyde mass murderer, whose early career in London is confused with Jack the Ripper . . .

Do any records of Wilhelm Blume still exist? It seems doubtful—the fire-bombing of Dresden destroyed most of the civic records, and the people who knew him more than sixty years ago must now all be dead. Yet Pauwels has obviously come across some garbled and wildly inaccurate account of Blume's career as Harry Whitecliffe. It would be interesting to know where he obtained his information; but neither Francoise d'Eaubonne nor John Kennedy Melling have been successful in persuading him to answer letters.

LEONARD GRIBBLE

The Shark Arm Case

In mid-April 1935 a couple of Sydney fishermen secured a bite that was larger than anything they had hoped to catch. Suddenly a very large fish was tangled in their lines.

'Hell,' one of them exclaimed, 'this feller must be over ten feet long!'

He was right. Their catch was all of fourteen feet from nose to tail. When landed it lay gasping and shuddering in the sunlight of an Australian autumn day. They had caught a tiger shark.

Within hours of their landing this catch the shark had been removed to the Sydney suburb of Coogee. By the 25th of the month the shark was attracting a crowd that daily filled the aquarium there. Visitors pressed forward to watch from a few inches the antics of the deadly maneater, who seemed oblivious to the interest being taken in it, and put on only a very dull show for the spectators. It flopped around in its tank, seeming to lack life and spirit.

As well it might. The shark had indigestion. It had swallowed something it couldn't stomach and later digest. But on the 25th it appeared to go into a violent piscatorial tantrum. April 25th is a national holiday in both Australia and New Zealand, Anzac Day, commemorating the Australian and New Zealand Forces who wrote a heroic chapter in the grim history of the First World War. On such a day Sydney was *en fête*. The Coogee aquarium was packed with sightseers, for whom the big attraction was the shark in its glass-sided tank. For most of the day the shark had given its customary apathetic display, but just before five o'clock it suddenly went into a series of aquabatic convolutions that held its audience enthralled. Some thought the big fish had gone mad as it churned the water to creamy foam.

With equal suddenness the thrashing motions ceased and before the amazed eyes of the onlookers the shark was violently sick. From its gaping mouth with its hideous paling of teeth was ejected a dark object about two feet in length. Washed to the surface through the bubbly pale froth was a human arm.

That arm must have remained in the shark's stomach, refusing to be digested, for more than a week since it had been caught and beached.

The Anzac Day performance by the shark in the Coogee aquarium was front-page news throughout Australia next morning. The newspapers explained how the police had arrived at the aquarium within half an hour of the amazing happening in the shark's tank. Aquarium assistants had separated the big fish from its vomit, and the obnoxious mess had been examined for further trace of a human diet, but none was found. The arm was the only human relic the shark had rejected. However, there was a possibility that other human pieces remained in the captive shark's stomach. So the doomed fish was killed and opened and a fresh exploration began among its unsavoury entrails. The smelly operation was time wasted. The sole evidence that a human being had vanished in the sea off Sydney was that disgorged arm with a length of sodden rope hanging from the wrist around which one end had been firmly bound.

The arm was in a remarkable state of preservation and a number of Australian fishery experts were asked to report on it. They did so with frank astonishment, for they were of the opinion that, in normal circumstances, the shark's gastric functions should have digested that massive snack within thirty-six hours at the most. Obviously the circumstances had not been normal, and they considered this was due to the shark's capture and captivity in the aquarium's large tank. The shark's digestive processes had been seriously interfered with and it had suffered acute growing indigestion, which explained its lethargic swimming display for the paying public.

While the experts were making up their minds the police were endeavouring to trace the arm's owner. They had one visual clue to help them. On the forearm was a distinctive tattoo picture of two boxers squaring up to each other.

The Sydney Criminal Investigation Branch soon discovered that surprisingly many Australians had been reported missing,

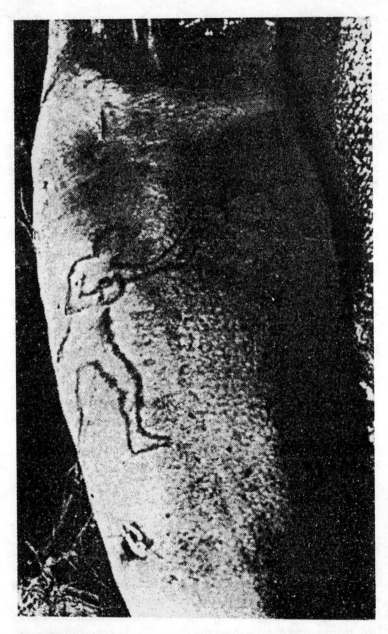

The tatooed arm

each with a boxing tattoo on his forearm. Scientists in the Sydney police laboratory peeled skin from the fingers at the end of the arm. This had to be done in a way that, owing to the waterlogged condition of the flesh, meant paring away minute fragments, which then had to be put together in a kind of jigsaw pattern to reveal the original arrangment of loops and whorls. When this work was completed, the result was checked with the fingerprint files of the C.I.B., where a regulation copy of those re-formed fingerprints was found. The victim was a man with a record. His name was James Smith. It was also on record that his wife had reported her husband missing.

At this stage some of the initial horror experienced by the Australian public when the arm was vomited by the shark was replaced by a keen interest to know what had happened to Smith. Had he been drowned in an accident at sea or did the police have a murder mystery to solve?

First they had to be sure in which direction they were moving and they had Mrs Smith formally identify her husband's arm. Smith had been a big man of forty-five. He had worked on construction jobs and at one time had been an engineer. He had also made money in lean times by working as a billiards marker, and his record showed that he had also worked as a navvy in a road gang.

His widow told the police that he left on a fishing trip on April 8th.

'Alone?' she was asked.

'No,' she told the police. 'He was going with another man, but he didn't mention the man's name.'

'Can you suggest who this man was?'

She shook her head, and as she did so she looked scared and her mouth tightened at the corners.

The police began a search of the beaches from which James Smith could have set out with a companion on a fishing trip. They found nothing belonging to the dead man and no evidence of his having encountered violence. The search was extended when they secured the help of divers from the Royal Australian Navy, who went down in the waters where the captured shark had swum. They came up with nothing. Pilots of the Royal

Australian Air Force flew low over the beaches and shallow waters on observation patrols. They too found nothing of help to the police.

Apparently the remains of James Smith, apart from the arm recovered from the tiger shark's tank, had vanished beyond recovery. Someone came up with the belated suggestion that Smith might have committed suicide by tying the rope attached to his wrist to a heavy weight and jumping overboard. But suicide didn't fit the picture the police had of James Smith from his record.

However, there was help from an unexpected quarter for the puzzled police. There were available in Sydney at that time no less than three experts who could provide valuable opinions as to how the missing Smith's arm came to be severed from his body.

One of these was Dr Palmer, a medico-legal expert who had worked previously with the police. Another was Dr Coppleston, a man who had made a close study for years of shark bites. The third expert was a Britisher, who as Sir Sydney Smith was later to become Emeritus Professor of Forensic Medicine in the University of Edinburgh, and a valued consultant with the police in many famous murder cases, including those involving Sidney Fox the Margate matricide and Dr Buck Ruxton the Lancaster wife murderer.

Sir Sydney later recorded the part he played in the Shark Arm case, as it became known. He said:

'The identification of the arm as Smith's was not disputed, but the question was raised whether it might have been bitten off by a shark while he was still alive. This, of course, would have been in favour of accidental death or suicide. Although I had nothing officially to do with the case, I was asked to examine the arm and express an opinion on this point. I found that the limb had been severed at the shoulder joint by a clean-cut incision, and that after the head of the bone had been got out of its socket the rest of the soft tissues had been hacked away. In my opinion, it was certain that it had been cut, and not bitten off by a shark. The condition of the blood and tissues further suggested that the amputation had taken place some hours after death.'

The inference was that Smith had been killed and his carved-up body later dropped in the sea, to be disposed of by the sharks of the coast of New South Wales. Sir Sydney added:

'This opinion fortified that already expressed by Dr Palmer and Dr Coppleston. I was told that Dr Coppleston was an expert on shark bites, of which he had seen a great number.'

The police concluded that Smith had quarrelled with his unknown companion. The quarrel had resulted in violence and Smith died as a result. When the detectives investigating the case learned indirectly that Smith had left home to travel to a seaside cottage, where he expected to join his companion, they went to the cottage and found it deserted. Local inquiries informed them that a tin trunk and a mattress were missing from a room in the cottage.

It was arguable that Smith might have met his death inside the cottage, and that a killer with a corpse on his hands would look to the most ready means of disposing of it. A mattress offered a convenient chopping board for dismemberment as the soft material would soak up the blood, thus aiding the butcher.

The police came upon a boat that was said to be the property of the cottage's owner. More inquiries informed them that three mats usually kept in this boat were missing, as was a coil of rope that seemed to match in size and texture the piece of similar rope found tied to the wrist of the tattooed arm. At this stage it was not difficult for the police to consider most of the cut-up body rammed tightly into the missing trunk, with the notorious arm left over. Unable to conceal it, the killer might have closed the trunk and locked it, then lashed the arm to one of the trunk's handles. The trunk and the attached arm could have been carried to the boat after dark, together with the blood-soaked mattress. The boat could have been taken out to sea and the trunk and mattress thrown overboard with the three mats that had been stained during the trip to the shore. Later the killer could have returned with the boat, believing that James Smith had vanished with a dark secret.

Then the unexpected had intervened. Due to the action of the waves and sea currents the tattooed arm tied to the trunk had been washed loose and attracted the attention of a prowling tiger shark, who had followed the tin trunk down through the water and snapped at the arm, severing the rope extending from the wrist. Jonah-like, Smith's vividly adorned arm had arrived in the belly of a big fish. Completing the Biblical parallel, the big fish had later disgorged its indigestible piece of humanity.

With the remainder of James Smith crammed into the locked tin trunk, which presumably lay at the bottom of the sea, it was understandable that the Navy divers and Air Force pilots had found nothing to report. Yet coincidence played a strange part in the Shark Arm mystery.

The only part of James Smith's anatomy to carry any distinguishing mark was that tattooed arm. Off the Australian coasts there are thousands of foraging sharks. Yet the one caught by the two fishermen was the tiger shark that couldn't digest the arm of a trunk crime victim. Moreover, that shark was the only one that, put into an aquarium, was sick and so allowed the arm to be resurrected in the most incredible and startling manner.

The Sydney police had been doing more than build theories after investigating the seaside cottage. They checked on Smith's very recent past and learned that some of his jobs had not been entirely legal. One at least had been very illegal. This was his employment as a crew member of a fast launch named *Pathfinder*. The craft was known to have been dodging Sydney Harbour revenue patrols for some time and had the reputation of a smuggler's vessel. She was believed to be running drugs, either opium or heroin, picked up from certain liners standing offshore. Such illicit cargoes were run to secret landing-places along the coast.

The phantom-like *Pathfinder* had made rings in the night round the Customs craft sent to intercept her until the first week of April, when the smuggler had unaccountably sunk. It could have been the victim of a rival smuggling gang, which was likely, or it could have gone down after an accident, which was unlikley.

But the foundering had left James Smith without a job, a man who knew a great deal about a number of hard-grained characters who preferred their identities to remain a secret and unassociated with their illegal activities.

It was an accepted fact of international Customs life that in the 1930s Sydney was a clearing house for regular cargoes of opium picked up in Chinese ports and intended for ports of the western seaboard of the United States. All Chinese craft were thoroughly searched when they docked in such a port as San Francisco, but a passenger on a ship sailing from an Australian port could most likely pass through the American Customs with an opium-filled suitcase worth many thousands of pounds. So fast launches like the *Pathfinder* were used at night to collect the opium or other drugs from ships arrived from China, and later to deliver it to someone on an Australian ship or cruise liner that had stopped at an Australian port.

Not surprisingly, along the Sydney waterfront gang rivalry among the smuggling crews sparked into vicious warfare. Launches were sunk by rival crews, cargoes of treated opium hijacked, men murdered and fed to the sharks.

Everything pointed, in the eyes of the Sydney police, to James Smith being the latest victim in this smugglers' war. They set out to find the owner of the sunken *Pathfinder*. It was a long and involved process. But where the Customs people had failed they succeeded. The man's name was Reginald Holmes and his ostensible business was boat-building. He lived at a place called McMahon's Point. When the police found him he readily agreed that James Smith had worked for him.

'I hired him to look after *Pathfinder*,' he told them. 'He did a good job and I was satisfied.'

'He left when *Pathfinder* was sunk?' a detective asked.

'That's correct,' Holmes agreed. 'I had no other suitable work for him. But I was sorry to lose him.'

'Why?'

'Well, for one thing, I think he was being blackmailed.'

That was a bright new angle. Holmes claimed he did not know the reason for blackmailing Smith, though he suspected it had something to do with his lost launch. But he volunteered the opinion that the man who might have been putting pressure on Smith was Patrick Brady, who owned other launches that were familiar along the coast, and could have been the man Smith was going to join on a bogus fishing trip at the deserted cottage.

When the inquiring detectives spoke to Mrs Inie Holmes she began crying and admitted that her husband had confided to her that he thought Brady had killed Smith and disposed of the body.

To prevent Brady avoiding arrest on a more serious charge he was promptly arrested on a minor charge of forging a licence certificate he held. When the detectives returned to the deserted seaside cottage at Cronulla, now known to be owned by Brady, they had come full circle in their inquiry.

Three days later a police launch observed a speedboat being driven by a man whose face was a mask of blood. The launch gave chase, whereupon the speedboat turned and tried to ram it. A signal was sent to other police craft. One of the most notorious sea chases in Sydney Harbour continued until the growing number of pursuers finally caused the speedboat's driver to make a false move and he was captured.

The man whose face was covered with blood pouring from a bullet wound above his eyes was Reginald Holmes, who had pointed the finger at Brady. When he talked again to the police he sounded like a deranged man. He claimed that as he left his home a stranger appeared and fired at him, hitting him in the forehead. He had started running and did not stop until he reched the shore and his speedboat. He had taken off to avoid being murdered. When the first police launch started after him he thought it was a boat with the gunman aboard. He had tried to lose it, and when he found he couldn't he had attempted to ram it. By this time he was faint and light-headed, and when he again tried to run he barely knew what he was doing.

The police accepted this story with marked scepticism, but behaved almost as strangely as Holmes. They passed him a towel, told him to wipe his face, and go home. If someone really was gunning for Holmes the target was being set up again.

The date set for the inquest on James Smith was June 13th. At one in the morning a patrolling constable at Dawes Point observed a car parked without lights under the arch leading to Sydney's famous bridge. He found a man slumped over the wheel. When he switched on his torch he saw blood on the man's clothing and in his lap. A police surgeon announced the dead man had been shot twice, once in the chest, once in the groin. The shooting had been a close range, probably no more than three feet. The real shock came when the victim was identified.

The dead man in the car was Reginald Holmes, who had not escaped the second attempt on his life.

The medical report said that Holmes had been dead about three hours when found. On the pavement beside the parked car was found a cartridge case. This suggested that Holmes had driven a passenger to that dark place under the Sydney Bridge arch, who when set down turned and fired twice through the car's window.

Patrick Brady, held in custody, had a perfect alibi.

A few hours later the inquest on Smith opened and dragged on for a remarkably unproductive twelve days, now that Holmes was unable to appear, until the coroner received instructions to terminate the hearing from the Australian Supreme court who had come to the belated conclusion that the inquiry could not be legally conducted since a single limb was not a complete body. There have been a number of famous murder cases where this concept of the law did not apply, but on June 25th, 1935, Mr Justice Halse Rogers ruled that it did.

The police reacted by charging Brady with Smith's murder, for they believed they knew very well what had happened to the latter.

Brady was brought to trial three months after the abortive inquest had been summarily closed. It had not been reopened during those three months. The police were in a dilemma. If they had arrested Holmes instead of freeing him after picking him up from the speedboat he would have been alive to appear as a Crown witness. But Holmes had been murdered, and he too had not had an inquest held on the cause of his death. That was a formality the police were keeping until after Brady's trial. But in the circumstances there was at best only a fifty-fifty chance of convincing a jury who had already been presented with a ready-made reasonable doubt by the Supreme Court.

The trouble was the police were losing face and could not continue to do so.

So the trial opened, but to everyone in Australia it was plain that the prosecution was fighting a losing battle. The police had found no new evidence to offer to bolster their case against the prisoner, and it was the already well-aired testimony of the thirty-nine witnesses at the abortive inquest that made up most of the case against the accused when Patrick Brady stood for trial before Justice Sir Frederick R. Jordon.

As for the prisoner, to the spectators he did not appear unduly alarmed about the outcome as he viewed the proceedings from the dubious oasis of the dock. He had aggressive counsel who demonstrated that they were quite prepared to tear wider any holes they discovered in the prosecution's case.

It was the evidence of Mrs Inie Holmes that proved a real challenge to the defence counsel. For she had gone on record at Smith's inquest as claiming that her husband had told her, 'Brady did it. He put the body in a trunk, took it out in his boat, and dumped it overboard.'

But with Holmes dead the words he was alleged to have said were at best hearsay, and the defence proved that it was very able to deal with hearsay. The only other move by the prosecution that made the defence consider its tactics was the presentation of testimony by several persons who claimed, in not very certain tones, they had observed Smith in Brady's company on the day it was believed he had disappeared.

The prisoner did not look particularly bothered by this evidence offered by the prosecution, but his counsel deemed it expedient to put him in the witness box so that he could tell his own story. This was risking the effect of possible tough cross-examination, but the defence gambled on the prosecution having at that stage a few shots left in its locker. Brady was put up for questioning and to impress the united gaze of the jury.

In reply to his counsel he readily admitted that James Smith had visited him at his seaside cottage at Cronulla on April 8th. Then the confident-looking prisoner sprang a bombshell in court. Led carefully by his counsel, he declared that the visit by Smith had not lasted long. Smith had left the cottage that evening.

He paused as though for effect, knowing that he had the full attention of everyone present, and leaning forward like a man who is impressed by his own words he added, 'But he didn't leave alone.'

There was the sound of a collective gasp of surprise. Brady then cleared his throat and announced that James Smith had left his cottage in the company of another owner of a fleet of launches.

'That man was Albert Stannard,' he declared firmly.

The prosecution was caught flat-footed. It needed only one glance at the faces of the jury after that statement from the witness box to know that Patrick Brady would walk from that court a cleared man.

And so it proved.

The prosecution had nothing to set against this claim, and it could not be disproved. But possibly what weighed most with the jury was the fact that Brady had been in custody at the time of both attacks on Holmes, who had been Smith's employer, and it was not unreasonable to suppose that master and man had earned the enmity of the same persons.

After the jury had found him not guilty Brady was released, leaving the police still with a double murder to solve. All the trial had achieved was to underline the fact that Smith and Holmes had most likely been victims of the same rival interests. For the police it meant going back even beyond square one. They had no chance of surprising a guilty peron into an admission. Each new person interviewed in the case had all the right answers to the questions asked. The only chance of getting at a well-covered truth seemed to be to induce someone to talk.

That meant offering money.

Reward notices were posted. The total cash offered was a thousand pounds. No one stepped forward to claim any of the reward money. Information, it seemed, was not for sale. In the meantime hundreds of men were switched to continuing inquiries in the case. Superintendent Prior, a very frustrated police official, told them, 'I want a clue. Any clue. Something that will take us to the solution of this case. No clue will be considered too small or too unlikely.'

One of the fresh pesons thoroughly investigated was the Albert Stannard named by Brady in court. Another was a man who had been seen frequently in Stannard's company. This second person was a labourer, a big, powerfully built man well known in the area around the Sydney docks. His name was John Patrick Strong, and it fitted him. He was said by some to be employed by Stannard as a bodyguard.

The police spent three weeks building a case against this pair, who were placed under a twenty-four-hour surveillance. At the end of those three weeks, with the year 1935 reaching its closing month, Superintendent Prior decided they had a case that could be brought to court. Stannard and Strong were arrested and charged with the murder of Reginald Holmes.

Neither was really taken by surprise, for both had lived too long with the police as close companions. The trial opened on a warm December day and Sydney's Central Criminal Court was crowded.

However, if the throng in shirt-sleeves and summer blouses expected drama and suspenseful excitement from a case that had been stamped originally with a hallmark of horror and now had an aura of underworld secrecy about Sydney's wharfside gangland and its drug-smuggling activities, they stifled in the heat only to leave the courtroom feeling an acute sense of anticlimax. The prisoners produced alibis which the police could not break. Some new faces in the array of police witnesses wore worried frowns when questioned, but most of the so-called new evidence was threadbare and inconclusive. The Crown, in fact, seemed to have a weak case, and this was manifest when the jury failed to agree and the judge dismissed them and ordered a new trial.

By this time the whole affair had developed into a dreary spectacle of blindfolded Justice having lost her scales. She still seemed to be groping for them when the second trial opened. It became a repetition of the first, and achieved only one firm result—this time the jury made up their minds unanimously.

They acquitted the prisoners.

For the third time in a row the Shark Arm case had resulted in the local police demonstrating an incompetenece that seemed alarming to a great many Australians. For when Stannard and Strong were cleared of murder by the second jury the incredible case was virtually over. The police made no effort to start it all over again. They had shot their bolt and it had landed nowhere near the intended target. They could be forgiven for feeling the case would be better forgotten than remembered.

Yet for more than thrity-five years the Sydney Shark Arm case has been one that offered a grim challenge to any who studied it. In a number of respects it is unique in its curious sequence of events and the amount of coincidence displayed. While commenting on his personal reactions at the time the case was front-page news Sir Sydney Smith felt impelled to say, 'It is a trite saying but true that fact is stranger than fiction.'

It can also be more horrifying both demonstrably and by implication, for in the Shark Arm case the conspiracy of silence was more effective than the conspiracy of violence, which had resulted in two murders—and perhaps others not uncovered— and the conspiracy of silence was never broken because there were those living who had too much to lose and murder was a cheap price to pay to retain a menaced security.

Rough usage in the courts had not completely obliterated that dubious hallmark of horror.

C. J. S. THOMPSON

The Mystery of the Poisoned Partridges

How did a brace of partridges which had been cooked and served for dinner become impregnated with strychnine was a problem that was presented to a Coroner's jury during the inquiry into a remarkable poisoning case at Blackdown Camp near Aldershot?

In June, 1931, Lieutenant Chevis, a young artillery officer, was occupying a bungalow at the camp where he was engaged on his military duties.

He was very popular in his regiment and was happily married; his wife having a flat in London, she often joined him with their two children at the bungalow at Blackdown.

On Saturday, June 21th, 1931, a brace of partridges was ordered from a poulterer at Aldershot and they were delivered at the bungalow in a van. They were placed by the cook in an open meat-safe kept outside the building, and there they remained until they were required for dinner in the evening.

Late in the afternoon some friends called to see Lieutenant Chevis and his wife, and after having cocktails they remained chatting for some time.

After they had left, Lieutenant and Mrs Chevis sat down to dine early, as they intended to go to the Military Tattoo which was taking place that night.

The dinner was brought in by the batman, who placed the roasted partridges before Mrs Chevis who was seated at the table, and she proceeded to serve them. Lieutenant Chevis took one mouthful and exclaimed: 'It tastes horrible!' and he refused to eat any more. He asked his wife to taste the bird to see if she found anything wrong with it. She just touched it with her tongue and said it tasted 'fusty' and could not get the taste out of her mouth for a long time afterwards.

Lieutenant Chevis then ordered the batman to take the birds away and have them destroyed. Fifteen minutes later he was taken violently ill. He lost the use of his legs and terrible convulsions followed. A doctor was sent for and the lieutenant was at once removed to hospital, where he died in great agony early on the following Sunday morning.

Mrs Chevis was also taken ill shortly after the meal and was seized with severe pains. She was medically treated and eventually recovered.

The Coroner was notified and inquiries were at once set on foot by the police.

A further element of mystery was introduced into the case when it was learnt that a telegram had been received by Sir William Chevis, the father of the deceased man, on the day of his son's funeral. It had been handed in at Dublin and contained the words: 'Hooray. Hooray. Hooray.' On inquiry it was found that the form was signed on the back with the name 'Hartigan' and the address of a well-known Dublin hotel. It further transpired that no one of that name was known at the hotel, nor had any person called 'Hartigan' been staying there.

Another strange fact connected with the telegram was, it had been sent off before any announcement of the tragedy at Blackdown Camp had appeared inthe Press. The matter was taken up by the police of the Irish Free State who, it was stated, had found that a man answering the description of the person who had handed in the telegram in Dublin had purchased strychnine from a local chemist.

The inquest on the body of Lieutenant Chevis was opened on June 23rd, but was adjourned until July 21st for the analyst's report. On August 11th it was resumed before a crowded Court by the Deputy Coroner for West Surrey.

In opening the proceedings he remarked that the evidence would clearly indicate the partridge as the means by which the poison had been conveyed. It was, however, a most unfortunate thing that both the partridges had been destroyed, especially the one served to Lieutenant Chevis, by his orders.

On the day of his funeral a telegram had been received at the house of his father, Sir William Chevis, who lived at Bournemouth, which contained the words: 'Hooray. Hooray. Hooray.' It was not signed, but on the original form being obtained for inspection there was found on the back a signature and address which read: 'J. Hartigan. Hibernia.' Although inquiries had been made by the Dublin police and every possible effort made, no trace could be found of the sender of the telegram, nor could his identity be established.

A photograph of the original telegram was published in the *Daily sketch*, and on August 2nd, a postcard was received addressed to 'The Editor', purporting to have been written in London on August 1st. It read:

> DEAR SIR,
> Why do you publish the picture of the Hooray telegram.
> J. HARTIGAN

This was followed by a further postcard addressed to Sir William Chevis and posted in Belfast on August 4th. It read:

> It is a mystery they will never solve.
> J. HARTIGAN.   Hooray.

'To add to the mystery,' the Coroner continued, 'the contents of the telegram were known to me before the last hearing, but it was deemed inadvisable to reproduce it at the last adjourned hearing. Although we thought this was assured, the telegram was published without consulting me or my officer.

'The great handicap in this case is that the bird was destroyed. Had that not been done the case was a simple one.'

Captain Chevis, brother of the deceased officer, was then called, and said that the 'Hooray' telegram arrived at 5 p.m. on June 24th, the day of his brother's funeral.

He did not know anyone in Dublin likely to send a telegram of the kind or anyone answering to the description which the telegraph clerk gave of the sender. His brother had never been in Ireland in his life.

Mrs Chevis in her evidence said she had given all possible information in connection with the inquiry. There were no telegrams belonging to her husband which might throw any light on the case.

Describing what took place at dinner on the evening of the tragedy, she said that her husband had two glasses of sherry after tasting the partridge, which he got for himself. Bulger, the batman, would have removed the dirty glasses and the cook would have washed them. She did not move them. The partridge she had on her plate tasted 'fusty', but there was no bitter, sharp or offensive taste. Both the partridges were cooked together in a tin and they were basted in the same fat.

She only took one mouthful and it was vaguely unsavoury. She was absolutely sure that her husband told Bulger to burn the partridge. He was very anxious that the dog should not get it. She knew no one of the name of Hartigan and no one in the household knew anyone of that name. Lieutenant Chevis, as far as she knew, had no friends or relatives called Hartigan.

Dr J.H. Ryffel, analyst to the Home Office, was then called and described the results of his examination of the contents of the stomach of the deceased man and of other articles removed from the bungalow. The latter included sink-water from the drains of the bungalow, a basin containing dripping, a vegetable dish containing peas and potatoes, an empty tin, a packet of gravy mixture, some anchovy sauce, a bag of flour and a tin of carbolic. He also examined some material from Mrs Chevis after she had been taken ill. This and similar material from Lieutenant Chevis wre mixed together and gave a yield of strychnine corresponding to a total in the amount received of .3 of a grain. The material from Lieutenant Chevis contained a large amount of strychnine. He also found a small amount of strychnine in the dripping and more in the gravy, which was very bitter. There was no strychnine in the water or other materials.

'I concluded,' continued Dr. Ryffel, 'that the total quantity of strychnine associated with the partridges amounted to at least two grains. This is an extremely rough calculation and would depend on what other materials were employed. The total quantity would depened on the proportion of the bird eaten, which I understand was very small.'

In his view if only a small proportion of the bird had been eaten the quantity in the bird was very considerable.

The minimum fatal dose of strychnine was half a grain.

Dr Ryffel added that he had received three partridges taken from the cold stores of the company who sold the partridges to Lieutenant Chevis, but none of them contained strychnine.

The Coroner asked witness: 'Supposing this bird had picked up strychnine when alive, could it have been absorbed sufficient to show the amount eaten by Lieutenant and Mrs Chevis?'

'I do not think so,' replied Dr Ryffel. 'The only thing would seem to me that if a partridge had taken a large amount of strychnine material in its crop, after it was in cold storage the amount might have diffused into the bird.' He understood, however, that the crop was cleaned at the shop before the birds were sent out and would not be included in the cooking. He did not think the bird could have absorbed the amount of strychnine into its own substance because it would be dead long before. On the other hand, if strychnine was injected into the substance of the bird it would stay there and stay during the cooking. But this is not strychnine taken by the bird in life. It is strychnine inserted into it afterwards.

'Strychnine itself is very insoluble, but it would be slightly soluble in fat, and two birds basted in the same fat would certainly give a proportion of strychnine on the second bird after cooking.'

In answer to further questions, Dr Ryffel said: 'Strychnine has to be absorbed from the intestines and when it is taken, as in this case, with a large amount of fat, the absorbtion is much slower than if taken by itself. The fact that Mrs Chevis's symptoms did not come on till later would point to her having less and to the fact that she did not pass her food on as rapidly as her husband. Strychnine could be fatal within two hours, but in the case of Lieutenant Chevis it was fourteen hours, because he was kept alive by artificial respiration and he ultimately died of failure of respiration.'

A police-inspector of Camberley said he searched the bungalow and found nothing in writing connected with the case. He had searched the Poison Registers of chemists in Frimley, Farnborough, Bagshot and Camberley, but found no evidence of any sales of strychnine.

A brother-officer in the Royal Artillery stated that Lieutenant Chevis was very popular and as far as he knew he had no enemies. He saw Lieutenant and Mrs Chevis on the day of the fatal meal and they both appeared in perfect health and quite happy.

Nicholas Bulger, batman to Lieutenant Chevis, said he did not serve any drinks at dinner that night. Mrs Chevis served the partridges and he handed the vegetables. He came from the south of Ireland, but he did not know anyone of the name of Hartigan. He removed the bird and took it into the kitchen and gave it to the cook. Mrs Chevis told him to destroy it; not to burn it. When he took it to the cook, he said: 'This is to be destroyed,' but she put it on the fire.

Mrs Yeoman, the cook, said that the safe in which the partridges had been kept was outside the bungalow and had no lock. She noticed nothing unusual about the birds. She had no friends in Ireland and did not know anyone of the name of Hartigan.

The manager of the firm who sold the partridges said they came from Manchuria. They had sold Manchurian birds for years and never had any complaints. They were delivered to the bungalow in a covered van which was kept locked.

The Coroner then summed up and said there was no doubt that Lieutenant Chevis died from asphyxia following the poison cased by eating the partridge. There was no evidence to show how the strychnine came to be in the birds. He had sifted all the evidence and could find nothing to lead him to any conclusion as to whether this was a case of accidental death, a foul murder, or whether it was a case of negligent dealing with things served up to eat as amounted to manslaughter.

The proper verdict was asphyxia following strychnine poisoning caused by eating partridge, with insufficient evidence to show how the strychnine came to be in or on the partridge. The jury, after a consultation of five minutes, returned with an open verdict.

What is the solution of the mystery involved in this extraordinary case? Misadventure may be ruled out, as even if the partridges had picked up strychnine in Manchuria, it could not have been absorbed into the flesh of the birds. It is also most unlikely that a poison such as strychnine could have got into the partridges by accident. It must, therefore, be concluded that the strychnine must have been deliberately introduced into the bires by some person with the object of killing both Lieutenant Chevis and his wife.

The Home Office expert in his evidence said he concluded that a considerable quantity of strychnine must have been present in the birds, and as the flesh was so strongly impregnated with the poison it would appear as if a solution had been injected.

Strychnine hydrochloride occurs in small white crystals, the maximum dose being one eighth of a grain. It is only soluble in about forty parts of water, but it dissolves in about eighty parts of alcohol. Its taste is characteristic and extremely bitter. Sprinkled on the back of a bird, even in the form of a powder, it would not be absorbed into the flesh. It is a drug so readily recognisable from the taste that even an enemy would hesitate before using it to murder an unsuspecting person.

An obvious question arises; does a clue lurk in the cruel telegram sent from Dublin to the father of Lieutenant Chevis? How did the sender of that message know of the tragedy before it was published in the Press? There could have only been one object in sending it, and that was to express the sender's delight that the murderer had succeeded in his purpose.

No motive can be assigned for the perpetrationof the crime, but the fact that the brutal telegram was addressed to the victim's father shows that the sender knew the anguish it would cause.

Taking all the circumstances known into consideration, one is led to the conclusion that the murder was the work of a homicidal maniac who had a fancied grievance against the family.

Armed with a hypodermic syringe charged with a solution of strychnine, which could be made from the tablets sold for that purpose, he would watch for his opportunity. The meat-safe was open to anyone outside the bungalow, and it would be but the work of a moment to inject the contents of the syringe into the birds and to slip away without being seen. The strychnine would thus be absorbed into the flesh of the birds and the cooking afterwards would assist it.

That murder was intended there can be no doubt. Whoever the unknown miscreant may have been, he was never traced in spite of all the efforts of the police, and the mystery of the murder of the unfortunate young officer remains a mystery still.

JULIAN SYMONS

The Yarmouth Murder

1. THE BACKGROUND

Herbert John Bennett, who was to be hanged for strangling his
wife on Yarmouth beach, was born in Gravesend in 1880. He
was the son of a cement works foreman and had little schooling,
but it is clear that he was from the first a boy of precocious
intelligence. He had sold newspapers and had worked as a
grocer's assistant when, at the age of sixteen, he met a girl three
years his senior, named Mary Jane Clarke. The girl lived with
her grandmother, and at first their meetings were clandestine—
young Bennett walked from Swanscombe to Northfleet on
Sundays to meet her as she came out of chapel. She had a pretty
tinkling skill on the piano, and when she set up as a music teacher
he was her first pupil.

She became pregnant and, when he was still no more than
seventeen years old, they were married. The ceremony was to
have been performed in Northfleet Church, but this was
forbidden by Bennett's father, who pointed out that his son had
made a false declaration of his age. This did not stop Bennett:
when they were married in Leyton Registry Office he declared
himself to be twenty-one, and one of the witnesses signed the
register in a false name. The child Mary Jane expected was
stillborn.

They lived for a few months with her family, and then set
up on their own. It is important to consider the kind of life they
lived: important because such a consideraton shows that Mary
Jane was from the beginning of their life together an active
accomplice in several extra-legal schemes. They moved from one

228

part of London to another, making a living by selling violins, which they bought for 4s. 6d. each and then advertised as 'Excellent Strad models' which would be sacrificed for a sum that varied between 1 and 2 guineas. Mary Jane called on many people who advertised for secondhand violins and told them that she was a poor clergyman's daughter, or a widow selling a precious relic. She must have played her part well for, as she told one of their many landladies, it was a profitable business, and she felt a bit sorry for the people she fooled. It was presumably with money from the sale of these violins that Bennett, early in 1900, bought a grocer's business at Westgate, and settled there with Mary Jane and the baby girl who had been born rather more than a year before. But they did not settle for long. Eight days after Bennett had taken over the shop, it was destroyed by fire. His insurance claim for £390 was compromised for £208, and he got some £450 more for the damaged stock, his horse and cart and piano, and some other stock which he had bought on credit, and for which he never paid.

The record so far is a not unusual one of swindling on a minor scale, with a suspicion of arson. But now occurred a curious incident, which does not fit the pattern. They left Westgate after collecting the insurance money, sent the baby to stay with Bennett's grandfather at Gravesend, and booked passages for South Africa as Mr and Mrs Hood. The single fare for the two of them cost nearly £50. They stayed four days in Cape Town— and came back to England. What they did in Cape Town was never discovered, and the object of the trip remains unknown. The South African War had begun a few months earlier, and Cape Town was full of Boer sympathizers. Bennett's counsel at this trial, Edward Marshall Hall, propounded the ingenious theory that Bennett had been engaged as a Boer spy. Certain aspects of Bennett's later conduct lend colour to this idea, but it is basically improbable. The Boers got all the information they needed from friends in Britain, and even if they had employed Bennett as an agent, there could have been no possible need for him to visit Cape Town. It seems more likely that the Bennetts thought themselves in line for some profitable piece of rascality in South Africa, and perhaps even carried it out.

In early May the pair were back in London, passing under the names of Hood and Bartlett, as well as Bennett. One of their landladies, Mrs Elliston of Wickham Lane, Plumstead, remembered Mrs Bennett engaging rooms about the 12th May. She went away, and that evening Bennett came. He stayed two nights alone, and then Mary Jane arrived with the child and a parcel. He asked her why she was so late.

'You knew the time I should come,' she said. 'Why did you not come to meet me? What with carrying the baby and the luggage, I could not get here any sooner.'

'Damn you, and the baby too,' Bennett replied.

They appeared to Mrs Ellison to be on bad terms. Bennett talked to his wife unkindly, and once Mary Jane told the landlady that he had smacked her face. Mrs Elliston heard not only that opening altercation, but a good deal more. She heard Bennett tell his wife to go out and look for a house at Bexley Heath. 'I have a berth at Woolwich. From to-night I do not wish to live with you again,' he said. After another quarrel, Mrs Elliston heard Mary Jane say to him: 'Herbert, I will follow you for the sake of the baby, and if you are not careful I can get you fifteen years.'

'I wish you were dead,' Bennett said. 'And if you are not careful you soon will be.'

Mrs Bennett left the Plumstead house about the middle of June. Bennett had gone a day or two earlier. During the month they had been there Mrs Elliston could not remember one kind thing that Bennett had said. Their next landlady, Mrs MacDonald, however, said that they seemed on good terms and generally appeared happy, although she had heard Mrs Bartlett cry once.

Later in July Mary Jane took a house, 1 Glencoe Villas, Bexley Heath, and paid a quarter's rent in advance. Here she used again the name of Bennett, and when the estate agent asked for a reference, produced one signed by a certain 'W.A. Phillips', which had been written by Bennett himself. Bennett, who had worked for three weeks at the Co-operative Society in Woolwich and was now employed at Woolwich Arsenal, visited his wife occasionally, but he lodged with a Mrs Pankhurst in Union Street, Woolwich.

On 1st July Bennett went up to London with a fellow employee at the Arsenal named Stevens and there, through a girl friend of Stevens's, he met an attractive parlourmaid named Alice Meadows. A friendship sprang up immediately between the young parlourmaid and the thin, dark, handsome Bennett. They met on Thursdays and Sundays, and exchanged affectionate letters. Bennett told her that he had been a grocer's assistant, but he lied in relation to almost everything else. Alice Meadows believed that he was a single man, and that he had a cousin named Fred, who lived with his wife and child at Bexley Heath and whom Bennett went to see occasionally. When they had known each other for a month, Bennett suggested that they should go together to Ireland when she had her fortnight's holiday. Alice, who considered herself almost engaged to him, agreed.

At the end of July Bennett was getting thirty shillings a week from his job at Woolwich Arsenal. He was supporting his wife and child at Bexley Heath, paying rent to Mrs Pankhurst, taking out Alice Meadows twice a week, and urging her to come away with him for a week-end to Yarmouth before the Irish holiday. It is pertinent to ask: where did he get the money? This was no problem to Alice Meadows, who believed that her lover had been left a lot of money by his mother and also that he carried on a legitimate and profitable trade in secondhand violins, but it must be a serious question for those who know that the first story was untrue and that the sale of violins had been given up some weeks earlier. This question was never answered at Bennett's trial; its vital importance will be discussed later.

On Saturday, 4th August, Bennett took Alice Meadows to Yarmouth. Her friend Miss Treadwell had given Alice the addresses of some lodging houses in the town, and Bennett wrote to one or two of them. The trip, however, was made in style, and there was no question of staying at a lodging house. They travelled first-class in the train, and he took rooms—separate rooms—at the Crown and Anchor Hotel. They walked about the town a lot, Alice Meadows said, and passed the Rows—the dark, narrow lanes intersecting the main streets of Yarmouth. They were horrible-looking places, Bennett said, and remarked that he would not like anybody belonging to him to stay there. The girl remembered those words later.

They came back on Sunday, and the following Thursday was Bennett's birthday. Alice sent him a telegram. It was not the only telegram he received on this day. One came to his lodgings at Woolwich, and there Mrs Pankhurst opened it. She read: 'Try to come home M very ill.' She took this telegram to the Arsenal, and asked Bennett what was the matter. He told her that his cousin at Bexley was ill, and that evening he went off on his bicycle to see her. The telegram was sent by Mrs Bennett's next-door neighbour at Glencoe Villas. We do not know the nature of Mary Jane's illness, but when Bennett returned to Woolwich the next morning (without his bicycle, but now carrying a lady's umbrella) he told Mrs Pankhurst that his cousin was very ill with influenza, and that she was not expected to live.

At the end of the month, on 28th August, Bennett and Alice took their trip to Ireland. Before they left he gave her an engagement ring, and they fixed June as the month of their marriage. They travelled around the country together—perfectly respectably, as she insisted—seeing sights and staying at hotels. Bennett spent money freely. Alice was now introduced to Mrs Pankhurst as Bennett's intended wife. Then, perfectly happy, she went back to her parlourmaid's position at Bayswater.

Such is the background of the drama. Before considering in detail what happened after Bennett's return from Ireland, it is proper to say that he had got himself into a corner from which no easy exit was possible. There is every indication that he was as much in love with Alice Meadows as she was with him, and Mary Jane was an impermeable block in the way of their happiness. There could hardly be a simpler or a stronger motive for murder.

2. THE MURDER

On Saturday, 15th September, Mary Jane left Glencoe Villas. She told her neighbour, Miss Lilian Langman, that she was going for a holiday. 'My old man is going to take me, after all,' she said. 'We're going to Yorkshire.' She took as luggage a brown bag and a brown paper parcel, and she was accompanied by the baby. Miss Langman noticed that she was wearing when she left a long gold chain. The exact nature of this chain was to become crucial in the case.

That evening Mary Jane arrived, not in Yorkshire but in Yarmouth, and came to the door of Mrs Rudrum, in the Rows. This was one of the addresses given to Bennett through Miss Treadwell, and before his visit with Alice he had written to Mrs Rudrum, who had been full up at the time. An unidentifiable man turned into the Row with Mary Jane, but when Mrs Rudrum opened the door she stood there alone with her baby. She said that her name was Hood, asked for a room, put the baby to bed and went out. When she came back she was a little the worse for drink, and rather confiding. She was a widow, she told Mrs Rudrum, and came from York. Her husband had died three months before the baby was born, and she had been brought down to Yarmouth by her brother-in-law. This brother-in-law, she explained, was extremely jealous, and inclined to follow her about.

For the rest of the week, until Friday, Mary Jane was in every evening by nine o'clock. She told Mrs Rudrum that she was expecting a letter and on Friday evening, while she was out, one arrived. On this evening Mary Jane did not come back until about 10.45 at night. She explained that she had lost her way. But had she? She was with a man that evening. Mrs Rudrum's daughter Alice saw her standing at the bottom of the Row and heard a man say to her: 'You understand, don't you, I am placed in an awkward position just now.' Then Alice Rudrum heard the sound of a kiss.

On Saturday, Mary Jane went out in the morning, stayed in during the afternoon, and then went out again at about 6.30 in the evening. She was wearing a long gold chain, five rings, and a gold brooch. She was also wearing a silver watch, and had a purse with a good deal of money in it. At nine o'clock that night Alice Rudrum saw and spoke to her outside the Town Hall. Almost an hour later the manager of a 'snug', a man named Borking, saw a man and woman, whom he identified as Bennett and his wife. Mary Jane Bennett was not seen again alive.

An artist's impression of the trial

What had Bennett been doing while his wife was in Yarmouth? On the evening of Friday, 14th September, he came up from Woolwich to Bayswater and told Alice that he wold not be able to see her becuase he had to go down to Gravesend to see his grandfather, who was ill. On Saturday he telephoned to say that he would not be up from Gravesend in time to go with her brother on the river on Sunday, but he arranged to meet her at 3.30 on Sunday afternoon, outside the house in which she worked.

Did Bennett take Mary Jane down to Yarmouth, and was he the man seen at the end of the Row before she knocked on Mrs Rudrum's door? There was some conflict on this point. The waiter at the Crown and Anchor remembered him as a man who had stayed that Saturday night, and had left to catch the 7.20 train to London on Sunday morning. This train, however, got in to Liverpool Street at 11.47, and a certain Mrs Lenston, who lived with Alice Meadows's mother in Stepney, said that Bennett had come to the house at about 11.30 on that Sunday morning. Mrs Meadows herself had talked to him at about twelve o'clock.

On Monday, Bennett went back to work at the Arsenal, and during the course of that week he saw two friends from the Co-operative Stores. One of them asked after his wife and child. They had both died in South Africa of a fever, Bennett said. 'Don't say much about it, as I feel it very much,' he said to them. 'She was my right hand.' On Thursday he met Alice, and told her that he would be unable to see her on the following Sunday because he was going to Gravesend again with his cousin Fred. On Saturday he told his landlady, Mrs Pankhurst, that he would like to keep up her mother's birthday, as she was the same age as the Queen. Later that day, however, she saw him with a time table in his hand, and he said he was gong to catch a train. He left that afternoon, wearing a light grey suit. He did not return that night.

Where did Bennett go on that Saturday? The waiter at the Crown and Anchor identified him as a man who had stayed there on Saturday night. He arrived at about 11.30 and left, again, on Sunday morning to catch the 7.20 train to London.

At about eleven o'clock on that Saturday night a man named

Mason and his girl were sitting in one of the secluded hollows on the South Beach. They heard another couple walking near them, and heard them sit down. Then a voice cried, 'Mercy, mercy', and a woman moaned. About ten minutes later Mason and his friend left the beach. They passed by the man and woman. The woman was lying on her back, but the man turned and looked at them. It was a dark, moonless night, and they could not see the man's face clearly.

At six o'clock on Sunday morning a bathing machine boy found the body of a woman on the beach, dead, lying on her back. She had been strangled by a mohair bootlace, drawn so tightly round her neck that it was embedded in the flesh. The knot in which it had been tied was an unusual one, consisting of a reef knot with a granny over it. The face was scratched and bruised, and it was obvious that a desperate struggle had taken place. The doctor who examined the body found bloodstains on the underclothes.

It was not difficult to trace Mary Jane in her character as Mrs Hood. The report that a woman lodger was missing from the Rudrums' house sent Inspector Lingwood of the Yarmouth Police round there at once. In Mrs Hood's bedroom he found a small purse with a latchkey, the return half of a first-class ticket from Liverpool Street, and a gold brooch with 'Baby' on it. He found two pieces of baby's clothing showing a laundry mark, '599'. He found a photograph of Mrs Hood and the baby. It had been taken by a beach photographer on the preceding Thursday, and in it the woman had a gold chain round her neck. Inspector Lingwood discovered that Mrs Hood had gone out wearing a chain and a watch, and these were missing from the body.

The beach photograph was widely circulated, and a lookout was kept for the watch and chain, without result. Police all over the country investigated people who had used the laundry mark 599, paying particular attention to the places in which Mrs Hood had told Mrs Rudrum that she lived. These enquiries also had no result. Five weeks after the murder a coroner's jury found that an unknown woman had been murdered by an unknown man.

The accused

Bennett, in the meantime, had been behaving in a way that was to have disastrous consequences for him. On the Sunday after the murder Alice Meadows met him in Hyde Park just before one o'clock. She was surprised, because he had told her that he must be in Gravesend to look after his grandfather. Now, however, he said that his father, sister and other relatives were there, and that he had come away to see her. He was wearing a grey suit and a bowler hat, which was very unusual for him on a Sunday. She asked him to come and have dinner at her mother's, but he said he was going to Woolwich.

He did indeed go there, and saw Mrs Pankhurst. She noticed that he was wearing the same grey suit that he had on the previous afternoon, and said, 'You have never been to see Alice in those clothes.'

'Rats to Alice,' he replied. 'She does not mind how I am dressed.'

On Monday he wrote a letter to Alice (it was dated the 23rd, that is Sunday, but was evidently not written on that day):

My own darling Alice,

I received your kind and loving letter this evening, and was quite pleased to hear from you, as it cheers me up. I arrived home quite safe but was not at all happy. I am glad you had somebody to pass the time away with, dearest, as you would have felt very miserable after seeing me as you did. I shall be very glad indeed, my darling, when you do not have to leave me at all, for I feel quite miserable now that I have had to wait so long to see you.

I shall be up on Thursday evening, dearest, all being well, as I am now on day work, and I hope I shall keep at day work as it is much better.

I have been to Bexley to-night, dear, and am sorry to tell you that grandfather passed away this morning, at 3.30 a.m., and is to be buried on Monday next, when I shall not be able to attend as I must not lose any more time at present.

I hope you are feeling better, darling, and I shall be glad to see you out of the place altogether . . . Give my love to mother and all at home when you write. Hoping they are all quite well, I must now close, my dearest, as it is getting late. Hoping to see you on Thursday when I shall have lots of news.

With kindest love and kisses, I remain your most loving and affectionate
Herbert

The grandfather had now been eliminated, and Bennett wore black trousers and a black tie to mark his passing. At the same time he disposed of the cousin, telling Mrs Pankhurst that he had given £15 towards his passage to South Africa. He visited Glencoe Villas, collected some of his wife's clothes, and told the neighbour, Miss Langman, that Mrs Bennett was ill up in Yorkshire. He wrote to the landlord terminating the tenancy of Glencoe Villas, and saying that he was going to America.

Bennett and Alice had fixed the wedding date for June, but on the Wednesday after Mary Jane's death he asked if she would marry him at Christmas. At the same time he gave her a gold pickaxe and shovel brooch, the first of several gifts made to Alice of things belonging to Mary Jane. He told Alice that he had bought his cousin's furniture, adding that 'they had gone straight away to South Africa'. On the Sunday following, Alice agreed to marry him at Christmas, and told him that she was going to buy a black coat and skirt. Bennett said that his cousin had a 'nice blue coat and skirt' and gave it to her. He presented her also with a sealskin cape, a piece of lace, a tablecloth, a piece of dress material, and a silver brooch. All these were things that had belonged to Mary Jane.

On 17th October, Alice gave up her job, and at about this time he told her (he was sadly mistaken) that he would hear no more abut his cousins, who had now become plural, and of both sexes. He took her to Charlton, showed her a house which she liked, and paid a deposit on it. Early in November he was at her mother's house for tea when Alice's sister mentioned that they had not yet caught the Yarmouth murderer. This was the first time that Alice had heard of the case. Bennett said nothing, but held out his cup of tea for another lump of sugar. He was in all things, as Alice Meadows was to say afterwards, a polite, kind and gentle young man.

The break in the case came when Mrs Rudrum, talking it over with her daughter Alice, remembered that the letter which had come for Mrs Hood on Friday bore a Woolwich postmark. Mrs Rudrum told this to the police, and special attention was paid to the Woolwich area. The police now looked for anybody in this area who used the mark 599, and who had stopped sending clothing to the laundry. These enquiries were also fruitless, because Bennet was still sending his washing to the same laundry.

It was not until 5th November that a certain Mrs Bennett was reported missing from her home in Bexley Heath, and the laundry mark was linked with her. Chief Inspector Leach of Scotland Yard learned that Bennett had worked at the Co-operative Stores, and at the Stores he heard a curious story from an employee named Robert Allen, who had been friendly with Bennett.

Allen had met Mrs Bennett, and identified her when the Inspector showed him the beach portrait, although he had apparently not previously connected her with the missing Mrs Hood. In October, Bennett had met Allen in the street, and told him that he had a bicycle for sale. A few days later Allen went to Glencoe Villas which, Bennett told him, was his cousin's house. There Bennett showed him a piano, which was also for sale.

'Is your wife here?' Allen asked.

'She is not here. She is down home,' Bennett replied. A little later he improved on this. 'I have no wife, but I am about to be married,' he said. Who was the lady introduced to him as Mrs Bennett? Allen wanted to know. But he got no satisfaction. Bennett reiterated that he had no wife, but that he was going to be married shortly. They returned to the question of the piano, and Allen agreed to pay £23 for the piano and the bicycle. Bennett said that he had paid 15 guineas for the bicycle alone, and showed a receipt for this amount. When Allen wrote to the manufacturers, however, they said that this was untrue. Allen accused Bennett for forging the receipt, and refused to pay anything more than his original £6 deposit.

When Inspector Leach heard this tale, he asked Allen to introduce him to Bennett. They met Bennett as he left the Arsenal, and Leach was introduced as Mr Brown. He put his arms round Bennett. 'I am a police officer,' he said, 'and I arrest you for the murder of Mrs Hood on Yarmouth beach.'

'I do not understand what you mean.'

Leach, accompanied by a sergeant, took his prisoner to Woolwich Police Station. There Bennett said: 'I have not been to Yarmouth. I have not lived with my wife since January, when I found a lot of letters from another man in her pocket.' He was shown the beach photograph, but said that he did not clearly recognize the woman.

The arrest had been made on uncommonly slender grounds, but a search of Bennett's room at Mrs Pankhurst's provided much evidence against him. In a portmanteau with the *Avondale Castle* label on it were found a silver watch and a gold chain, two pearl necklaces, fourteen letters from Alice Meadows, a receipt from the Crown and Anchor for the period of his stay there with Alice, a revolver and cartridges, a man's and a woman's wig, a false moustache, collars marked 599, and a receipt for Glencoe Villas. The watch and chain were shown to the Rudrums, who indentified them as those worn by Mrs Hood. They also remembered the name Bennett, and now found the original letter sent by Bennett asking for lodgings. The handwriting, they said confidently, was the same as that on the missing letter sent to Mrs Hood.

3. THE TRIAL

Bennett's arrest was the signal for a newspaper campaign of vilification unequalled in this century. Feeling in Yarmouth was high against him, and on his first appearance in custody, at Yarmouth Town Hall, a crowd of angry men and women tried to get hold of him, and when they found this impossbile, howled, hooted, whistled, groaned, and shrieked abuse. This popular feeling was exacerbated in particular by the *Evening News* and the *Daily Mail*. 'His thin lips nervously twitched as the charge against him was read', the *Evening News* said, differing from the *Daily Mail*, which stressed his absolute composure and added that his appearance was not unpleasing:

> He has a good forehead, with wavy, dark brown hair, a long nose which is straight except for slight tilt at the end, brown eyes which are a trifle near together, large unshapely ears and a slightly receding chin. He had neglected to get his hands clean before coming into court.

The *Evening News* told much of the story, in advance of the prosecution case being presented in court. They got hold of Allen, and printed an account of his relations with Bennett; they also

The beach photograph with the chain

interviewed Mrs Elliston (who discussed the case with a *Daily Mail* reporter too), and another landlady named Mrs Cato, who said that while they stayed with her the Bennetts had realized £5 to £6 a day by the sale of violins. She added that, when they had been talking of a murder, Bennett had said, 'There's only one way to do a job of that kind. Strangle them. It's quick and silent.'

Throughout, the *Evening News*, like several other papers, assumed Bennett's guilt. In the course of an interview with Alice Meadows, the reporter described her as 'prostrated with grief and hesitating between love and duty, doubtful as to whether to screen the man she loves from the merciless clutches of the law, or whether to aid justice in its demand that the woman done to death on the sands at Yarmouth be avenged.'

Bennett's case was thus almost irretrievably prejudiced from the start. The evidence of the watch and chain seemed only to set the final stamp on a case already made hopeless by the double life he had been leading, and by his conduct after Mary Jane's death. Yet the process of erosion carried on by Bennett's counsel, Marshall Hall, during the trial, undermined much of the prosecution case in a way which the astute Charles Gill, who led for the Crown, cannot possibly have foreseen; and Marshall Hall's defence of Bennett, although it was finally unsuccessful, must rank among his greatest achievements as an advocate. He was able to speak with such passion and eloquence because of his own belief in Bennett's innocence, a belief which was shared by the junior counsel and the solicitor. 'My God, I believe that man's innocent,' said the junior counsel, Thorn Drury, after a first interview with Bennett in prison. 'Of course he is innocent,' Marshall Hall said coldly, when Drury communicated his belief.

Marshall Hall's tactics were simple. He attacked the prosecution case at all points, throwing doubt on either the integrity or the intelligence of every witness. The most damaging single point against Bennett was the discovery of the watch and chain in his portmanteau. This was buttressed by the evidence about his September visits to Yarmouth, and his behavior after Mary Jane's death. The affair with Alice Meadows provided a perfect motive. With regard to this, Marshall Hall could do little more than stress Bennett's kindness and gentleness, and the fact that 'he never took advantage of me, behaving at all time as a gentleman', as Alice said. There the motive unshakably was, and Marshall Hall's suggestion that both Bennett and Mary Jane had the idea that their marriage might be void because of the irregularities connected with it was really flung out as a gesture, which he hardly bothered to elaborate.

With much of the other material, however, Marshall Hall was able to do a great deal. Mrs Elliston, for instance, the Plumstead landlady who had given evidence about Bennett's bad behaviour to Mary Jane, must have wished herself out of the witness box soon after the beginning of the cross-examination:

Marshall Hall: Do you read the *Evening News* and the *Daily Mail*?
Elliston: I have been worried too much to do so lately.
M.H.: Did you see a statement of yours about November last?
Elliston: I saw it in the papers.
M.H.: Did you read the statement as an account of what you knew about this case in the *Daily Mail* of November 12th?
Elliston: I saw it in some evening paper.
M.H.: Were you one of the first people to recognized the photograph of the deceased as being Mrs Bennett?
Elliston: Yes.
M.H.: Were you much visited by people representing newspapers?
Elliston: There were only one or two.
M.H.: Did you speak freely to them?
Elliston: I did not say much to them.
M.H.: Did you tell them this, that when Mrs Bennett arrived at your house she was richly dressed and wearing a quantity of jewellery?
Elliston: I did not say she was wearing a quantity of jewellery; I said she was dressed well, but not richly dressed. I said her bodice was lined with silk but not her dresses. I said she had a lot of jewellery. She had gold spectacles, ornaments in her hair, a gold bracelet and rings.
M.H.: Did you say her underwear was covered with lace?

Elliston: I saw her underclothes were good and had lace on them.

M.H.: Did you say to the reporter that her purse was observed to be well filled with gold;

Elliston: Yes. She had plenty of money.

The Judge: What were they paying you a week?

Elliston: Ten shillings a week for the apartments.

M.H.: Did you tell the press that you did not believe the story that they had come from South Africa?

Elliston: I did not say I did not believe it.

M.H.: Did you say they did not look like people who had come off a sea voyage?

Elliston: I do not remember.

M.H.: That must have been an invention of the gentlemen of the press?

Elliston: I suppose so.

M.H.: Did you see an account, purporting to be an account of what you had said to a reporter, in an evening paper?

Elliston: I read something in an evening paper, but I do not know when it was.

Marshall Hall suggested here, as he was to do with other witnesses, that the importunity of newspapers had led Mrs Elliston to say things she knew to be untrue. Her husband was a police constable and had seen Bennett on the night of his arrest.

M.H.: Did your husband actually go to the police station to see Bennett the night he was arrested?

Elliston: Yes, he went there to identify him.

M.H.: Knowing that on 6th November this man had been arrested on a charge of murder, on 11th November you were gossiping about this case to a newspaper man?

Elliston: I did not think it would do Bennett any harm.

M.H.: (holding up a copy of the *Evening News*): And you as a woman will say that you did not tell the man what appeared in the paper?

Gill protested and the Lord Chief Justice, Lord Alverstone, intervened to protect Mrs Elliston. But no protection could erase the effect created by Marshall Hall, that she was a woman who would say anything for the sake of a little notoriety.

With another landlady, Mrs Pankhurst, Marshall Hall was gentler. She, too, was a prosecution witness, but she had been favourably impressed by Bennett, whom she described as a peaceable, quiet, orderly young man. Marshall Hall tried to induce her to agree that she was not sure whether or not Bennett slept in her house on the night of 22nd September, but her certainty that he did not return could not be shaken. She remembered positively, she said, because she had made up the bed of only one lodger on the following Sunday morning, and that had not been Bennett. She had also sent up her little boy with a cup of tea that Sunday morning, and he had brought it back because Bennett was not there.

It was difficult, also, to touch the witnesses who had given evidence of Bennett's behaviour after Mary Jane's disappearance, for it was beyond dispute that he had told lie after lie. Marshall Hall did what he could, but Cameron and Parritt, Bennett's friends at the Co-operative Stores, refused to confirm his statement that he had been with them on the night of 22nd September, and insisted that the occasion he referred to was the following Saturday, the 29th. He had more luck with Allen, who had been engaged in the bicycle and piano transaction, when he pointed out that Allen had paid only £6 on a sum total of £23:

M.H.: You owe him £17?

Allen: There is that to pay over the piano and bicycle transaction.

M.H.: Have you said that if Bennett worried you for the money you would prosecute him for fraud?

Allen: No.

M.H.: Did you say the cycle receipt was forged?

Allen: Yes.

M.H.: Do you want to have your revenge on this man who had swindled you over the bicycle by having him arrested in the street?

Allen: I had no idea of having revenge.

M.H.: You got the piano and the bicycle and you propose to keep them?

Allen: I have them still, and I do not know what I shall do with them. I had an expert to examine the piano and he said it was not worth the price.

M.H.: And yet you agreed to buy it?

What Bennett had said in London, however, was not the real heart of the case. It was his presence in Yarmouth on the night of the 22nd and his possession of the watch and chain that were the really damning things. In Yarmouth, Bennett had been recognized by the distillery manager Borking, by a fisherman's wife in the snug at the time, by the waiter at the Crown and Anchor, and by a newsagent at the railway station on Sunday morning. Marshall Hall questioned all these identifications. Borking, an amateur artist, had identified Bennett by his steel-grey suit, his heavy moustache, and his square cut 'clerical' waistcoat. Of these, only the suit was identified correctly, for Bennett had no more than a slight moustache, and when seen in London on Saturday and Sunday was wearing an ordinary waistcoat. Borking said that he had made a sketch of the man in the bar, and had also sketched the braiding on the woman's dress, but these sketches were not produced in Court. The fisherman's wife, Mrs Gibson, had seen Bennett twirling his moustache:

M.H.: Does not every man with a moustache twirl it?

Mrs Gibson: Not the way he did.

M.H.: When you saw the prisoner in the dock on 24th November, you at once said it was the man?

Mrs Gibson: He was wearing a heavier moustache.

M.H.: I think you told the police the moustache looked heavier at Borking's?

Mrs Gibson: Yes.

M.H.: Can a man make his moustache heavier at will? (Laughter.) Have you talked this case over with anybody?

Mrs Gibson: No.

M.H.: When you went to the police-court, did you at once tell the police you recognized the prisoner?

Mrs Gibson: No.

Reade, the waiter at the Crown and Anchor, also said that
the man who stayed there was wearing a heavier moustache,
and he had identified Bennett only (as Marshall Hall put it) after
'the Press had taken up the case, and sensational journalism had
sent its lying filth broadcast through Yarmouth'. The newsagent
who had seen a man with a very agitated and excited manner
waiting to catch the 7.20 train on Sunday morning, agreed that
this man was no more than 'very much like the prisoner', and
added that he appeared to be waiting for somebody. The
moustache in Bennet's portmanteau had been made of real hair
with a gauze backing, and could not be fixed over a genuine
moustache. Moreover, all these witness said that the man they
saw was wearing a trilby hat. Bennett habitually wore a
bowler, and according to Alice Meadows he was wearing a bowler
hat when she met him on Sunday.

In dealing with Mrs Rudrum, Marshall Hall made a more
serious accusation than one of mere inaccuracy. It will be
remembered that Mrs Rudrum had recalled that the envelope
received by Mrs Hood was postmarked Woolwich, and had
found the original letter sent by Bennett asking whether she
had a room free for his week-end with Alice Meadows. This
was not the limit of her discoveries. Just before the trial began,
she found a petticoat in a drawer on which 'Benet' was written
with marking ink. This had apparently been missed by the police
when they searched the house. After a thunderous but
inconclusive argument with Mrs Rudrum about the colour of
the envelope addressed to Mrs Hood (at the Magistrate's Court
she had said it was blue and now she said it was grey-blue,
which was in fact the colour of Bennett's sationery) Marshall
Hall turned with deadly effect to the finding of the petticoat
with the name Bennett incorrectly spelt. He asked Mrs Rudrum
to spell the name.

'B-E-N-N-E-T', she said and paused. Then she added the
other T.

M.H.: You said one 't' at first, then two; which is it?
Mrs Rudrum: I mean two 't's'.
M.H.: Will you write it down?

Mrs Rudrum: I cannot unless you tell me how to spell it. I am a very bad speller.

M.H.: Where did you find the petticoat?

Mrs Rudrum: Hanging up by the bed. It was afterwards put in a drawer and not produced again till I was asked for it.

M.H.: Just look at this petticoat. It has been torn or cut after it was marked, because the ink has gone through onto the piece which has been cut off.

Mrs Rudrum: Yes.

M.H.: You knew the police were searching everywhere to establish the identity of the woman?

Mrs Rudrum: Yes.

M.H.: Do you mean to tell me that the petticoat was hanging up in the woman's room when Lingwood came on 23rd September?

Mrs Rudrum: Yes. He saw it, I think.

M.H.: Did you not see that he was searching for all the clothes he could find?

Mrs Rudrum: You must remember that I was in a very excited state that morning.

The Judge: Can you explain how the petticoat, which was hanging up on a peg in the woman's room, was not discovered on the morning the search was made?

Mrs Rudrum: No, my lord.

With the most difficult point of all, the watch and chain, Marshall Hall scored his greatest success. The chain found in Bennett's portmanteau was a link chain, and Marshall Hall contended that it was not the same chain as that in the beach photograph. His cross-examination of Conyers, who had taken the photograph, was richly comic. Marshall Hall produced an enlargement of the photograph:

Conyers: I have been in the trade thirty-five years, and I know that is a bad one. (Laughter.)

Marshall Hall handed him another copy.

Conyers: Ah, that is a good one. It is a bromide print. I am speaking the truth, and that is a good one. (Renewed laughter.)

M.H.: Try to be serious, if you can.

Conyers: I am quite serious, and I will be serious.

M.H.: This is the chain found in the prisoner's portmanteau. It is a link chain and not of the rope pattern.

Conyers: I cannot say now that the chain is rope. It would be necessary to enlarge the photograph, and examine the chain in it and the real chain side by side under a glass.

The Judge: The difficulty I have is that the chain is not in focus in the photograph.

Conyers: Quite right (Laughter.) No amount of focus could alter the appearance of the chain.

Under further cross-examination Conyers said it would be impossible to make the chain in Bennett's possession look like the one in the photograph. The Judge, exasperated, intervened:

The Judge: Why do you say it is impossible to make the parts between the links look like that?

Conyers: I do not say it is impossible.

The Judge: You have said so. The jury had better look at it. You can stand down, Mr Conyers, unless somebody wants you.

Was the photograph out of focus, or was it really a different type of chain? Another prosecution witness said that the chain might be either of the rope or link pattern. Mrs Rudrum although not sure about the watch, said that she was absolutely certain that Mrs Bennett was wearing a link chain. At the time that the chain was found in Bennett's portmanteau she had been less sure, but under cross-examination she became more and more positive—rather too positive:

Mrs Rudrum: I was told by the police that they had found the chain.

M.H.: And you believed it, Mrs Rudrum?

Mrs Rudrum: No. One does not know what to believe.

M.H.: But you are now prepared to say it was the same chain?

Mrs Rudrum: Yes.

M.H.: You are prepared to back your opinion against your

honest doubt. Did you ever realize the meaning of the words,
'I indentify the watch and chain produced';

Mrs Rudrum: I never had the chain in my hands.

M.H.: Though you had doubts before, now that you have been
cross-examined you are positive?

Mrs Rudrum: Yes, I am.

M.H.: Are you equally positive as to the watch?

Mrs Rudrum: No.

M.H.: What made you doubt when you first went into the box?

Mrs Rudrum: It was the light.

M.H.: But the photograph has made you certain? (This was an
enlargment of the beach photograph.)

Mrs Rudrum: Yes.

M.H.: Are you as sure of that as of everything else?

Mrs Rudrum: Yes.

Her daughter Alice thought that is was not the same chain,
and would not swear as to the watch. A 'photographic artist'
called in by the police to photograph the chain became so
confused that in the end he was driven to say in despair, 'I do
not think anyone can say definitely what sort of chain it is.'
Marshall Hall then brought up his own battery of expert
witnesses, who were quite certain that the chain in the photograph
was of the rope, or Prince of Wales's, pattern, and that it could
not possibly be confused with Bennett's link chain. Their
evidence was not substantially shaken by Gill's cross-
examination. Finally Marshall called Mrs Cato who, it will be
remembered, had been susceptible to the blandishments of
newspapers. Mrs Cato now said that Mrs Bennett had had *two*
chains, one real gold (this was the one found in Bennett's
portmanteau) and the other imitation. She had also, Mrs Cato
said, had two watches. This obliging landlady added for good
measure that Bennett had treated Mary Jane most kindly, and
that she had been far from a good wife or an attentive mother.
It was now, however, Gill's turn to confront a witness with the
damaging things she had said in a newspaper interview. 'With
all her faults', Mrs Cato had told a reporter from the *Evening
News*, 'Mrs Bennett was a lovable little creature, and if ever

a woman was fond of a man she was fond of him. He treated her in a way to crush the love of any woman.' There was nothing in her newspaper story to suggest that Mrs Bennett had had two chains and two watches, and although she plaintively said that she had told this to the newspaper man, who had replied, 'That is all bosh', Gill's cross-examination was very damaging to her story.

So far, Marshall Hall had cast doubt on the prosecution case against Bennett, without positively attempting to explain his movements. Several of his own witnesses, like Mrs Lenston and Mrs Meadows, had a similar negative helpfulness. They said that Bennett had been with them at a time on Sunday, 16th September, which would have been impossible if he had caught the 7.20 train up from Yarmouth. But where, then, had he been, and where was he on the night of the murder, the 22nd? There was another crumb of negative help, or perhaps more than a crumb, in Alice Rudrum's story of the man who had kissed Mrs Bennett good night on Friday, 21st September, and had said that he was in an awkward position just now. This evidence helped Bennett, because he was certainly not in Yarmouth on that Friday night, but it was a positive alibi for the 22nd that Marshall Hall needed. Suddenly it seemed to be in his hands. A man named Douglas Sholto Douglas, a manufactuere of fancy goods, said that he had met Bennett in the early evening of the 22nd near Lee Green, and had been with him from about six to seven o'clock. If this evidence was accepted, it provided Bennett with a perfect alibi.

In his biography of Marshall Hall, Edward Marjoribanks says that he was doubtful whether to call Douglas: partly because the case had gone so surprisingly well, particularly in relation to the watch and chain, and partly because of the damage that might be done to Douglas's story under cross-examination. To resolve this difficulty Marshall Hall had a long interview with Bennett in the cells, and asked him with proper solemnity whether he had met Douglas on that day at Lee Green. Bennett replied that he had. Marshall Hall then left Bennett alone for two hours with a piece of paper on which was written 'I wish Douglas called' and 'I do not wish Douglas called', and asked him to return the paper with one of the phrases struck out. Bennett struck out 'I do not wish Douglas called': but he refused to go into the witness box himself to confirm the story, nor had he mentioned the meeting before Marshall Hall told him of it.

This was the story Douglas told. He had been out for a walk that Saturday afternoon, and on the way back to his house at Hither Green, at about six o'clock, he met a man who asked for a light. The man was wearing a grey suit and a bowler hat. Douglas had never met him before, and did not much care about talking to him now, but he found it difficult to get away with reasonable politeness. As they walked along the man talked about himself. He worked at Woolwich Arsenal; he travelled a good deal, and had recently been in Ireland; he said either that he lived or came from Bexley Heath. Talking in this way, or rather, with the man talking and Douglas mostly listening, they came to the 'Tiger' at Lee Green. 'I could not shake him off,' Douglas said. 'He was a respectable man, but not the sort of man I wanted to associate with. So I asked him to have a drink, as a polite way of shaking him off. As I was rather thirsty I had a glass of bitter and he had spirits.'

They came out of the pub, and parted. Before they did so, the man pointed to a house next to the 'Tiger' and said, 'A namesake of mine apparently lives there.' The place was a shaving saloon, and the name over the door was 'F.K. Bennett'. Douglas explained to Marshall Hall why he had not come forward until after the police-court proceedings in November:

Douglas: About the middle of November I saw the reports of the Yarmouth murder trial.

M.H.: What occurred?

Douglas: Well, when I found that the name of the man charged with murder was Bennett, when I read of the light grey suit, and that the man worked at Woolwich, I took him for the same man I saw when I was out for a walk on that Saturday, 22nd September. I thought I was justified in making further investigations. I learned afterwards that the prisoner had been in Ireland. All this made me think it was my duty to communicate with the police.

M.H.: Did you see the prisoner?

Douglas: Yes, I went to Norwich and saw him in prison. I did not speak to him nor he to me. I had a good look at him, both full-face and profile.

M.H.: And what was your opinion?

Douglas: I had do doubt that the prisoner was the man I met in the lane on 22nd September.

M.H.: Have you any doubt?

Douglas: I have not a shadow of a doubt about the man or the date.

M.H.: Have you the smallest interest in this case?

Douglas: No. The suggestion is perfectly absurd.

Douglas was a surprise witness, and Gill had no time to prepare his cross-examination. He concentrated upon three points: Douglas's professed difficulty in shaking off the man, his lateness in coming forward, and the possibility that he might have mistaken the date. On the first point he was ironical. 'A man you had never met before, and whose company you did not desire, was with you for one hour?' he said incredulously, and asked why Douglas had not walked out of the 'Tiger', or why he had not turned off on the road to it. Douglas reiterated that he did not want to be rude, and said that on this particular country road there were no turnings. On the question of the time at which he had come forward, Douglas openly said that in November he did not want his name or address in the papers; he was negotiating a partnership, and did not want anything to stop it. On the third point Gill could not shake him. Douglas said that he put shoots into pots on most Saturdays, and on those days he did not take walks because he was not fit to be seen. He had found pots with the dates 15th Septgember and 29th September on them, but none for the 22nd. He checked the date also by the fact that he had received a particular order on that Saturday, and took it out of his pocket in the pub to look at it.

Douglas was a good witness: yet his evidence had little effect, and Marshall Hall felt afterwards that it had been wrong to call him. In retrospect, it seems obvious that Douglas's story was not likely to convince the jury unless Bennett went into the box

to confirm it. About this point there is some obscurity.
Marjoribanks says in one place that Bennett refused to go into
the box, but in another that he was 'a man so wholly unreliable
that it would have been most hazardous to put him into the
witness box'. In a letter to his friend Sir Aruthur Pinero, written
after the trial, Marshall Hall gives another account:

> When I saw that wretched man Bennett on Friday morning ALONE I
> said to him this: 'If you will only go into the box and admit *everything* except
> the actual murder, I can get a verdict, but of course you must admit that
> when you saw the papers on the day after the murder you *knew* it was your
> wife, but that you were afraid to comunicate for fear of losing Alice
> Meadows.'
> His reply was: 'I cannot say that, because I was not in Yarmouth on
> the 22nd, and I never knew that the murdered woman was my wife till I
> was arrested.' I pointed out that this was hopeless,and he declined to give
> evidence at all.

Whichever of these slightly contradictory stories is right, nothing
Bennett said in the witness box could have done him so much
damage as his failure to enter it. Had he gone into the box he
must have given some explanation, however lame and
unsatisfactory, of his actions on 22nd September, after he left
Mrs Pankhurst's in the afternoon. In the end Marshall Hall was
reduced to saying that 'if he was not there on Saturday night,
did it prove that he was at Yarmouth, now that they knew that
he had a latchkey, and was sometimes in the habit of remaining
out all night?' But, as the jury must have thought to themselves,
if he had been out all night why did he not go into the witness
box and say so? A few years earlier, before the passing of the
Criminal Evidence Act, Bennett would not have been allowed
to give evidence,and because of that very fact Marshall Hall
might have got an acquittal. Now the Act designed to help the
prisoner undid him. It is hard to resist the conclusion that since
Marshall Hall would not or could not call Bennett, he should
not have called Douglas. By doing so he exposed very clearly
the yawning gap in his defence.

Through this gap Gill drove his horses. He reminded the jury
that 'absolutely no answer had been given to the vital questions
where the prisoner was on the nights of 15th September and of

22nd September'. It was strange, he said, that Bennett had never mentioned meeting Sholto Douglas and that no person had seen them in each other's company. Without impugning Douglas's good faith he pointed out that every statement he made could have come to his knowledge through reading the papers. The Lord Chief Justice, in his summing up, said that if they believed the alibi the case was at an end, but he emphasized the danger of relying on such a story 'which was wholly uncorroborated, in the face of other facts'. And again, the jury must have asked themselves: why did not Bennett come forward to corroborate it?

The most extraordinary development of the case was yet to come. After Marshall Hall had begun his closing speech for the defence he received a telegram from a Lowestoft stationer named O'Driscoll: 'Have Lowestoft police made report if not communicate at once most important.' The 'most important' evidence that O'Driscoll had to communicate was this. On the Wednesday evening after the murder a man had come into his shop. One of his boots was laced, while the other had the tongue hanging out. There were scratches on his face. He asked for a paper with a report of the Yarmouth murder in it, and said that he did not mind what paper it was so long as it had a good report of the murder. When he had paid his halfpenny for the paper O'Driscoll noticed that his hands also were scratched. He read the paper in the shop, and while he read it made 'a sort of groaning'. When he saw O'Driscoll looking at him, the man clutched the paper and ran out of the shop.

This evidence had been ignored by the Yarmouth police, presumably because they thought it absurd to assume that the murderer might have been running around searching for a report of the case four days after the murder. In court, however, O'Driscoll's evidence caused some stir. The prosecution recalled the doctor who had examined the body, who said that there was no blood or skin under the fingernails, as there would have been had Mrs Bennett scratched her attacker; but there was sand on her hands, and he agreed that this sand might have removed other traces. Gill did not bother to mention O'Driscoll in his closing speech, but the Lord Chief Justice referred to him in summing up, although he said that 'they ought not to allow such evidence as this to weigh upon their minds if in the end they were satisfied of the guilt of the prisoner'.

Lord Alverstone's summing up was, inevitably, very much against Bennett. The jury took 35 minutes to find him guilty. He was hanged at Norwich.

The problem presented by the Yarmouth murder is in a sense the reverse of that posed by the Porthole case. Had the jury in the case of James Camb given more weight to the South African witnesses they might, strictly upon the evidence at the trial, have found that there was a reasonable doubt of his being a murderer. In the Bennett case there can be no complaint against the verdict, for the evidence was overwhelming: yet an aura of mystery will always surround the case, and the circumstantial evidence against Bennett may have given a different interpretation from that accepted at the trial. There are too many loose ends for any writer interested in murder to be convinced of Bennett's guilt.

Where did Bennett's money come from? Who was the man Mrs Bennett talked to and kissed on Friday night at the end of the Rows? Was Bennett, who had not slept with his wife for some time, likely to have made a sexual assault on her? (The medical evidence was not positive on this point, but there was 'a desperate struggle', and the bloodstains on her underclothes were consistent with an attempted assault.) Above all, was it not stange that Bennett, after making himself thoroughly well known at the Crown and Anchor by two visits, should choose just this hotel to stay at after strangling his wife? I believe that it is possible to construct a story that will cover all these points plausibly, and will explain his conduct after the murder, while still leaving him innocent of the crime.

Let us begin with the assumption that the Bennetts had turned from fraud to blackmail. The violin game was over—too many people had tried to trace the elusive couple when they discovered how they had been cheated—but the idea that Bennett had settled down to humdrum honesty is against everything we know of him. Or, it may be added, of Mary Jane. It is natural that a woman presumed to have been brutally murdered by her husband should be presented as weak, frail, and under his influence: but there is no reliable evidence that this was true of Mary Jane Bennett.

She told Mrs Cato that she took the principal part in the violin swindle, and this is confirmed by the fact that she actually sold most of the violins. There is abundant evidence that, like Bennett, she was an habitual and accomplished liar. What is more likely than that, if Bennett found a likely subject for blackmail, he should turn to Mary Jane as a ready accomplice, or that she should welcome the chance of joining forces with him again? Why, if there was nothing to hide about the visit to Yarmouth, did she tell people in Bexley Heath that her old man was taking her to Yorkshire?

Bennett, then, brings his wife down to Yarmouth on Saturday, 15th September. He installs her at Mrs Rudrums's, and stays himself at the Crown and Anchor. This was an extraordinary thing to do, according to the prosecution story that Bennett had brought Mary Jane down to Yarmouth with the deliberate intention of murdering her. Why leave it for a week, during which she might well have confided to Mrs Rudrum that her real name was Bennett? And, if he was going to leave it for a week, why not at least return to London that Saturday night rather than leave a trail at the Crown and Anchor? This strange conduct becomes immediately credible, however, if he introduced Mary Jane on that Saturday evening to a prospective victim. He would not himself, of course, have been her husband but her brother-in-law—the 'jealous brother-in-law' Mary Jane vivaciously described to Mrs Rudrum in another series of lies. Mary Jane herself, no doubt, would have been a widow—a rather gay widow, with a small daughter.

Bennett then went back to London, leaving the acquaintance to ripen. Nobody ever asked the question: what did Mary Jane do during her week at Yarmouth? Let us accept that she was with the baby during the daytime. When she had put Ruby to bed she went out each night, returning 'not later than nine o'clock', according to Mrs Rudrum. Where did she go, how did she spend the evenings? And above all, who was she with on Friday night, when she came in at 10.45, and was seen by Alice Rudrum with a man who was certainly not Bennett? It is suggested here that she spent those evenings with a man to whom she had been introduced by Bennett, and that the climax—the demand for money—was to be made by Bennett on Saturday, the 22nd.

What were Bennett's intentions in all this? His conduct, and the remarks he made at this time, could be perfectly explained if he meant to take the money, leave Mary Jane stranded, and go away with Alice Meadows after bigamously marrying her. He was not a man likely to be worried by bigamy.

On Saturday, 22nd September, by this theory, Bennett did go down to Yarmouth. He did *not* meet Douglas, who was mistaken either in the date or in the man. We cannot know exactly what plan the Bennetts had made. It is most likely that he arranged to catch Mary Jane with her lover on the beach, and then reveal himself as her husband. But something went wrong. Perhaps the victim guessed something of the plan, perhaps he was truly a violent man whose sexual advances she had resisted all the week, and who now attempted to take her by force, strangled her and fled. When Bennett arrived on the beach he found her dead. Perhaps the watch and chain had been taken by the murderer as a blind; perhaps Bennett rashly took them himself (although this does not seem to fit what we know of him), and they were indeed the ones found in his portmanteau. His conduct afterwards was consistent. He knew that Mary Jane was dead, so that there was no obstacle to his marriage. It would have seemed to him mere common sense to give her clothes and belongings to Alice Meadows. Every lie he told was an act of self-protection. If he admitted to knowledge of his wife's death he would be putting his neck into a noose.

Could such a defence have been put before a jury with any hope that they would accept it? Certainly not. This is a theory that cannot be proved, and that depends upon a hypothetical blackmailee: yet it covers all the facts of the case, in a way that the prosecution's version of the crime did not; it plausibly explains the actions of Bennett and of Mary Jane; it is, very likely, as near as we shall ever get to knowing what really happened.

HAROLD T. WILKINS

The Monster
of Bruges

Our twentieth century—the age of two devastating world wars;
of relativity; the coming of interplanetary travel, still, however,
a long way off in the future; the diabolical hydrogen bomb and
the fearful weapons of inter-continental ballistic missiles; and
of the years ahead of which no man cares to take a long view—
has certainly seen no lack of mysteries as baffling as any that
were in the centuries before.

Some years before the Second World War, I was in that city
of slow time and the sound of dreamy carillons, where, if there
are not now 'grass-grown streets trodden by noiseless feet', there
is certainly a strange labyrinth of twisting medieval streets in
which it is easy for a stranger to get lost all night. I refer to
Bruges. I stayed at an ancient house not far from the Rue des
Tonneliers, right in the heart of this queer timeless old city, and,
there, I was told a very eerie story connected with some very
strange bones now in the 'dry' section of a certain Belgian
Medical Museum. This ancient house had formerly belonged
to the order of the Black Friars, or Dominican monks; but, about
1908, it had been acquired by a private person who let out flats
in it to artists, or to foreigners desiring to make a protracted
stay in this picturesque, old Flemish town. As would be expected
of a former monastic institution, the house had grim and massive
walls, many small rooms that had once been cells, tortuous stone
stairways, and very narrow passages.

But there had been complaints about the place. People came
and rented the rooms and flats, for which only a modest rental

was asked; but many of them packed up and left, some even before their period of paid occupancy had ended. There had been stories of eerie footsteps of something unseen ascending the stairs, not merely in the night, but in the day. One Englishman, who was about to come out of his door on a top storey, hurriedly shut it when he saw, in the dim angle of the stone passage outside, where only a crepuscular light entered even at sunny noon, what he called some 'damned inhuman', but vague and bizarre object, standing and waiting. He could not make out what it was, but it shuffled and padded off, leaving behind a horrible stench, as 'if it had come out of the Devil's own latrine!' There were also eerie raps on doors, and when the doors were opened, no one was seen there.

At last, the *patron* who saw that if these phenomena continued, he would be left with an empty house on his hands—since not even the most downright sceptic can be prevailed on to live and spend his days and nights in an old house which has 'something queer about it'—got in some builder's hefty men and had them break up the heavy stone flags of a very ancient and roomy stone cellar, which was believed to be the source of the phenomena. They did not find any coffins, or skeletons under the floor, nor any fruits of the clandestine amours of medieval monks and nuns, nor any sign that someone in the fourteenth or fifteenth century had by some means 'raised the Devil' and couldn't get him to lie down afterwards! But when the labourers were asked to apply their chisels, and picks and cowbars to the thick *walls* of this queer cellar, they opened up something on which no pathologist could express a decided opinion. They found, right in the middle of the thick cellar-wall, a sort of alcove in which were strange bones that did not all look human.

A surgeon, who was also a pathologist, was called in, and when he examined the bones, even he, hardened to macabre sights, shuddered. He said: 'This must have been some monstrosity, walled up untold years ago, and the bones all belong to the same uncanny being, *Nom du diable* . . . I confess I am unable to express any opinion on the origin of this horrible thing; nor can anyone now say if the monks knew anything about it.'

All one can say is that the monstrosity was not an infant, but adult; and whether or not it was the fault of some nasty amour of the unnatural type denounced in the books of the Pentateuch, or the remains of some horrible thing teleported to Bruges from some world in space, it is beyond the wit of man to determine. All *I* can say, besides this, is that the Flemish gentleman who told me this story, and who now owns the old house, assured me that there are now no raps on doors by an unseen thing, nor charnel-house stenches; but that all is now as holy and quiet there, as the nave of a church consecrated with holy water. I had no inclination to test his assurance; but, after cogitating 'Who had done the walling-up, and when?' I made tracks for a cheery pavement café off the *Grande Place* and called for an extra large glass of strong schnapps. It is obvious that a number of persons unknown could have told a most hair-raising story about what went on in that ancient cellar!

LEONARD GRIBBLE

In and Out of the Eagle

It was nine years after the passing of the Criminal Evidence Act
of 1898 that a man charged with murder for the first time gave
evidence on his own behalf, and in so doing won a historical
verdict of 'Not guilty'.

Which meant that someone got away with murder.

Emily Dimmock, who had led a complicated emotional and
sex life and had passed herself off as a Mrs Phyllis Shaw, was
murdered on the night of September 11th, 1907. The discovery
was made sometime around the middle of the morning of the
12th by another Mrs Shaw. This woman was the mother of a
son named Bert who lived in a house in St Paul's Road, Camden
Town. Bert Shaw occupied furnished rooms and paid rent to
a landlady named Mrs Stocks, who opened the front door in
answer to the mother's double knock.

Mrs Shaw had called to see her son, who was employed as
a dining-car cook by the Midland Railway. Usually he worked
on trains which took him north from St Pancras and brought
him back in time to reach home between eleven o'clock in the
morning and noon.

Bert had recently married, and at the time Mrs Shaw paid
her morning call in September to St Paul's Road she was still
looking forward, howbeit with mixed and dubious feelings, to
meeting her daughter-in-law for the first time. That meeting was
to be delayed for a short while after her arrival, but when it finally
came about the result was to be cataclysmic and the world of
Mrs Shaw was to be virtually destroyed.

The same shock wave was to ruin several other little personal
worlds.

'I've come to see my daughter-in-law,' Bert Shaw's mother told Mrs Stocks.

I don't think she's up,' was the landlady's comment, uttered with disapproval for such dilatory ways.

'Oh.' Mrs Shaw was slightly nonplussed by the news. 'Perhaps I'd better go up and tell her I've come.'

The two women moved into the house and Mrs Stocks closed the front door. Mrs Shaw, once inside, was in no hurry to mount the stairs and meet a stranger she had roused from bed. She remained chatting for some minutes with the landlady, and the two were still talking when Bert Shaw arrived home.

'Hello, Mum,' he said, kissing his mother. 'I didn't know you were coming.'

'Took everybody by surprise,' said his mother. 'Your wife isn't up yet, Bert.'

Bert Shaw looked at Mrs Stocks, who nodded.

'I'll go up,' she said. 'If she isn't up the door will be locked and she'll have to open it.'

However, his banging on the door of their furnished apartment brought no response from the woman within. He came downstairs, looking angry and sullen.

'She won't answer, Mrs Stocks. Can you let me have a spare key?'

'There's one somewhere. I'll see if I can find it.'

A few minutes passed with mother and son enduring an uncomfortable silence, then the landlady reappeared and handed Bert Shaw a key.

'I'll want it back,' she insisted.

The man took the key and returned up the stairs, followed by his mother, holding her skirts above her ankles and panting a little from the exertion. Mrs Shaw watched her son insert the key in a dark-painted door. He pushed the door open and entered, to bring up short with an oath. She crowded after him, and up the stairs came a very curious Mrs Stocks, full of anticipation that was to be more than adequately justified.

The door from the landing had opened on to a parlour, which was in a state of upheaval. It was as though someone had ransacked the room. Cupboards were open and their contents

Phyllis Shaw, alias Emily Dimmock

strewn about the floor. Some drawers had been thrown into the centre of the room and left upside down.

'Good God, what's happened?'

He was asking the question when he rushed at he closed door of what was the bedroom, but again Bert Shaw's progress towards tragedy was delayed. The door to the bedroom was also locked, and the key was missing. He rattled the door-handle, then beat a panel with his fist.

'Phyllis!' he shouted. 'Open the door!'

There was no sound of movement on the far side of the door. Mrs Shaw looked at Mrs Stocks. The landlady's face wore a grim look and the mother's gloved right hand stole to her mouth. She was suddenly fearful.

Swearing, Bert Shaw drew back and threw himself at the bedroom door. Mrs Stocks started to protest at this savage misuse of her property, but she bit off the sound. There was a wrenching of woodwork and the door burst inwards. Bert Shaw was catapulted into the bedroom and into a scene of horror.

The clothes had been stripped from the large old-fashioned double bed. They lay in a twisted pile in the middle of the room, flecked with blood. On the floor, a short distance away from the bed was a large bright pool of drying blood. Some of the blood had coursed like a miniature river across the floorboards to the wooden skirting, where another pool had formed.

The angry and confused husband tore at the pile of bedding and stared at the face of the woman he had told his mother he had married, a woman who had arrived with him at the house in St Paul's Road and announced she was Mrs Phyllis Shaw. The face was white, for it had been drained of all colour by the horrible gash extending across the woman's throat from under the lobe of one ear to the other, giving the lower half of the features the expression of a terrifying and horrible grimace. The murdered woman was nude. She lay on her stomach on a twisted sheet that was glued to her body with her own blood.

Bert Shaw stared at the wreck of the woman he had brought to this house as his wife. Even Mrs Stocks, who had not taken to Phyllis Shaw, did not know that the dead woman had never legally owned that name. She had not married Bert Shaw. She

had come with him and said she was his wife because doing so
was a change from streetwalking.

Her real name was Emily Dimmock.

Staring down at her remains Bert Shaw realised what a
damned fool he had been. He didn't have to be told that some
man from the woman's past had found her and he had been
someone seeking vengeance for some past misdeed. To Bert Shaw
it all seemed obvious.

He staggered away from the horror in the middle of the room,
muttering brokenly. He had understanding that was frightening
in its clarity. She hadn't given up the life of the streets. She had
been bringing clients home while he was at work, without even
Mrs Stocks knowing. The landlady usually went to bed early
and her bedroom was at the rear of the house. She wouldn't
know what went on in the top front.

It was Shaw who called the police to the house and who
summoned a Dr John Thompson to inspect the slaughtered nude.
Dr Thompson was the police surgeon for that division of the
Metropolitan Police area. The surgeon was particularly intrigued
by the lack of any sign of a struggle. There were no scratches or
bruises, and the expression on the drained face above that frightful
throat gash, which had almost severed the head from the trunk,
was not one of terror. Almost it was one of composure, suggesting
that the killer had taken his victim quite unawares and before she
could react to the knowledge of danger overtaking her.

Yet the police surgeon found one curious detail that puzzled
him. This was the position of the dead woman's left arm. It
seemed to him to have been forced back into a position which
was quite unnatural and not one the woman would have
assumed. It was a position that would have been painful to endure
if one wished to sleep with the arm so twisted and raised. Dr
Thompson was intrigued as to whether such a position had been
given the left arm before the woman's throat had been cut or
afterwards, when the body had been tumbled over on its stomach.

The weapon used by the killer had been sharp and, in the
medical man's opinion, heavy. The killer had been a person of
considerable strength, and from the depth of the grim incision
one of harsh determination. Emily Dimmock had been

slaughtered like a sheep with its throat cut. The windpipe, the jugular vein, and the carotid artery had been slashed through, and the pharynx deep down to the spine. In fact, the head remained on the pale shoulders merely because some muscles and tendons had escaped the heavy slash across the throat.

When Dr Thompson examined the corpse in the early afternoon the body was chilled and the limbs rigid. He made a note that *rigor mortis* was more advanced than he had expected. He had a brief sum in comparative arithmetic to work out, taking into his reckoning the temperature of the room when he arrived, the excessive amount of bloodletting, the character of the wound and the body temperature of the victim.

He decided that the killer had done his work on Emily Dimmock most likely between four and six o'clock that morning, while Bert Shaw was somewhere on the other side of England.

When the police searched the room they found other bloodstains that seemed to conflict with the surgeon's first opinion. For instance, two large congealed stains were found on the washbasin stand and a third on a water jug kept on the stand. There was water in the basin, and this was stained a pale red. One of the woman's garments, a petticoat, had been thrown over the back of a chair when she undressed. Blood had been splashed over it.

What added to the confusion of effect was the clean state of a towel that remained in its original fold over the handrail of the washbasin stand. Blood had not been splashed on it and the murderer had not used it to rinse or dry his hands. If the murderer had poured the water from the large floral jug into the washbasin, in order to rinse his hands, he had done so without leaving any blood on the jug's handle. This seemed puzzling, expecially as the towel had not been used.

The room had been gloomy even at midday with the sun pouring late-summer brightness into the street outside, for the venetian blinds had been drawn when Bert Shaw forced his way into a bedroom that had been turned into an abattoir. When the ribs of the blind had been turned sunlight streaked the room with surrealist stripes, and one bar of golden brightness fell across a sewing machine.

A postcard album was balanced on the machine. It was open, and some of the cards had been detached from their corner slits and had fallen to the floor.

Bert Shaw was asked about that postcard album, and told the police that he had no idea why it had been brought into the bedroom.

'Phyllis always kept it on the table in the front room,' he told them. 'She seemed to value it. I don't know why, but she did. She really took care of it.

To him she was Phyllis, the girl who had posed as his wife, and he did not speak of her as Emily. However, he had something else to tell the police. The killer had been a thief. With him had gone some of Bert's possessions, including a silver cigarette-case on which were inscribed his initials, A.S., a gold watch of an indeterminate number of carats, a silver watch-chain with a fashionable Edwardian charm attached to it, and also the dead woman's purse, which presumably had contained money.

The killer had taken the wedding ring from the dead woman's left hand, but had departed without pocketing two other gold rings, which remained on top of a chest-of-drawers, in full view of anyone standing in the middle of the room.

The state of the parlour suggested that Mrs Phyllis Shaw had entertained her killer. On the table near the middle of the room were four empty stout bottles. Used cutlery and plates pointed to two persons having sat down to a meal.

Mrs Stocks was asked if she knew her female lodger had a visitor to supper. The landlady was indignant.

'If I'd known that sort of thing was going on in my house I'd have had her out in the street where she belonged,' was the woman's crisp assurance to the questioning police.

The police could only start a full-scale inquiry with Bert Shaw himself. Although the man could not be considered as a suspect, it was without doubt he who could give them the best lead in the early stage of the inquiry. He knew most about the woman he had allowed to pose as his wife, what she had been, whom she had known, possibly whom she might have known. Bert Shaw had a bad time helping the police, and in his own view he had only himself to blame. He should have known better than to set up a home with Emily Dimmock.

The police checked, for the record, his whereabouts at the time of the crime. Twelve hours before the murder he had been at home with her in St Paul's Road. Then he had gone to St Pancras to catch the dining-car train to Sheffield, and had worked in the company of the regular dining-car crew.

Mrs Stocks was asked about the hours after four o'clock the previous afternoon.

The landlady had observed the woman she knew as Mrs Shaw out in the garden taking down a row of washing from the communal clothes-line. The woman piling her dried wash into a basket had her hair in curlers. That was not long after Shaw had gone off to work. At seven o'clock the two women had met again when the upstairs lodger came down on her way to the garden. Mrs Stocks had noted with the disapproval of a woman whose own life was neatly organised, and who had a sense of the fitness of things in her surorundings, that the curlers were still decorating Mrs Shaw's hair.

From this it could be assumed that the curlers were being kept in position to afford the maximum effect when ultimately removed. However, as the investigation proved, this was not done before eight o'clock, the time when Mrs Stocks heard the front door slam.

That had been her lodger leaving. Emily Dimmock, in the opinion of the police, had left to keep an assignation, one not likely to be with a female friend. It was an easy opinion to form.

Mrs Stocks retired to bed at her usual early hour and enjoyed her normal good night's sleep. No sounds of cries or disturbance awoke her before her customary hour for rising. She had prepared and eaten her breakfast and begun her day's housework by nine o'clock, when she went to the Shaw's door and rapped on it.

'I didn't get any answer,' she told the police, 'but that didn't surprise me. She never rose early.'

She explained that she had heard no sounds from upstairs before the arrival of Bert Shaw's mother.

It was obvious that the police would have to look elsewhere for information about the dead woman. They had some background details from a very subdued Bert Shaw, and with these as a starting point they quickly extended their inquiry.

Filling in the dead woman's background did not prove any difficulty. Emily Dimmock was a woman who had mixed a good deal in her own rather wide-ranging circles. She had taken up with Bert Shaw, who was attracted to her physically, as a means of having a fresh base from which to operate as a streetwalker. She had become a prostitute at an early age for the reason that she enjoyed the attention of males who were prepared to flatter her and had an inbuilt dislike for work of the kind she considered drudgery.

In fact, Emily Elizabeth Dimmock was a fairly common social phenomenon of her times. She was a child of a large working-calss family in Walworth, in south-east London. In point of fact she was youngest of a brood of fifteen children who lived their childhood in the purlieus of the Old Kent Road where Marie Lloyd was the reigning queen of the variety halls.

The youngster who found she could get along very well without morals until she met a man who showed her, too late, the danger of the life she had chosen, was both tall and slim. She had a figure that can best be described as feminine. It was what wholly enthusiastic novelette writers of the day described as a very good one, by which they inferred that, tied into the very restricting corsets of the era, a female figure was induced to appear eye-catching with elaborate curves and platforms and clefts. Emily Dimmock seemingly knew not only how to wear the whalebone-ribbed foundation garments that emphasisied her youthful femininity, but how to shed them with a flourish. She had a dress sense that was largely flair. Somehow she had contrived to learn how to play the piano, perhaps by ear, for she also had a good singing voice.

On her behalf it must be admitted that she did make an effort to tread the ways of irksome virtue. As soon as she left the over-crowded shelter under the parental roof south of the Thames she journeyed to middle-class East Finchley, where she lived in and dressed as a maid-of-all-work, which proved very much less than to her liking. She was still little more than a girl when she began a nomadic existence, travelling with her crammed

Gladstone bag from one address to another until she reached central London and settled down at an address in Bidborough Street, across the Euston Road from St Pancras Station.

The house in Bidborough Street was one of those that for a generation or two had been described as disorderly. In short, Emily Dimmock had moved into a brothel. It was run by a man named Crabtree. Her Bidborough Street period taught her all she needed to know about handling men in order to separate them from the money in their pockets. When she was experienced even by Crabtree's standards she moved on, having decided there was a greater percentage in free-lancing than in keeping a heavy-handed ponce in booze and baccy as well as certain home comforts.

It was during this free-lance interval that she acquired the hobby of collecting postcards and inserting them in an album. The cards were sent her by former clients, and they came to her from many countries throughout the world, especially from Service personnel who had purchased her favours while on leave.

When she met Bert Shaw her way of life was no secret. Their attraction was animal and mutual and in the language of a different age they decided to shack up together. He because she solved the tiresome problem of celibacy for a young man with no great future prospects, and she because she was sufficient of an opportunist to try to grab the best of two different worlds. She would be kept and protected as a married woman, but would be able to continue her promiscuous adventuring in the hours Bert Shaw was inverting their marital roles and slaving over a hot stove for the Midland Railway.

While she was honest with him about her past, she kept her intended future, and the revenue it would produce, a secret from him. After all, even a bogus husband has no relish for wearing the horns of a genuine cuckold.

The police very quickly established that she had a nightly haunt for picking up a client during Bert Shaw's absence. If, after a few drinks, she liked the man and he appeared generous she took him back to St Paul's Road and closed the front door quietly before showing him the way upstairs. Mrs Stocks invariably co-operated by sleeping through the coming and later the going.

This favourite haunt was the Rising Sun, a public house in Camden Town. For nine months she continued living this profitable and to her gratifying double life until it ended brutally and abruptly on the night of September 11th, 1907. At the time of her death Emily Dimmock was twenty-three.

It was at the Rising Sun that the detectives making inquiries heard of a ship's cook named Robert Percival Roberts. On the Sunday before the Wednesday when she was murdered Emily Dimmock had picked up Roberts as a new client. He had plenty of spending money as he had just been paid off after a long voyage. Apparently he considered he had received value for his money because he also spent the nights of the Monday and the Tuesday with her. The police traced Roberts, who told them he would have spent the night of Wednesday also with her, but she already had another client booked. He was able to prove as good an alibi as that other cook, the bogus husband, for the fatal Wednesday night, which encouraged the police to lose interest in him, but not in something he told them.

He related how, on the Wednesday morning, when he was preparing to sneak out of Mrs Stocks' house, a couple of letters were thrust under the landing door to the Shaw rooms. He picked them up and handed them to the woman. One, as he remembered, was an advertising circular. The other was a letter which she tore open and read hurriedly. Afterwards she showed him part of it, thereby proving that she had the prior date and so could not accommodate him.

The ship's cook remembered one pertinent question in the scrawled lines thrust in front of his face and also the signature.

The question was 'Will you meet me at the Eagle, Camden Town, 8.30 tonight, Wednesday?' The signature was 'Bert'.

The writing was in purplish indelible pencil. So was the writing on one of the hundreds of postcards she possessed and prized. It was one she took from the chest of drawers and showed him. It was a postcard of a woman with a child. The writing on the other side had apparently been scrawled by a wag. It read: 'Phillis [sic] darling, if it pleases you meet me at 8.15 p.m. at the' followed by a crude drtawing of a rising sun. It ended, 'Yours to a cinder, Alice.'

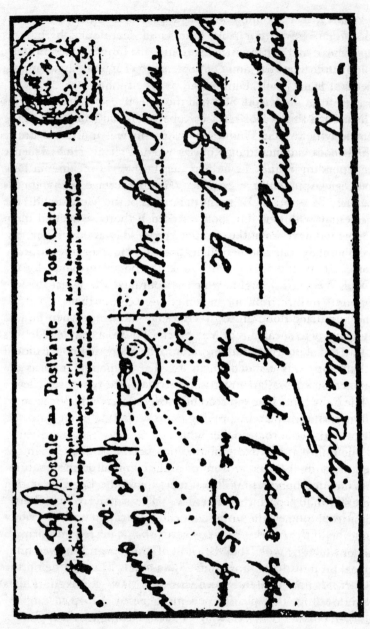

"Can You Recognise This Writing?"

What Roberts remembered was that letter and postcard appeared to be written in the same hand. He handed her back the postcard and with some surprise saw her strike a match and hold it to the circular and the letter. She dropped the burning sheets of paper into the grate and returned the postcard to the drawer from which she had taken it.

No. 29 St Paul's Road had another lodger who paid a weekly rent to Mrs Stocks. This was a widow, Mrs Alice Lancaster, who had already told the police she was the person who pushed the letters under the Shaw door. The fact that she lived in the house suggested to the police that the name Alice had been chosen specially to avoid arousing Bert Shaw's suspicions should he accidentally happen on such correspondence. The charred fragments were raked from the grate. A few words were decipherable. They were sufficient to confirm the ship's cook's story.

Search was made for the card signed Alice. It was not in the drawer described by Roberts. The inference was that the killer who had turned out cupboard and drawers and gone through the post-card album had finally found it before leaving.

In this the police were drawing a natural but false conclusion as Bert Shaw was able to prove. Cleared by the police, he decided to leave St Paul's Road and a regrettable incident in his past. While he was packing his bags he moved the newspaper lining a drawer in the chest. The movement revealed the missing card. He turned it over to the police who soon had Roberts identify it.

The Police at last had something concrete to work on. They went through the postcards in the album and found three more with identical handwriting to the one signed Alice, but when they were shown to people who had known the murdered woman none admitted they knew the writer. The cards were photographed and copies sent to the Press. The national newspapers requested any reader who recognised the writing to tell the police. The national appeal produced a vast number of responses, but none helpful. The *News of the World* went one better than its competitors. It reproduced the Alice postcard with an offer of a reward of a hundred pounds to anyone who could provide information which led to the identifying of the mystery handwriting.

The offer appeared on Sunday, September 29th. It was seen by a Ruby Young, who lived on the other side of London in Earl's Court Road. She cut out the newspaper illustration, but before she could post it she received a visit from a young man she knew very well whose name was Robert Wood. He was an engraver who thought of himself as an artist, just as Ruby Young thought of herself as an artist's model. They lived in a sort of mock La Bohème that had never occurrred to Puccini.

'That's your handwriting,' the girl told Wood, who did not bother to deny it.

'So you know I'm in trouble, Ruby,' he said. 'Will you let me tell you?'

With the certainty that she could collect a hundred pounds any time she approached the *News of the World*, Ruby Young waited. She was told how on a Friday evening a short time before Wood had been in the Rising Sun in Camden Town when a young woman with a quick smile asked him for a penny for the nickelodeon. He gave her a coin and bought her a drink, which was a pointer to how Emily Dimmock opertated to make contacts.

This girl in the pub had told him her name was Phyllis, and when a boy entered selling postcards she asked him to buy one for an album she said she kept. But Wood said he had better cards in his pockets. They were several he had bought while in Bruges. He showed them to her and she selected one of a woman with a child. The woman returned it to him and asked him to send it to her when he had written something pleasant on it as a memento. He told Ruby Young he had written some words making an appointment, and was about to add his name when he was stopped.

'Put Alice,' said the woman.

He had done so, and then found he had no stamp. He pocketed the card and promised to post it later. Not long afterwards he left the Rising Sun. The woman calling herself Phyllis was still inside.

According to Wood that wasn't the end of the episode. The next day, by chance, he ran into the woman again and apologised for forgetting to send her the card. He posted the card the next day, Sunday, and on the Monday evening saw the woman once

Robert Wood, finally acquitted of the murder

more in the Rising Sun. He bought her a drink. When she had finished it she rose to leave.

'I'll be back shortly,' she smiled.

But she was still absent when he rose to go, tired of waiting. Outside, he turned to cross the street and saw her at once. She was talking to a lame man when she caught sight of him. She turned away from the lame man, calling, 'I'll see you when the pub closes,' and hurried to join Wood, who took her back to the Rising Sun, bought her a couple of drinks, and then left.

'That's the last time I saw her, Ruby. I swear it.'

Despite her doubts Ruby Young allowed herself to feel convinced. She had known Wood for a considerable time and had been intimate with him over a period of more than three years, though the first fine careless rapture of their association was almost a forgotten memory. She knew he had a glib tongue and instinctively felt she should mistrust what she had heard. But she found she could be generous to a man who had meant much to her. She told him she would not claim the reward and would not go to the police.

Robert Wood must have considered he had perfomred exceptionally well to be so convincing.

Unfortunately for him others could recognise his handwriting, and one was a foreman at the factory where Wood worked as an engraver. He too challenged Wood, who told him the story that had passed muster with the sentimental Ruby Young. To bolster his plea with the factory foreman the young man begged him to keep what he knew to himself.

'My father's health is in a bad state,' he explained. 'If he learns I've been consorting with prostitutes it could kill him.'

The foreman allowed himself to be persuaded and joined the conspiracy of silence. Because of this the Press publicity campaign failed.

However, Wood at times could be too glib for his own good. He had a friend named Lambert who was assistant to a bookseller in the Charing Cross Road. A week after the murder, on the 20th, Wood met Lambert and said something that made the bookseller's assistant think hard.

'I've seen Mr Moss, the head man at the works,' Wood

volunterred gratuitously, 'and he's been talking about the Cambden Town murder. If he says anything to you, will you tell him that we met and had a drink, but leave the girl out?'

This remark caused Lambert to recall the last time he had seen Wood. It was on the night of the 11th. He had gone into the Eagle public house, opposite Cambden Town station, not long after nine o'clock and found Wood talking to a strange young woman with her hair still in curlers. There had been a breezy introduction without names and the woman had pointed to her curled hair apologetically and said she had just run out for a few minutes. Lambert had no doubt that the woman was one who sold her favours for cash. He left after finishing his drink and forgot the incident until Wood's request brought it back to his mind.

He realised Wood had been talking to the woman who had been murdered in St Paul's Road. He in turn challenged Robert Wood, and was told about the aged father and assured that Wood could, as he phrased it, 'clear myself'.

Lambert knew the Wood family. He felt sorry for them. For that reason another member joined the conspiracy of silence.

But Wood's luck could not continue in such a fabulous fashion. It was inevitable that the silence was broken some time. This was sooner than Wood might have expected, for the detectives had already the description of a young man who had been buying Emily Dimmock drinks in the Rising Sun on Monday, September 9th. Moreover, Emily Dimmock had confided to a woman friend that she was rather scared of him, though she did not explain why.

The police had also taken a statement from a carman, named McCowan, who had walked along St Paul's Road about a quarter to five on the morning of the 12th and seen a man leave No. 29. The carman had not seen the other man's face clearly, but he had been quick to notice a distinctive walk, which curiously jerked at the man's shoulders. All of which made the police anxious to find a man they very much wanted to question. The trouble was, however, they still had no idea of where to find this wanted man.

Meantime Ruby Young told a woman friend of what she had

promised Robert Wood, and added that he had requested her, if necessary, to provide him with an alibi for both the Monday and Wednesday nights. The friend was told this as a thrilling secret. She in turn shared her secret with a man she thought would appreciate it.

She was right. The man was a journalist.

He had no compunction in visiting Ruby Young and frightening her into telling him what she knew. He arranged a meeting with her later at Piccadilly Underground Station. She kept the appointment and so did the journalist who was accompanied by another man. The second man was Inspector Neil of Scotland Yard. In time Neil was to join Francis Carlin as one of the Yard's original Big Four, and just as Carlin, a famous catcher of murderers, failed in Chelsea, so Arthur Neil, famous as the detective who trapped George Joseph Smith of the Brides in the Bath notoriety, failed in Camdem Town.

But there was a difference in the failures. Neil did arrest a man he believed was a killer.

His belief stemmed from the moment he heard the frightened Ruby Young's hesitant story. Wood was arrested by Neil as he was leaving the factory premises of the London Sand Blast Glass Works in the Gray's Inn Road. The time was six-thirty in the evening of October 4th. Neil made no mistake in identifying the man he wanted because he had Ruby Young meet Wood.

Wood was taken by cab to Highgate police station, where after receiving the customary caution, he made a statement that followed the line of the story he had told Ruby Young and the factory foreman. He added the false alibi he had asked the woman to provide and so trapped himself, for he did not know that she had told the Yard man of his request.

The next day Wood was put into an identity parade and was picked out by several women who claimed they knew he had been friendly with Emily Dimmock for more than a year. When asked to walk McCowan instantly picked out Wood as the man he had seen leaving the house in St Paul's Road.

Wood was formally charged with Emily Dimmock's murder.

The inquest was held and at the conclusion of the evidence the jury returned a vercict committing Wood for trial. By the

time the case opened at the Old Bailey before Mr Justice
Grantham, exactly three months after the finding of Emily
Dimmock's nearly decaptiated body, the interest of the general
public had swung widely towards sympathy for the prisoner. The
directors of the firm that had employed him put up a thousand
pounds for his defence.

'He is incapable of such a monstrous crime,' one of them told
a reporter.

Sir Charles Mathews, who opened for the Crown, made great
play with the obvious, that the prisoner had tried to suborn
witnesses and had endeavoured to tamper with potential
evidence, as well as lying to the police in claiming a false alibi.
A point he made much of was the woman's hair when she was
seen in the Eagle by Lambert, for he claimed that the curlers
in it were proof that she had not gone out to interest a stranger
in her looks, but to meet someone well known to her. There was
great play about the handwriting on the postcard, admitted by
Wood, and that on the burned fragments, which was identical.
Even more play was made of the meeting in the Eagle, where
the two were not well known. The suggestion was that Wood
had set up the meeting there because he intended murdering
the woman. Then in walked Lambert, a veritable *deux ex machina*.
Sir Charles Mathews made out a storng case.

However, the defence was led by an advocate to whom strong
cases were merely a challenge to prove they concealed an inherent
flaw. This was Marshall Hall, who began by atacking the police
and gave one of their chief witnesses, Sergeant Grosse, a severe
legal mauling, particularly on the important detail of the light
in St Paul's Road at a quarter to five on the morning of
Steptember 12th. Having done that, the famous advocate
destroyed much of the value for the Crown of McCowan's
evidence, forcing the unhappy carman to admit the man he had
seen could have been a casual pedestrian and not someone who
had just left No. 29.

Ruby Young received the same harsh treatment when she was
asked, with little chance for considering all its implications, to
reply to the following question from a legal luminary who had
given it long and careful thought:

Sir Edward Marshall Hall

'With regard to that arrangement, have you ever though that, regarding the evidence of Dr Thompson, who places the time of murder at three or four o'clock in the morning, the alibi Wood arranged with you from 6.30 to 10.30 p.m. on the previous evening to the murder would be a useless alibi for the murder, but a perfect alibi for the meeting of the girl?'

She could only mutter that she hadn't considered the possibility.

When the Crown produced a number of rather disreputable witnesses Marshall Hall told the jury that calling prostitutes and brothel-keepers was a manifest demonstration of the weakness of the prosecution's case, and went on to hammer at his claim that Wood had no motive for murdering Emily Dimmock, that the stolen articles had not been traced to him, nor had the murder weapon. The prosecution's case was as flimsy, in effect, as the few scraps of charred paper which the murdered woman had destroyed, not the prisoner. He admitted Wood's lies, but brushed them aside as the product of a natural fear because the prisoner had known the murdered woman and feared publicity because of her reputation. He even produced a witness named Westcott, a railway worker, who walked with an athlete's shoulder jerk.

It was undoubtedly Marshall Hall's day when he sat down, and the judge realised this when, in his summing up to the jury, he said, 'In my judgment, strong as the suspicion in this case undoubtedly is, I do not think that the prosecution has brought the case home near enough to the accused.'

These words brought applause from the public in the well of the court. The effect of this helped to make the jury's task easy. They returned a verdict of 'Not guilty', which was a signal for crowds outside the court to demonstrate their pleasure as they blocked all roadways. Ruby Young had to be smuggled out of the building to avoid a section of the crowd that was suddenly voicing intense hostility towards her as someone believed to have sold a lover for a promised reward, which was quite untrue.

Also, Ruby Young did not receive any reward money. She vanished. So did Robert Wood, after changing his name.

The police arrested no one else for the murder of Emily

Dimmock, so someone got away with her murder. Was that someone a man who stood trial, was acquitted, and afterwards changed his name? It is a question many have pondered and argued, and probably will continue to do so as long as unsolved crimes remain a challenge.

Unquestionably Wood was lucky in his defence, for the claim has been made that in his advocacy on Wood's behalf the famous barrister reached a persuasive peak he never subsequently attained. He even persauded the judge and Mr Justice Grantham was a hard man to convince.

Or perhaps the Crown's counsel failed.

If Robert Wood did not get away with murder, then the person who did was some unknown whose anonymity was never pierced because Emily Dimmock covered up for him with her coded postcards. In this case he could have been a former client who resented her living with another man as his wife and arranged to have his own showdown with her. Perhaps she realised this but was confident that, once in bed, she would get a fresh victory on her own terms. Sexually she had no inferiority complex.

Which might have been her undoing.

Her very capacity for making men want her might have determined one to end a grim charade in which he could never turly dictate the terms to a thoroughgoing wanton. A condition that could be ended by a knife slash. Most likely while the victim slept.

GUY H. B. LOGAN

How to Dispose
of a Human Body

The greatest difficulty with which a murderer is confronted is
the disposal of the body of the victim.

All kinds of methods have been employed by assassins, from
Catherine Hayes to Patrick Mahon, but only that entertaining
scoundrel, Landru, appears to have thought out and adopted
a plan which was so secure as to have enabled him to destroy
entirely the remains of the many confiding ladies who put their
lives and property into his keeping.

French murderers, of whom Voirbo and Avinain may be taken
as samples, have shown a preference for the dismemberment
process, afterwards casting the human fragments into the Seine,
and Kate Webster, of Richmond notoriety, found the Thames
very convenient and handy for the same fell purpose. Greenacre,
like Sheward, of Norwich, cut up the body of his victim, and
distributed the remains in places where they were quickly found,
to be afterwards pieced together. Cook, of Leicester, destroyed
the body of his creditor, Mr Pass, by fire, a process which has
had many copyists, and Deeming, Edgar Edwards, and others,
resorting to the device of the Mannings in 1849, simply huddled
their victims into graves previously prepared. So, too, did John
Holloway, a little under-sized ruffian who had tired of his wife,
at Rottingdean, Sussex, and Walter Miller, the Chelsea double-
murderer. The doyen of this class, head and shoulders above
the rest for greed, cunning, ferocious cruelty and malignity, was
that fiend incarnate, young Troppmann, who, in 1869, converted
a clover field at Pantin, near Paris, into a private cemetery.

None of these, however, succeeded in 'getting away with it',
as one might say. They were all wrecked by the discovery, either

285

of the bodies intact, as in the case of Deeming, or of the mutilated remains, as in the instance of that hard-faced, raw-boned Irishwoman, Kate Webster, and even Landru, of whose victims hardly a trace was ever found, ended his adventurous and picturesque career on the scaffold. He was, nevertheless, a cool and resourceful criminal, of whom it can truly be said that he only once lost his head—and then for ever.

Nor have trunks and boxes proved at all efficacious as a means of concealing great crimes. That amazing American, H.H. Holmes, whose real name was Mudgett, showed a certain amount of ingenuity when specializing with a trunk, and there was the later case of a man, Robinson, who deposited the body of the woman he had slain in the parcels' office at Charing Cross. These, however, had been anticipated by that extraordinary villain, Lacenaire, who had planned to pack the body of the bank-porter he had decoyed to his room in a basket for conveyance to a quiet spot in the country where it could be otherwise disposed of. One would say of this method at the first man who resorted to it was a genius, and the others idiots.

Attempts have been made to conceal a murder by setting fire to the house with the body in it, though even this method has its risks. The fire has been discovered and put out before the body could be consumed, or, as in an American case, the skull has been found with a bullet in it. John Lee, of Babbacombe, the 'man they could not hang', endeavoured to burn down Miss Keyes's house, with Miss Keyes's body convenient to the fire, and Garcia, the Spanish sailor on tramp, resorted to a similar device after slaughtering the Watkins family at Llangibby, near Usk.

The elements, in fact, have not been at all favourable to murderers faced with the necessity of concealing 'the body'. Water has rejected the victim's remains, fire has failed to destroy them, and they have been recovered from unhallowed graves. Hanging may or may not be a deterrent, but I can well believe that the difficulty of disposing of the body has kept many a potential murderer from translating his homicidal tendencies from the sphere of contemplation to the region of actuality.

The case of the German baker, one Urban Napoleon Stanger,

whose strange disppearance created much stir in London about
a century ago, suggests, however, that someone may have hit
upon a means of disposing of a human body without risk to
himself. After a careful study of all the circumstances in that
strange case I can come to no other conclusion than this: that
murder was certainly committed, but the authorities were unable
to make a capital charge because they could not produce the
corpse. Whoever did away with U.N. Stanger—and suspicion
was directed against two persons—took very good care to wipe
that unfortunate tradesman so completely out of existence that
not even a hair of his head remained to bear witness against the
murderer. How his death was accomplished we cannot tell, but
it was the general impression at the time that Stanger had been
baked in his own oven, and that Mrs Stanger, his wife, had
assisted to dispose of him in that drastic manner.

Mr and Mrs Urban Napoleon Stanger were natives of
Kreuznach in Germany. They had married in 1868, and came
to London two or three years later with a view to bettering their
condition. The man was by trade a baker, and with his small
savings he started in business for himself, opening No. 136 Lever
Street as a bakery.

Lever Street is in the parish of St Luke, Whitechapel, and
is, even to this day, a rough street in a rough neighbourhood,
but in 1870, when the Stangers came to live in it, it had as
unsavoury a reputation as any thoroughfare in that quarter. Its
inhabitants were, for the most part, foreign jews, drawn from
the criminal classes of many countries, whose small businesses
served as a cloak for concerns that were much less innocent. It
was a densely populated neighbourhood, and Stanger's trade
was a good one. It enabled him to save money, and there is no
doubt that he was comparatively well-to-do when in November
1881 he vanished from human ken.

The Stangers, so far as was known, bore exemplary characters,
or certainly the man did. It might be said of him in the words
of the poet, that he 'wore the white flower of a blameless life',
that his bread was up to standard weight and of good quality,
that he was industrious and thrifty, and kept clear of debt and
difficulty.

Of Elizabeth, his wife, one cannot be so sure. Perhaps in her younger days, before a lazy and self-indulgent life played havoc with her face and figure, when, as a maiden, she frolicked in the market-square of her native Kreuznach, this good lady may have possessed some charm and fascination, but, if so, she lost them on reaching the middle age. One does not like to be ungallant to a baker's wife, but candour compels the admission that Mrs Stanger was a coarse, stout, hard-featured matron, whose appearance, whatever qualities of heart and mind she may have possessed, was singularly unprepossessing. This was not imnpoved by the cheap jewellery she affected or the gaudy garments with which she loved to adorn her ample person.

For the rest, she was sullen and secretive, rather scornful of her meek little baker, and somewhat apt to waste Urban Napoleon's money.

Although he never complained, and outwardly, at least, appeared to be on good terms with his assertive spouse, the baker, in the opinion of his neighbours, had 'rather a life of it', and they also declared that the woman had been heard abusing him 'in good set terms', as Shakespeare says, on many occasions. The shop prospered, bread being the staff of life all the world over, but there appears to have been no great harmony in the domestic circle above stairs.

Mrs Stanger was one of those persons who are industrious by fits and starts. Sometimes she would serve behind the counter for days on end, 'from early morn to dewy eve', and at others she sulked upstairs, doing nothing at all, it was said, except gaze into space and sip brandy, a tipple for which she appears to have had a weakness. At such times she had been known to pelt the baker with his own loaves, which, at the best, is not significant of either affection or esteem.

The Stangers kept one maid, who, besides helping in the housework, occasionally served in the shop, an errand-boy, and a journeyman-baker, one Christian Zentler; but, as the two latter did not sleep on the premises, the actual household consisted of only Urban Napoleon, his wife, and the maid.

A compatriot of the baker, a man named Franz Felix Strumm, lived near by, and the two were friends. Strumm was himself a master baker but he had no shop or business of his own, and, being hard up and in debt, he was glad to assist Stanger in the baking, and thus earn a little much-needed money. He was a married man, but that fact did not prevent him from casting sheep's-eyes in the direction of Mrs Stanger, who reciprocated in kind. Strumm became a constant visitor at 136 Lever Street, and the attentions he paid his friend's wife were of such an intensive character as to provoke the wonder and indignation of neighbours, who, ordinarily, would not be suspected of moral scruples.

Whatever the relations between Mrs Stanger and the ardent Strumm, who, it is to be suspected, had rather an eye to the bakery than the lady, they were not a romantic or attractive pair. If Mrs Stanger was coarse and heavy-looking, Strumm had the aspect of a villain. He had a long and heavy face, a hooked nose, a short, dark beard, and an expression of cunning and malice impossible to describe. Furthermore, he was of heavy frame, slow in speech and movement, with sombre eyes which spoke of hidden passions and veiled insolence. 'I may be doing the man an injustice,' wrote one who saw and watched him in court, 'but he looks to me to be capable of any atrocity.'

Such was the position of affairs on the 12th November, 1881. At just before midnight on that date, Christian Zentler, on his way home, passed along Lever Street, and saw four men standing on the pavement outside Stanger's shop. They were the baker himself, Felix Strumm, and two friends of theirs, Englishmen named Long and Cramer. They were talking together, and appeared to be on the best of terms. When Zentler had passed them by he happened to turn round, and he saw Long, Cramer, and Strumm go off, and the baker enter his house alone. He was never seen or heard of again.

The following day, on Zentler's arrival at the shop in Lever Street, Mrs Stanger alone was visible. She appeared, Zentler said, 'A little put out,' and she asked him to go round and beg Mr Strumm to come immediately, as he was urgently wanted. Zentler did so, and Strumm came at once. It was almost as though he expected some such summons. He remained there all day, but of Stanger there was no sign, and Zentler does not

How did they do it?

appear to have inquired after him. Perhaps he did, and was put off with some evasion. One or two persons came to see the baker on business, and these Mrs Stanger interviewed. She declared that private affairs had caused her husband to make a hurried visit to Germany, and added that the date of his return was uncertain. Strumm now came to the shop early in the morning and remained all day, and on or about November 26th he took up his abode there, Mrs Strumm being, apparently, complacent to the arrangement.

Naturally, all this set the neighbours talking, and curious and unfriendly glances were cast on Mrs Stanger and Strumm when they were seen together, arm-in-arm, on a fine Sunday. Urban Napoleon might be in Germany, though people only had his wife's word for that, but really, said the gossipers, there was no occasion for Mrs Stanger to advertise her relations with his friend in that brazen fashion. The delinquents themselves seemed unconscious of or indifferent to this censure, and Mrs Stanger, in particular, flaunted public opinion by being seen with Strumm on all possible occasions.

A little later on the residents on either side of 136 Lever Street got a surprise. The name U.N. Stanger vanished from the shop front, and that of F.F. Strumm took its place.

This added fuel to the fire of gossip and conjecture. It was discovered that Strumm was acting as if Stanger's property was his own, just as if the missing baker could never return to claim it, and people, scenting a mystery, took to staring at the shop in a manner that the inmates must have found disconcerting and embarrassing. It was rumoured that the baker had been murdered, and that certain meat pies, prepared by Mrs Stanger with her own fair hands, were composed of something that was not the flesh of any bull, sheep, pig, or even horse. In fact, Mr Stanger's remains, it was said, had been converted into twopenny pies, and were being sold to a deluded public by that personage's better half.

The police, however, appear to have taken no action, other than to 'move on' the children and others who blocked the pavement before the shop. It was no business of theirs, discounting as they did, the meat-pie story, and if Stanger chose to go away and remain in hiding, it was his affair, and no outsider had the right to interfere.

In April 1882, however, there appeared in the Press, and on handbills and hoardings, the following announcement:

> Fifty pounds reward. Mysteriously disappeared, since the early part of November last, from his residence No. 136 Lever Street, City Road, Urban Napoleon Stanger, master baker, native of Kreuznach, Germany. Any person who will give information leading to his discovery will receive the above reward. Wendil Scherer, Private Enquiry Angent, 28, Chepstow Place, Bayswater.

The source of this advertisement is a little uncertain, but it was said to have been inserted by a relative of Stanger, who, calling at the Lever Street establishment, and being far from satisfied with the woman's replies to his repeated inquiries, had taken this means of bringing matters to a head.

For the strange affair had assumed a look that was decidedly ugly. If Stanger really went to Germany, at, according to his wife, a moment's notice, he had taken particular good care not to go near any of his relatives in that country. He had also left all his money behind, in order, as it would seem, that it might be seized by his wife and Strumm in his absence, as well as his business, which, by some singular process of acquisition, now belonged to the latter. No one had seen Stanger depart, and he had informed no one of his intention to go away. He had entered his house at midnight on February 12th, and had never been seen or heard of again.

The advertisement caused a profound sensation in Whitechapel, and, owing to it, the unaccountable self-evacement of Mr Stanger became a constant theme of discussion there and even father afield. All kinds of rumours were spread abroad, such as Strumm having been seen staggering along the City Road with a suspicious-looking sack early one morning, and of a cry or scream heard in the Stanger house at about one o'clock on the morning of November 13th.

Strumm, however, still continued in possession of Stanger's shop and business. When pressed to throw some light on his friend's disappearance, he would answer he 'was in hiding somewhere, being so deep in debt.' This was demonstrably false, for Stanger had enough money saved up to settle all his debts a hundred times over. The position became so threatening, and the resentment of the populace so strong, that Mrs Stanger, unable to face the general suspicion and curiosity, left the shop, and took up her abode—with Mrs Strumm, of all people—in another part of London.

So matters remained throughout the Spring and Summer of 1882, with Strumm in sole possession of all Stanger's effects, and the baker himself still missing and unaccounted for. Private inquiry and an exhaustive search threw no light upon his strange disappearance, nor could anyone be found who had seen the man since November 12th, 1881.

In October 1882, nearly eleven months later, however, the police took action. Strumm and Mrs Stanger were arrested. The former was charged with forging and uttering a cheque for the payment of £76 odd, and, also, with conspiring, together with one Elizabeth Stanger, to defraud George Geisel and William Evans of the sum of £76. Geisel and Evans were the executors under the missing baker's will, and they had, it may be assumed, taken action in order to show that Strumm was fraudently dealing with the testator's property, and to bring the matter of his disappearance into the open. The Worship Street police court was crowded when the prisoners were brought up to answer the charges, and reporters from all over the country, scenting an elucidation of the mystery, attended the hearing.

Neither the appearance nor the bearing of the two accused persons impressed observers favourably. The female prisoner was loquacious and defiant, the man sullen and stolid. They exhibited no outward sign of shame, or trepidation—they had, perhaps, the best of reasons for knowing that no murder charge could be brought against them.

Christian Zentler merely stated in his evidence that he had seen Stanger enter his house alone at night on November 12th, and had never set eyes on him since, while a near relative of Stanger's who had come expressly from Germany to bear witness, swore that neither he nor any other relative had seen or heard of the master baker since.

Strumm repeated his statement that Stanger had, in his opinion, gone abroad to escape his creditors, and that he, Strumm, had often lent him money. The prisoner's own circumstances before he went to live in Lever Street, however, gave the lie to that, and it was also proved that Stanger had between £400 and £500 in the bank at the time of his disappearance. He was not at all the sort of man to go away, and leave that money for others to dispose of. Strumm's statement, in fact, only served to strengthen the suspicions against him, and the public hostility, in which Mrs Stanger shared, rose to a dangerous height when the terms of Stanger's will became known.

He had left all his furniture, personal effects, the good-will of the business, and the entire income derived from realizing all his estate, rent, and personal, investing the proceeds in mortgages, to his wife, conditionally, that she did not marry again or cohabit and live with any other man. The implication of this was that Stanger strongly suspected the relations already existing between the woman and Strumm, and had taken what seemed to him at the time the most efficacious method of putting a spoke in their wheel. It more or less accounted, too, for Strumm, unable to profit by the baker's disappearance in any other way, having seized his business and forged his signature to cheques and securities.

He could only have done this with the connivance of Mrs Stanger, whose plan it was to have him acquire everything belonging to her husband so that she could defy the conditions of the will and go to live with Strumm afterwards.

The pair were committed for trial, but subsequently on some legal point of law the proceedings against the woman were abandoned, and Felix Strumm appeared alone in the dock, at the Central Criminal Court, to take his trial for forging a mortgage deed having relation 'to the property of Urban Napoleon Stanger, missing since 12th November, 1881.' Mr Justice Hawkins presided, and Montague Williams, Q.C., appeared for the prisoner, who presented the same appearance of suppressed savagery which he had revealed at the earlier inquiry. Mrs Stanger was the principal witness.

No one who listened to this woman's testimony entertained

the least doubt that she had lied from beginning to end. Her one object was to clear the prisoner and to blacken her husband's character. According to her sworn evidence, the latter was a spendthrift. How he wasted his money she could not exactly say, but somehow he got through it, and he would not have been able to carry on the business but for Strumm, who contributed large sums of money to its maintenance.

She further declared that her husband did not disappear on the 12th of November, 1881, as supposed, but either on the night of the 19th or early on the morning of the 20th. What actually happened, she said, was this:

In the morning, in response to an urgent message from her husband, Strumm had come to the house, and, after some talk, had promised to lend Stanger another sum of money. They also made arrangments to go into the country together the next day, Sunday, as they often did.

After tea, her husband went for a walk, and she remembered hearing him talking with two or three other men, about midnight, outside the shop. He had finally bade them good night, and, entering the house alone, joined her in the sitting-room. She had been drinking, was excited and upset, and they had a few words when she upbraided him with spending his money and neglecting his business. He was in a quarrelsome mood and perhaps she provoked him. One word led to another, and then he said suddenly:

'I have often told you I would leave you, and now I will go. I am tried of your scoldings and reproaches.'

This so upset the amiable Mrs Stanger, the devoted, faithful wife, that she burst into tears, went upstairs, and 'so to bed,' as the little diarist was fond of saying. She left her husband below, and never saw him again.

On getting up in the morning she discovered that he had carried out his threat, and, not knowing what best to do, she sent for that friend of the family, Mr Strumm, and asked him if he would look after the business for her. This that kindly, disinterested tradesman consented to do, and, the better to carry out his promise, he had gone to live on the premises. She had never compromised herself with Felix Strumm, he was merely a good friend, and Strumm's wife knew all about it and approved. As to the forged documents, it was she and not Strumm who had signed her husband's name. She had been, she added, in the habit of signing cheques and various documents for her husband, and she had seen no harm in what she had done. Anyway, Strumm was innocent as the babe unborn.

This was the gist of her evidence, but she became confused under cross-examination, and involved herself in a maze of contradictions. She could not be absolutely sure of the date of her husband's disappearance; she thought is was November 19th, but it might have been the 12th. She said that, now she came to think of it, her husband followed her upstairs that night, that the quarrel had been continued, and that he left her in bed at half-past one, and that she did not see or hear from him again. She stood down at last, a thoroughly discredited witness.

The jury brought in a verdict of Guilty against Strumm, who then stood up, and denounced judge, jury, witnesses, and his own counsel in one burst of malice and rage. White with fury and fear he declared that he was innocent, that his advisers had bungled the case shamefully, that he was the victim of a conspiracy on the part of Stanger's relatives and that there was 'no justice in vile England for a foreigner.'

Unmoved by this outburst, Hawkins, who believed that both man and woman should have to answer a much graver charge, proceeded to pass the severest sentence in his power.

He said:

'Franz Felix Strumm, you have been convicted of a very wicked forgery, and you have not improved your position by throwing unmerited abuse upon your legal advisers. I am to punish you for the forgery you have committed, and to take nothing else into consideration, except the fact that you have committed the forgery under circumstances that have been disclosed by the jury. In all those circumstances I feel it my duty to condemn you to be kept in penal servitude for ten years.'

'Thank you,' said the prisoner impudently, 'I am very much obliged to you.'

He would have liked to say more, but the warders on either side of him closed in, and he was removed, still muttering his protests, to the cells below. He requested to be allowed an interview with Mrs Stanger, who had been, he said, 'mein goot vriend', but this was not permitted. He proved an intractable and violent convict, and was constantly in trouble, so much so, indeed, that he was compelled to serve the full ten years. On his release he joined that oddly assorted couple, Mrs Strumm and Mrs Stanger, in Germany, and I have heard that he died at Frankfort in 1896.

It is impossible to resist the conclusion that Urban Napoleon Stanger was done away with. He was never seen or heard of again, and it is ridiculous to suppose that, if his disappearance was a voluntary one, he would have gone off without settling up his affairs or letting anyone know of his intention. The man who wishes to cut himself adrift from home ties and old associations takes very good care to provide himself with the means to live, and Stanger did not do that. He went off, if his wife's story was true, with no more than he had on him at the time, and left behind him furniture, clothes, papers, securities, and money in the bank. Strumm and the woman dealt with his property because they knew he would never return to claim it. how the body was made away with no one can say, but Strumm was a baker, and the oven, a large one, was very handy and convenient.

Little Mysteries No. 8

ERLE STANLEY GARDNER

Is This the Perfect Crime?

When a German plane unloaded its bombs over the British suburb of Everton, the explosion blew the police into a quandary.

On its face, the case is simple enough. The bomb demolished a concrete wall, exposing a buried steel cylinder which had been hermetically sealed. The explosion, however, blew off one of the ends of the cylinder. Some time later, examining this cylinder, police discovered gruesome evidence of an ancient crime.

Or was it so ancient?

In this steel cylinder, some seven feet long, some two feet in diameter, reposed the skeleton of a Victorian Beau Brummell. At least, so the available evidence would seem to indicate at the time.

The clothes were expensive garments cut in the style of a bygone era. Moreover, as though to clinch the case, there was a diary dated 1884 and 1885, a railway ticket dated June 27, 1885, and a post-card dated July 3, 1885.

The body was that of a man six feet tall, twenty-five to thirty years old, a well-formed, dashing young Victorian dandy, who doubtless had endeared himself to many of the impressionable beauties of the period. And that very popularity had, in all probability, led to his death.

But not so fast! Dr Charles Harrison, senior pathologist of Liverpool University, examined the body and, although he conceded the clothing went back in style to a period some sixty years ago, he advanced the startling suggestion that the body itself had not been dead more than ten years.

Now the police must choose between two possible theories.

In the one case, the crime is relatively simple. Some sixty years ago, a murder was committed, quite probably in a fit of jealousy. Then the body was disposed of with a cunning skill which has concealed the crime until the murderer himself has gone to his own reward.

But the testimony of Dr Harrison opens up another possiblity, one that makes our current mystery novels seem tame by comparison.

Let's consider that possibility from the standpoint of a fictional detective in our current mystery novels. We can fancy our detective pacing the floor, hands thrust in his pockets. 'You will note,' he observes to an associate, 'that there were certain papers found with the corpse—diaries for 1884 and 1885, a railway ticket dated June 27, 1885, and a post-card from Birmingham dated July 3, 1885.'

'Then the murder must have been committed some time in the summer of 1885,' the associate asserts.

'Not necessarily,' our detective points out; 'remember the testimony of Dr Harrison. Obviously, when documentary evidence is found with a body, we may assume that the murderer either didn't know such evidence was in the pockets of his victim's garments, or did know, but decided such evidence couldn't possibly incriminate him. Then, there is the third possibility that the documents were planted.

'Observe that the railway ticket is dated in June of 1885. A person buying a railway ticket either travels on it or takes it back for a refund. Yet here is a post-card from Birmingham dated over a week after the date on the ticket.

'It is interesting to speculate on these significant bits of evidence. Everything is possible. Suppose that as late as 1935 someone wished to dispose of a hated rival. We are probably justified in supposing that the murderer was a close associate of his victim. There was a masquerade, and the murderer suggests to his victim how clever it would be to attend that masquerade dressed in the raiment of the dandy of some sixty years ago.

'One can image what happened after that. The raiding of

ancestral trunks in some half-forgotten corner of the attic. One can even visualise the expression on the murderer's face as he handed his victim an old diary, a railway ticket, an old post-card. 'Here, put these in your pocket. Bring them out at an opportune moment. No question about it, Bill, you'll be a riot. You'll be the life of the party.'

'The victim puts the articles in his pocket, smiles fatuously at himself in a mirror.

'Perhaps in that mirror he catches a glimpse of the motion behind him. Perhaps he tries to duck to one side, but he is too late.

'After that, it only remains for the murderer to seal the body in a steel cylinder, embed it in concrete. He has committed a perfect crime. The chances are no one will ever discover the skeleton; but in case anyone does, the evidence will indicate the forgotten crime of a bygone era.

'And so,' our detective goes on, 'I think we'll search the society columns of 1935 and find the fashionable masquerades . . .'

'The fashionable ones?' the assisant asks.

'Yes, yes,' our detective says impatienty, 'obviously this young man was of good family. Remember he must have had access to trunks that were in an ancestral attic because he was six feet tall. The garments fitted him perfectly. It's not easy to get clothes of the Victorian era. It's doubly difficult to get clothes that would fit a tall and slender young man unless, perhaps, he had inherited those characteristics from his ancestors, as well as a mansion spacious enough to contain trunks. Moreover, we had better bore a hole in that steel tank and send the shavings to be analysed. Metallurgy has made strides in the past sixty years, and we can tell the date when . . .'

Easy enough when one is writing fiction.

Sources and Acknowledgements

'The Axeman of New Orleans' (originally 'The Axeman Wore Wings') from Robert Tallant: *Ready to Hang* (New York: Harper and Row, 1952; London: Kimber, 1953, as *Murder in New Orleans*), copyright © 1952 by Robert Tallant.

'The Hand in the Sand' by Ngaio Marsh, from *My Favourite True Mystery*, ed. Ernest V. Heyn (London: Heinemann, 1956), copyright © 1956 by the Estate of Ngaio Marsh. Reprinted by permission of Aitken & Stone Limited.

'The Green Bicycle Case' (originally 'The Death of Bella Wright'), from Edmund Pearson: *More Studies in Murder* (New York: Smith and Haas, 1936).

'Death of the Black Dahlia' by Craig Rice, from *My Favourite True Mystery* (op. cit.), copyright © 1956 by the Estate of Craig Rice. Reprinted by permission of Scott Meredith Literary Agency, Inc.

'The Case of the Movie Murder' by Erle Stanley Gardner, from *True Magazine*, 1946, collected in *Los Angeles Murder*, ed. Craig Rice (New York: Duell, Sloan and Pearce, 1947), copyright © 1946 the Estate of Erle Stanley Gardner, renewed 1974. Reprinted by permission of Thayer Hobson & Company.

'The Mystery of the Missing Arsenic' by Nancy Mitford, from *Picture Post*, 1953; collected in *A Talent to Annoy: essays, articles and reviews 1929-1968 by Nancy Mitford*, ed. Charlotte Mosley (London, Hamish Hamilton, 1986), copyright © 1986 by the Estate of Nancy Mitford. Reprinted by permission of Peters Fraser & Dunlop Group Ltd.

'The Head Hunter of Kingsbury Run' by William Ritt, from *Cleveland Murders*, ed. Oliver Weld Bayer (New York: Duell, Sloan & Pearce, 1947), copyright © 1947 by William Ritt.

'Who Killed Madame X?' by Anthony Berkeley, from *Great Unsolved Crimes* (London: Hutchinson, n.d.).

'Pierre Torture' from Frederic Boutet: *International Criminals Past and Present*, translated by William Mostyn (London: Hutchinson, n.d.).

'The Mystery of the Village Beauty' from Elizabeth Villiers: *Riddles of Crime: fourteen murder mysteries that were never solved* (London: T. Werner Lawrie, 1928).